A Child
Is Being
Beaten

A Child
Is Being
Beaten

Violence Against Children,
An American Tragedy

by Naomi Feigelson Chase

McGraw-Hill Book Company

Düsseldorf   Madrid   Mexico   Montreal   Panama
New York   St. Louis   San Francisco   Bogota
Paris   São Paulo   Tokyo   Toronto

First McGraw-Hill Paperback Edition, 1976

3 4 5 6 7 8 9 MU MU 7 9 8 7

Designer: Ernst Reichl

Reprinted by arrangement with Holt, Rinehart and Winston

Library of Congress Cataloging in Publication Data

Chase, Naomi Feigelson.
   A child is being beaten.

   Bibliography: p.
   1. Child abuse—United States.   2. Child welfare—
United States.   I. Title.
HV741.C38   1976   362.7'1   76–25577
ISBN 0–07–010685–1

To my parents and my children and to Gordon

AUTHOR'S NOTE   The names of most of the professionals in this book—doctors, social workers, etc.—are real, as are the names of those people mentioned in Chapter 9, "Where Are They Now?", who have either been convicted for their crimes or, like Lee Harvey Oswald, are well known for their alleged acts. Other names, places, and identifications have been changed to protect privacy.

Contents

A Child
Is Being
Beaten

Introduction

CHILD ABUSE is the deliberate and willful injury of a child by a caretaker—hitting, beating with a belt, cord or other implement, slamming against a wall, burning with cigarettes, scalding with hot water, locking in a dungeon, hog-tying, torturing, even killing. It involves active, hostile, aggressive physical treatment. Child neglect is more passive negative treatment characterized by a parent or custodian's lack of care and interest, and includes not feeding, not clothing, not looking after, not nurturing. The legal definitions vary in different states; so does the degree of harm done to the child.

I've heard many otherwise loving parents screaming out of anger, frustration, or desperation, "Stop that, or I'll kill you." Until I started to research this book, I never paid much attention. Then, one night at a party, I heard a doctor, a warm, normally affectionate man, terrify his three-year-old son by joking, "If you don't cut that out, I'll throw you out the window." I thought of pictures I had just seen of children whose parents *had* thrown them out the window to their death. The doctor didn't mean it. The other parents did. As I said, there are differences of degree. We live in a culture of violence. And none of it helps the children.

I had my first experience of child abuse in the Pittsburgh public schools, though I viewed it then as simple sadism. Miss Steiner, my third-grade arithmetic teacher, was a stout middle-aged lady with bobbed gray hair that peaked like a bluejay's. For all I know, she had a secret, unfulfilled passion for mathematics that had once fired her heart, but what kept her going when I

1

knew her was her relish for humiliating children. In Miss Steiner's class, you stood up to recite the multiplication tables, the entire class at rigid attention. If she caught you talking, you would have to stand in the corner for the rest of the class period.

But her real triumph was to catch you chewing gum. If she did, she made you stick it on your nose. Then she would call on you for the answer to six times seven. Sitting with gum on your nose through an entire math period leaves no marks, but it's an ugly experience for an eight-year-old child. The clever ones swallowed hard before she caught them.

In junior high, at Linden School, the principal favored corporal punishment. Linden stood on a pleasant tree-lined street in a pleasant middle-class neighborhood. Most of the students were nice, clean, well-disciplined children, who did their homework at home and behaved in school. The "bad" kids in my class were likely to be boys, likely to be tardy, likely to talk in class, to throw spitballs and paper airplanes, to snicker when the teacher's back was turned, to balance, when she turned and faced them, on the thin wire of disrespect. Not ideal, perhaps, but hardly a blackboard jungle.

Still, if you misbehaved at Linden, you were sent down to the principal's office and if the principal, Miss Caroline Patterson, thought you were bad enough, she hit you repeatedly on the backside with a big wooden paddle.

Miss Patterson was tall and large, with straw-colored hair pulled back in a bun. Every day she wore the same navy blue suit and white blouse with a bow at the throat, concealing, I was sure, a belt of snakes and her Amazon girdle. Her office was dark and she sat with her back to the door at a huge desk within a hand's reach of her large wooden paddle.

Miss Patterson never paddled any nice little white middle-class Jewish girls like me. But she did hit many other children.

That was close to twenty-five years ago, and Miss Patterson was bush-league Dickens. But children are still hit by teachers in my old home town as they are in schools all over the country. Jonathan Kozol's description in *Death at an Early Age* of the nasty caning of small black children in the Boston public schools—caning until their hands bled—is an ugly picture of child abuse that is generally kept behind school doors.

In 1974 a pattern of repeated beatings in one New York City school made front-page news when a teacher who had been writing the school superintendent about it for months finally gave up and went to *The New York Times*, taking one of the wooden paddles that had been used. The superintendent suspended him for going outside school channels. The *Daily News* took a poll of its readers and found them, five to one, in favor of corporal punishment. Ex-Governor Rockefeller said he thought it was a good thing, too. Surprisingly, New York State Senator Marchi, who usually favors law and order, introduced a bill to outlaw corporal punishment in New York schools.

Teachers often take a very cavalier attitude toward hitting small children. *Time* magazine, in a 1972 story on corporal punishment in schools around the country, quoted one school principal as saying that paddling was a useful warning to a child, "like giving him a traffic ticket." I was appalled to read that. Would the principal say the same thing, I wondered, about hitting an adult? Why is it we dismiss so cavalierly physical violence against children that would be called assault and battery if directed against adults?

My early experience at Linden showed the same thing that much of my research for this book shows: poor children are more likely to be mistreated than rich ones, and it is frequently the practice if not the policy of our public, tax-supported institutions to abuse them.

I never heard anything about child abuse when I was a child, and until recently I did not hear much as an adult. Like most parents from time to time I have experienced very angry if not violent thoughts about my children, and on one occasion when I was furious at my then ten-year-old son I took a favorite trophy of his and threw it to the floor. Of course it was irreplaceable and broke to bits. I was not only ashamed and sorry, I knew I had wanted to do it. It never occurred to me that I was experiencing the same feelings of rage, frustration, inability to cope, hopelessness, and helplessness that cause many parents to harm their children, sometimes severely. I do know now that like most mothers I could have used a lot of help when my children were little because, despite my B.A. and my M.A. and even my teaching experience, I knew nothing about caring for a child. Unfortunately, many if not most young mothers today—rich, poor, black, white—don't know anything either.

When an editor at Holt suggested child abuse as a subject for a book several years ago the idea alternately depressed, horrified, and fascinated me. I recalled the brutal stories of the English couple on the moors who tortured and killed a dozen or so children some years ago. Was their behavior only an extreme sickness of two individuals, or was it an exaggeration of a national cultural pattern?

I knew that in New York City alone there were almost 30,000 children whose personal circumstances were so grim that the city became responsible for their lives and fortunes. I had worked for the city and the thought of having it responsible for anyone's destiny was appalling. Were those children the victims of family disasters or, somehow, like the children at Linden who got hit with a paddle, victims of public policy?

Along with those questions, I was puzzled at the recent outbreak of articles and books about child abuse and neglect, making it the latest social-welfare cause. That, in itself, seemed worth investigating. The unusual amount of attention from the press and from professionals—doctors, lawyers, social workers, politicians—was seemingly more than the numbers of abused and neglected children would warrant. Lumping together abuse and neglect—a new trend in courts, legislatures and in the media—has inflated numbers, which are in any case "iffy," and has obscured many of the differences between the two. It has also called more attention to the issue because child abuse is at first glance more horrifying and more sensational than the passive, indifferent behavior to children that we call neglect.

Abuse makes the front pages more often. It sells more papers. It creates a sense of public outrage that builds support for legislation that requires reporting of child abusers and neglecters.

What is it all about? Why the recent outcry? Is child abuse and neglect a recent phenomenon? A growing one? And is it the doing of sick individuals or sick societies or both? The diagnosis is important since that determines the cure.

The thesis of this book is that child abuse is a serious social problem that goes back to the beginnings of history. It seems that every society we know of has had a policy, implicit or explicit, for dealing with mouths it couldn't feed, often by infanticide. And particularly in recent modern history, societies have had policies, most of them shameful, for dealing with the children of the poor. In the last few years, for a number of reasons, none necessarily humanitarian, child abuse has replaced welfare, the multiproblem family, and the culture of poverty as the latest description of what's wrong with the poor, thus allowing professionals new reasons for inspecting, punishing, and regulating them. It gives the courts new reasons to take their children away. It gives social workers a new vocabulary and vocation as the old methods prove useless. It stimulates new funds for research. Most important, by defining the problem in terms of individual rather than social pathology, as the bulk of the professional literature has done, it allows us to concentrate on "treating" the sick individual rather than changing the sick society.

The problems of child abuse and child neglect today are real, serious, and symptomatic of increasing family and social disorganization. The question is, Who is responsible and what can we do about it? And why do we look only at the poor and only at individual families? Why do professionals ignore the question of institutional abuse of children—in schools, in custodial institutions, in foster homes, in children's detention centers—where the evidence is clearer and the numbers larger of children repeatedly abused? How many Willowbrooks, that infamous Staten Island lockup for retarded children, do we have and need? When legislators press for increased reporting of child abuse, why don't they insist on or at least include reports of institutional abuse?

If we are serious about protecting children, we will have to look at violence against children in the context of a violent society that sanctions social and institutional neglect. We will have to look at our attitudes toward the young and the whole spectrum of physical violence that we use in dealing with and disciplining them.

It is a curious phenomenon in Western capitalist countries, not only in America but in England and even in New Zealand where a recent study shows child abuse and neglect to be most common among the Maori and Polynesian populations, that the guilty are the people at the bottom—the black, the brown, and the poor.

It's clear that when we talk about child abuse and neglect in America we are talking about the poor, usually the black poor. Is this because they are more violent, more neglecting, because their life is more stressful and frustrating or because it is an open book to welfare departments and sociologists? Or is it all of the above?

Are our dual educational system, our two-class system of health care, our legal discrimination, our racism, our welfare and day-care and foster-care policies the result of ignorance and benign neglect? Or are they social policy? Is it the mother, the father, the children, the family, or the society that needs help? Who is responsible for the beaten child?

1

It
Started
with Eve

"You want to know about child abuse?" asks the young lawyer. *"Here's a good one, a case I lost. I don't know how to label it. Under child abuse? Parental neglect? Institutional unconcern? Social disregard? You tell me. The child's name is Janine. Janine Fraser. Society's child.*

"Janine is a black, Protestant girl who was abandoned by her mother at the age of seven. Her father had abandoned them both long before that. Her mother finally just gave up. Left her.

"They put Janine in a child-care institution in New Jersey. 'Child care'—that's a laugh. At the age of twelve, Janine outgrew the age limit at that particular institution and they sent her to Bellevue Hospital in New York. Don't ask me why. They just sent her.

"Actually, Janine liked it at Bellevue. She wanted to stay there. But of course they wouldn't keep her because they're a hospital, not an institution for needy—I should say 'needing'— children. They had her in their psychiatric unit for a while but then they said, 'This girl is O.K. She doesn't need to be in a psychiatric ward. She needs foster care.'

"Bellevue recommended she be placed in a foster home. But the Department of Social Services just couldn't find one for her. She was too old. She was considered difficult because she'd been in Bellevue. She was too black. So they sent her to a mental hospital, Rockland State. This is done frequently. The kid's got to go someplace. Maybe she's not anxious to go to a hospital, but what's the alternative? Jail? She didn't do anything wrong. She was just abandoned.

"So she spent a year and a half at Rockland. They recommended placement, too. They said, 'Nothing's the matter with this girl.'

"At sixteen she was discharged to her mother. Well, her mother hadn't wanted her at seven and she didn't want her now. She kicked Janine out. The cops picked Janine up walking around the streets at night and told her they were going to take her to the city's Juvenile Center. That terrified her. She'd heard it was horrible and she refused to go.

"So the cops said they'd have to take her to Bellevue, then. That was O.K. with her because she liked Bellevue.

"When she got there, some sympathetic social worker at Bellevue called me and said, 'Here's this sixteen-year-old girl who's been shunted from one institution to another since she was seven. Can't you do anything for her?' I brought an action against the city in her behalf. But meanwhile, Bellevue said, 'The girl's not sick and she's not crazy, so we can't keep her. She'll have to go to the Juvenile Center.'

"Well, she didn't have any chance at that point. She went to the Center. The girls there were tough, street tough. She's not. She'd spent her last nine years in institutions.

"Various agencies promised to take her and didn't. Finally she told me that if June fifteenth came and she was still in the Center she was going to kill herself. The fifteenth came and she tried to commit suicide."

The lawyer closes the file. *"What can I do?"* she asks. *"It's awful to say, but it might have been best if she'd succeeded. As it is, she's now back at Bellevue. And for the third time, they won't be able to keep her. As a matter of fact, it's just possible they'll send her back to Rockland."*

WRITERS of natural history once told us that, unlike humans, animals killed only to eat or to protect their territory or themselves. They did not kill their own kind and they were, supposedly by instinct, fiercely protective of their young. We know better today. We know from people who have studied animals in the wild as well as those who have observed them in the laboratory that many cherished ideas about animal behavior were dictated by our romantic concepts about animal versus human nature. Freudians might call our outmoded concepts denial or wish fulfillment. At any rate, we have discovered that much so-called recorded natural history, from Pliny on, is distinctly untrue.

Many of our shattered fantasies center on the so-called mother instinct. Experiments have shown that under stress, rats, among others, will neglect and abandon their young. Monkeys removed from their natural habitat and placed in unfamiliar surroundings will bite and even eat their own litters.

It's not just stress that makes animals turn on their own kind. Although Pliny and others described lions in the wild as gentle, noble creatures, more recent and closer observers tell us that lions will go on wanton killing binges, murdering any animal that crosses their track. At such times, they not only kill more than they can eat, but will abandon, kill, and eat their own young.

And they are not sacrificing parents. According to Boyce Rensenberger, who has tried to give us a more realistic picture of leonine life, adult lions satisfy their own hunger first, often by cannibalizing their own kind. When prey is scarce, the adults will take what food there is, leaving their cubs to starve. A fourth to a third of all lion cubs reportedly die because adult lions have monopolized the food. A like number die because their mothers have abandoned them. So much for the mother instinct. Male lions will kill and eat lion cubs in a neighboring pride. And in prides where the males have been killed by invaders, the females will also turn on their cubs.[1]

Certainly new information about animal behavior raises old questions about mothering instincts, both in animals and humans. It makes us think about survival and stress and to what extent, when survival is a question, both humans and animals give nature an assist in keeping the population within bounds. It also raises questions about behavior the whole herd participates in—in humans this is called culture—as compared to the deviant, or exception to the rule. Jane Goodall has shown us two strikingly different examples in *In the Shadow of Man*: one, the remarkable chimpanzee Flo, who, were she human, we would call a supermom, and the other, her friend Fifi, whose cubs showed distinct signs of maternal neglect. In fact Fifi's history made Goodall suspect that this chimpanzee mother might previously have abandoned several cubs at birth.

It would seem that among both animals and humans, the instinct to nourish and the impulse to maim and destroy exist side by side. "A Child Is Being Beaten," one of Freud's best-known papers, describes what he considered the universal unconscious wish to hurt the young.[2] Indeed, although child abuse—from wounding and torture to selling and abandonment to outright murder—has received an unusual amount of attention in the last few years, the maltreatment of children is as old as humankind.

If we trace the thread back through the years, we discover that abortion, abandonment, and infanticide have been practiced in varying degrees since the beginnings of history, or as the Bible and mythology suggest, the beginnings of mythic time. It seems that, unlike animals, most humans have stopped short of cannibalizing their own children. But the theme of cannibalism, both implied and expressed in myth and fairy tale the world over, demonstrates the fear, the wish, and the conscious taboo.

In one popular type of fairy tale, the protagonists are children, often on their own, whose adventures include the possibility of being eaten. The happy ending usually includes a last-minute rescue, often by a parental figure, and a return to their own hearth and home. The tales may be about royalty ("Many years ago there lived a king and queen and their daughter . . .") or about ordinary folk ("Once upon a time there was a poor woodcutter . . ."), but the experiences of the children and the motives of the parents—particularly the evil motives of step-parents—are remarkably alike.

Hansel and Gretel, for instance, are put out of their house by their father at their stepmother's insistence because there's not enough to eat. Lost in the woods and eventually tricked into the witch's oven, they are just about to be cooked up in a tasty meal when their father saves them in the nick of time.

In the original version of "Snow White," the wicked step-mother tells the huntsman to bring back the girl's lungs and liver for her to eat. In the Walt Disney version, she asks for Snow White's heart. In "The Juniper Tree" the stepmother who wants her stepson's inheritance kills the boy and cooks him up in a stew. After he is buried, the child is magically transformed into a bird, kills the stepmother, and is reborn as a boy. Little Red Riding Hood, on her errand of mercy, escapes being eaten by the wolf in grandma's clothing, thanks to a passing hunter. In "The Three Little Pigs," which might be read as an allegory of children on their own, the clever child turns the tables, or in this case the boiling pot, on the hungry wolf. The tale ends with the wolf in the pot, which is where most meals begin. The poor Gingerbread Boy has to run forever because everybody wants to eat him.

Tales like these express and relieve two of children's most common fears, being abandoned and being eaten. The taboo against cannibalism is so strong that in most fairy tales the children are rescued. Russian fairy tales are an exception. The Baba Yagas simply eat the little ones and put their heads as a warning on stakes around the house.

Although the fairy-tale child usually escapes a nasty fate, in myths the plot is often carried to its grim conclusion. Medea, a prototype of the mother in "The Juniper Tree," takes revenge on her husband who abandoned her, by killing their children and serving them up in a meal for dad. In Roman mythology even the first parents are tainted. Saturn, father of the Roman gods, is a monster who devours his own children. Jupiter, the only child who escapes, later gives Saturn a drink that forces him to disgorge the others.

Some people read the story of Adam, Eve, and the apple as an allegory of cannibalism. David Bakan, a Canadian psychiatrist who has written about the theme of child abuse in literature and myth, is intrigued by that interpretation. Bakan was told as a child that the fruit of the tree of knowledge which Adam and Eve ate was really a baby. He believes many others have read it in the same way. Since "knowledge" or "knowing" is a common literary euphemism for intercourse, it follows that the "fruit" of knowledge can easily be interpreted as a baby.[3]

God's punishment of Adam and Eve supports the sexual taboo and perhaps adds to the unconscious resentment—at least in the Judeo-Christian tradition—against children. For taking sex only as a pleasure, God throws Adam and Eve out of Paradise, makes Adam work for his bread, and tells Eve she must henceforth bear children in pain. From the beginning the Bible makes it clear that women pay for sex with suffering. Children are first associated in the Bible with pain and penalty, as though cursed by their parents just as God cursed Adam and Eve.

While cannibalizing children is relatively rare in human history, infanticide as ritual sacrifice was unhappily common in biblical times. The boy Isaac's near-escape at the hands of his father, Abraham, is a familiar biblical tale. Told by God to sacrifice his best-loved son, Abraham laid his child on the altar and put the knife to Isaac's throat. When God was convinced of Abraham's piety, he allowed him to substitute a ram.

There are many similar stories. Children are used to test their parents' piety in other Bible stories as well as in Greek myth. They were also sacrificed in so-called national emergencies. King Saul, for example, tried to sacrifice his son Jonathan when he thought that might bring him victory in battle. Iphigenia, whose father Agamemnon sacrificed her to the gods so the becalmed Trojan fleet could set sail, is a Greek parallel. Saul's troops urged him to spare Jonathan. Iphigenia was snatched from the altar by the goddess Diana and spirited off.

The *deus ex machina* exists only in the imagination, but real, living children were frequently burned at the altars of various gods in biblical times. It is ironic that Solomon, whose canny solution for saving one child made his name synonymous with wisdom, burned as sacrifices scores of others.

Although denounced by the prophets, the sacrifice of first-born sons was ordinary enough in ancient Palestine. The Book of Chronicles specifically names the Moabite King Mesha, who burned his eldest son for the god Chemosh; the Ammonites, who offered their sons to their god Moloch; the Arameans who sacrificed their children; and along with Solomon, the Hebrew kings Ahaz and Manasseh.

Robert Graves says the commandment "The firstborn of thy sons shalt thou give me . . ." referred to infant sacrifice only, not to older children.[4] That is not a comforting observation. The prophet Ezekiel described that law as an evil statute that polluted Israel as punishment for idolatry. Eventually, animals and finally other tokens were substituted. The idea still survives in the ceremony of the ritual circumcision, the Pidyon Haben, where the first son is dedicated to God to bring good luck.

The practice of child immolation was so common in ancient Israel that some scholars think Hell was the name originally given to Gehenna or Ge-Hinnom, the valley near Jerusalem where children were sacrificed.[5] The valley, which was later turned into a garbage dump that burned continuously, has ever since been a literary image for the fires of Hell.

There are numerous references in the Bible to infanticide ordered by the king to nip a prophesied rival in the bud. In such stories, the hero is usually saved and hidden until he reaches manhood. Probably the most familiar is the Old Testament story of Moses. Pharaoh orders the slaying of all male Hebrew infants and Moses is saved only because his mother manages to hide him in the bullrushes where the Pharaoh's daughter finds him. For those Christians who read the Old Testament as prefiguring Christianity, we have the New Testament Herod ordering the deaths of all children two and under. This Slaughter of the Innocents, as it was called, from which Jesus is saved, heralds the beginning of Christianity. To push home the point, Innocent's Day used to be celebrated in most Christian countries by the ritual whipping of children.[6]

The same pattern is common in myth. The infant Oedipus was ordered killed by his father Laius when an oracle warned that the baby would grow up to threaten his life and throne. Rescued by an old family retainer, Oedipus survives to marry his mother. Like Pharaoh, Herod, and Laius, Nimrod, king of Babylon, fearing the birth of a prophesied conqueror, massacres 70,000 infant boys. To escape the edict, Nimrod's own wife fools him, disappearing to give birth to their son Abram.

Time and history is always on the child's side. The outcast hero always survives. He frequently grows up to kill his father or father substitute in a rage as both Oedipus and Moses did.

"Immurement," the practice of placing children in the foundations of walls or buildings, was a specially gruesome form of infanticide. A variation on the "emergency" sacrifice, it was often called for in founding cities to insure their prosperity. Joshua's curse on anyone who rebuilt Jericho was "he shall lay the foundation thereof in his firstborn and in his youngest son shall he set up the gates of it." According to the biblical account, Joshua's curse was fulfilled. Archeologists have found many jars with bones of newborns that had been buried under Canaanite house corners, thresholds, and floors. Immurement was an ancient practice in India too.

It is false vanity to dismiss these practices as products of the primitive mind. Female infanticide was permitted in China at least as late as the 1870s and in 1948 an article in *The British Journal of Psychiatry* noted that, "It was and still might be the custom for new pottery furnaces in the Kiang-si province (of China) to be consecrated with the secret shedding of children's blood." [7]

As to immurement, children may have been buried alive in the dikes of Oldenburg until the seventeenth century, and in 1843, when a new bridge was to be built in Halle, it was widely suspected that a child would be buried in the foundation.

Infanticide was practiced in biblical times to satisfy the perceived demands of religion and superstition. But throughout human history, a more common reason for infanticide has been population control.

Infanticide was a regular feature of Eskimo, Chinese, Scandinavian, Polynesian, African, American Indian, and Australian aborigine cultures. Anthropologist William Graham Sumner notes that in the Hawaiian Islands, children after the third or fourth child were customarily killed.[8] The Polynesians, according to James Frazer, reportedly used to kill two-thirds of their offspring, and so did the Tahitians.[9]

The Reverend J. Orsmond visiting Tahiti in the late 1820s

noted the relationship between infanticide and social class. Members of the higher, heavily tattooed social class were obligated not to kill their children, whereas the lower caste, those with small or fewer tattoos, were obligated to kill their babies after the first or second. It was considered a disgrace if they allowed the babies to survive.[10]

The able-bodied in a society, adults in the prime of life, must bear all their society's burdens, which include those too young to care for themselves and those too old. As Sumner describes their solution:

> It is certain that at a very early time in the history of human society the burden of bearing and rearing children, and the evils of overpopulation, were perceived as facts, and policies were instinctively adopted to protect the adults. The facts caused pain, and the acts resolved upon to avoid it were very summary and adopted with very little reasoning.[11]

Eugenics was another argument for infanticide. Seneca, Plato, and Aristotle all approved the killing of defective children and we know that the exposure of newborns in ancient Rome was rather common.

While the practice of killing newborn babies with congenital weakness or deformities may revolt the twentieth-century mind, we should remember that in such practices as infanticide and abortion there is a certain element of judgment as to what the welfare of society requires.

Infanticide as the only alternative for disgraced unmarried mothers is another persistent human theme. The killing of illegitimate children at birth was extremely common in Germany and in most of Europe as late as two hundred years ago, common enough for Goethe to use as a theme in *Faust* and for Frederick the Great to hold an essay contest on how to eliminate it. Unmarried mothers had few choices. If their maternity was discovered, they were excommunicated by the Church and lived as social outcasts. If they killed the child and were found out, the penalties were terrifying.

In eighteenth-century Germany, the most common punishment for infanticide was sacking. The victim was put in a sack and thrown into a river, frequently with a live animal or two in order to make the death more painful. In 1740, the year of his coronation, Frederick the Great, king of Prussia, substituted decapitation for sacking on the grounds that the former was more humane.[12]

The relationship between illegitimacy, infanticide, and the problems of overpopulation were a common theme elsewhere in Europe too. In Swift's "A Modest Proposal for preventing the Children of Poor People from being a Burden to their Parents and Country," the author suggests a satirical scheme for turning unwanted babies into "plump and fat" feed "for a good table," which would at least prevent "that horrid practice of women murdering their bastard children, alas so frequent among us, sacrificing the poor innocent babies . . . more to avoid the expense than the shame." [13]

Malthus, writing in 1798 about the dangers of overpopulation, ignored both infanticide and abortion as common practices of checks and balances. But Darwin, several years later, noted that they both "now prevail in many quarters of the world. . . . Infanticide seems formerly to have prevailed . . . on a still more extensive scale [and] to have originated in savages recognizing the difficulty or rather the impossibility of supporting all the infants that are born." [14]

The problems that Swift, Malthus, and Darwin concerned themselves with, the "difficulty or rather the impossibility of supporting all the infants that are born," persisted through the nineteenth century. It was a problem for the poor mother or family as it was for societies unwilling to feed large numbers of poor, often bastard, children. The problems were heightened by urbanization, industrialization, and the slow decline of the community and then the extended family itself.

A ballad called "Song of the Slums," popular in London in the late nineteenth century, is a sad reflection on the problem.

Up and down Pie Street
The windows made of glass

Call at number thirty-three
You'll see a pretty lass.

Her name is Annie Robinson
Catch her if you can
She married Charlie Anderson
Before he was a man.

Bread and dripping all the week,
Pig's head on Sunday,
Half a crown on Saturday night
A farthing left for Monday.

She only bought a bonnet box
He only bought a ladle
So when the little baby came
It hadn't got no cradle.[15]

The nineteenth-century English novelists, particularly Dickens, described in detail the plight of poor children in an increasingly industrialized society. Children were commonly beaten by schoolmasters and other adults, a practice described so often by Dickens that giving a child a beating became known as giving him "the dickens."

The enslavement of children in the factory system and the use of poor children as part of the industrial work force (see Chapter 3) became, increasingly, a way to exploit both the population and the cheap-labor problem. But infanticide persisted. An 1890 edition of the *Encyclopaedia Britannica* noted:

The modern crime of infanticide shows no symptoms of diminishing in the leading nations of Europe. In all of them it is closely connected with illegitimacy in the class of farm and domestic servants. The crime is generally committed by the mother for the purpose of completing the concealment of her shame and, in other cases, where shame has not survived, in order to escape the burden of her child's support. . . . The paramour sometimes aids in the crime, which is not confined to unmarried mothers.[16]

The encyclopedia was wrong in labeling the crime modern, but it indicates how widespread the practice was. In addition, so many infants farmed out for care, nearly all illegitimate, had died in the lying-in or baby-farming houses of London, that in 1871 the House of Commons called for their investigation and licensing. Farming out was, in fact, thinly disguised infanticide.

Like infanticide, abortion has become a persistent feature of human society, both spoken of throughout history only in whispers. The practice is not taboo, only the mention of it. George Devereux's cross-cultural study of abortion in primitive societies, published in 1960, concluded that *"abortion is an absolutely universal phenomenon and . . . it is impossible even to construct an imaginary social system in which no woman would ever at least feel impelled to abort."* [17]

Abortion and infanticide are similar in character and purpose. Abortion prevents child bearing; infanticide, child rearing. Sumner calls them "folkways which are aggregates of individual acts under individual motives, for an individual might so act without custom in the group." [18]

However, when many people observe a custom over a long period of time, the act changes character. It is no longer an "individual act of resistance to pain." When practiced over a long period of time, a custom testifies to common experiences and common ways of dealing with it. It is a judgment of expediency and policy, passed on from one generation to another. In the course of time, such policies affect the welfare of the group, its numbers, and its quality.

If abortion and infanticide are similar in purpose, we would expect infanticide to disappear in a society where abortion was sanctioned and widespread. It was startling therefore when an article in *The New York Times* in 1973 noted the recent increase in infanticide in Japan. [19] The article described the discovery of the body of a newborn in a railway station locker in Tokyo and, a few days later, another in Osaka. Evidently such incidents have been increasing in Japan from 2 in 1970 to 40 in 1973, and according to the *Times*, they are only part of a much larger wave of infanticide and abandonment. More than 100 babies were killed in Japan in 1973, in addition to the 119 children abandoned in Tokyo alone.

The Japanese have practiced infanticide for more than a thousand years. Infanticide became prevalent during Japan's feudal era, the seventeenth, eighteenth, and nineteenth centuries, as a means of population control, particularly by farmers, who killed their second or third sons at birth. The practice was called *mabiki*, an agricultural term that meant "thinning out." Unlike China, where it was customary to kill infant girls, Japanese girls were often spared because they could be married off, sold as servants or prostitutes, or sent to become geishas. The institution of the geisha saved large numbers of Japanese baby girls from death. Nevertheless, in two and a half centuries, between 1600 and the late 1850s in northern Japan alone, between 60,000 and 70,000 cases of *mabiki* were recorded each year.

Toward the end of the nineteenth century, as Japan passed from feudal to modern times, *mabiki* was prohibited, not because morality dictated it but because it was national policy to encourage population growth for industry and the army.

After World War II, infanticide reappeared in Japan and rose to a peak of 399 cases in 1948 and then dropped for the next ten years. In 1958, it began to rise again. Why has the phenomenon persisted while the means and motives of the people who practice it have changed? Since Japan was one of the first countries to adopt a liberal abortion law and contraceptives are widespread in Japan today, population control would not appear to be the cause of infanticide. The Japanese attribute infanticide and abandonment in Japan today to rapid urbanization and the resulting shift from traditional large families to the modern, nuclear family. One study of Japanese infanticides showed that most occurred in nuclear families. Another noted that as the family size decreases, the number of young mothers who lack confidence in their ability to raise children grows. Infanticide in Japan is not due to promiscuity (illegitimacy) or cruel stepmothers and is more likely in families where the mother spends a lot of time alone with the baby.

The study suggested that Japanese parents today are more

immature than they used to be and are more likely to kill or desert children than Americans, who are more prone to child abuse.

Throughout history, infanticide—whether as a sacrifice to the gods, as a eugenic device to weed out the sickly, a tool of population control to hold down numbers, or as the last resort of disgraced unmarried mothers—has been much more common than we have been willing to believe. Like it or not, the killing of children is a constant and important feature of human social history. While child sacrifice, according to Sumner, "expresses the deepest horror and suffering produced by the experience of the human lot . . . men must do it. Their interests demand it however much it might pain them." [20] Child sacrifice was common in ancient and biblical times, has persisted through what anthropologists call our semicivilized state, and in terms of history has barely ceased. Along with abortion, it has served throughout history as a recognized form of population control.

Infanticide and abortion represent the earliest efforts of humans to deal with the burden of children and overpopulation by resorting to immediate and sometimes brutal devices. The burden of children varies greatly with the condition of the people and their stage of development. For primitive people, perhaps even for civilized, overpopulation makes children a hardship to the parents, unless the people have strong neighbors and a need for warriors. The demand for boys as opposed to girls may likewise vary. In pastoral-nomadic life, it seems, many children were regarded as a blessing. In the life of the narrower family, children became more of a burden. Progress has made children even more expensive, so that progress itself has led to abortion and infanticide.

Although certain tribes practice infanticide because of female egoism, Sumner notes that the egoistic motive of mothers to refuse the strain of child bearing and child rearing could never alone suffice to make abortion and infanticide a folkway if it did not coincide with the interest of the group.

Abortion and infanticide are primary and violent acts of self-defense by the parents against famine, disease, and other calamities of overpopulation which increase with the number which each man or woman has to provide for. . . . They become ritual acts and are made sacred whenever they are brought into connection with societal welfare, which implies some reflection. The customs begin in a primary response to pain and the strain of life. Doctrines of right and duty go with the customs and produce a code of conduct in connection with them. Sometimes if a child lives a specified time of life, its life must be spared. Sometimes [infanticide] . . . is practiced only on girls. . . . Sometimes . . . confined to the imperfect infants. . . . Abortion and infanticide are so nearly universal in savage life . . . that exceptions to these practices are noteworthy phenomena.[21]

With such a long and documented history why is there such a silence about infanticide and abortion? What is the nature of this taboo?

Taboos are prohibitions, originally sacred prohibitions, against certain kinds of behavior. Taboos range from the trivial and apparently superstitious, like avoiding black cats, to the dietary, like avoiding pork, to the sexual, like prohibiting marriage or intercourse between certain blood relatives, to those regarding murder, the almost universal taboo against killing one's own kind. It is the last two taboos, which reflect the strongest passions and would be most disruptive to the society, that have caused us to erect the greatest restraints. Yet with some activities, like infanticide and abortion, the conflict between social need and moral revulsion has led to a displacement of the taboo from committing the act to talking about it.

In some cases the token taboo becomes a legal restriction. Since Roman times there have been laws against infanticide, and more recently as the illegal practice increased, there have been laws against abortion. Today the tendency is to recognize and legalize abortion, although the Church continues to fight it. The prophets of biblical times inveighed against infanticide, as did the prophets in the Koran. The Code of Hammurabi, some 4,000 years ago, provided that a nurse who allowed a suckling to die in her hands and substituted another would have her breast amputated. Tiberius ordered the death penalty for Carthaginian priests who sacrificed children in the fire to Moloch. The early Christian emperors all passed laws against infanticide, as did Henry II of France, James I of England, and Prussia's Frederick the Great.

The laws, it would seem, have seldom been effective. The needs of society to control its population or its inferiors has been too great.

However, the real taboo, as Devereux, Darwin, and others have implied, has been not so much to forbid the act, but to avoid mentioning it. In fact, until the very recent recognition of child neglect and abuse, there has been a long taboo of silence about the maltreatment of children.

If infanticide and abortion are needed instruments of social policy, why then the silence? The silence, I think, has to do with the fear of confronting what is often a parent's overwhelming feeling—the wish to be rid of Eve's burden.

The physical destruction of a child is the extreme reaction of parents to the stress of having children. We know, especially those of us who are parents, that the strains and obligations of child care call forth in all of us negative as well as positive feelings. There is no way to get around the fact that the existence of children adds another heavy stone to the weight of the parents' struggle for existence.

In the early years, especially, the relation of parents to child is one of sacrifice. The burden of nurturing and caring for the child's needs is one that in most cases falls wholly, directly, and without relief on the parents. Only in socialist societies is there much help from the state.

The interests of children and parents are to some extent antagonistic. The possibility of compensations, the parents' pleasure in and love for the child does not change the primary relationship between the two. One gives and the other takes.

In discussing the burden of child care and the way children interfere with the parents' life, the stress, limitation on sexual expression, sacrifice, and deprivation, Sumner says:

It may well be believed that if procreation had not been put under the dominion of a great passion, it would have been caused to cease by the burdens it entails. Abortion and infanticide . . . show how early in history of civilization the burden of children became so heavy that parents began to shirk it and also . . . show the rise of a population policy which is one of the most important programs of practical expediency which any society can ever adopt.[22]

The maltreatment of children, taboo or not, has throughout history been a frequent instrument of social policy as well as a persistent and terrifying human fantasy, and remains so today.

The fact is, the laws against it have by and large proved futile in the past. We have no reason to expect that the laws against child abuse and neglect will have any greater effect today. As long as poverty and illegitimacy exist, children who become a burden to the parent or a burden to the society are going to be killed, enslaved, harmed, or abused. If we care about helping the children, we will have to take a broader look at children in our society.

2

Children
Are Niggers

We are sitting in the office of Children's Protective Services in a
large suburban county. The building is new and spotless, the
director young and earnest. He says that most of the people they
see are poor and on welfare, but lately they are finding more and
more kids in trouble from families that are well-off. "I'll give you
some examples," he tells me. "We were called recently by the
police who answered a burglar alarm in midafternoon at a very
fancy suburban estate. The two-year-old, who was at home with
her five- and seven-year-old brothers, had tripped the alarm. The
mother was at the decorator's in the city. We sent someone out
to stay with the kids. When the mother got home, she was very
defensive. 'I'm not on welfare,' she said. 'What are you
bothering me for?' But she had a lackadaisical attitude toward
supervision, which we are finding very pervasive.

"Teenagers out here are a gray area. From the preventive
aspect, the judge would prefer to see us involved rather than the
court. It really stuns me as a parent, but some very sophisticated
people don't see the connection between leaving kids alone for
long periods of time and the possibility of acting-out behavior.

"Another family the police alerted us to were a fourteen-year-
old boy and sixteen-year-old girl left alone for weeks while their
parents were in Florida. The parents live in a very fancy section
of town in an eighty-six-thousand-dollar house. It turns out the
girl may have been better off with the parents away. They were
very sadistic with her, locking her in the basement when she
wouldn't behave, things like that. Eventually we got them to
make separate living arrangements for her.

"We don't really provide intensive services. We can't. We investigate reported cases and try to provide coordinated services, but we're trapped between our limited resources and increasing needs. We've just had to gear ourselves to crises; get in, provide some help, get out. We've geared ourselves to that because we have no choices.

"The hospitals here, especially the private hospitals, are very bad. They'll transfer suspected abuse to the county hospital to avoid responsibility.

"Day care here is mostly for working mothers, though a lot more could use it. One of the things we've found effective is our homemaker service. The criteria for need is the disorganized, overwhelmed parent who's having trouble managing kids and a family, or maybe is home due to physical or mental illness. With homemakers we can reduce the number of kids who have to be placed by about half as much. By the time you figure putting three kids in foster care, giving them medical and clothing allowances, you're also saving money. But we're very short on homemakers.

"You know, I'd say the most common problem is the young, immature parent who got married or became pregnant early, and is now overwhelmed. That's the major portion of our case load. Parents who can't manage. Well, the answer to mismanagement should not be removal of the children.

"Then I'd say there's a high percentage of parents who are alcoholics, a small percentage on drugs, and enough that are mentally ill. That's not a major portion of our case load, but it consumes a major portion of our time. The state mental hospital is dreadful. It's a revolving door. Someone's hospitalized, gets poor care, is out soon, is worse after. The hospital assumes that they can care for their kids, but that's a pretty faulty assumption. They go in medicated, come out more so.

"The lack of supervision is especially pressing in the one-parent household. The press of employment, social life, the problem of raising kids alone, and the need for release—it's really tough. That, plus the disappearance of the extended family and the lack of real neighbors. The families we get tend

to be more and more isolated. We had a woman here, divorced, four or five kids, she was going for her degree in social work and working at night. While she worked, her sixteen-year-old had pot parties. But she was admirable in some ways, trying to make it on her own.

"What the courts call chronic neglect is a form of isolation, sticking to oneself. Single parents especially tend to do that. If you lead a more conventional life, it's easier to socialize. Very few single women have friends or parents around. We say, 'How can you leave the kids alone?' They say, 'I have no one. What can I do? Money's a problem. The next time I want to go out, I'll call you and you can come and baby-sit.'"

A SOCIETY's attitude toward children is part of a whole texture of values that may vary greatly from one culture to another, even among neighboring peoples. For example, anthropologist Margaret Mead has described the gentle, nonviolent Arapesh of New Guinea who love and cherish children, while the nearby Mundugumor, a fierce and aggressive people, practice infanticide and treat harshly even those children they allow to survive.[1]

The Arapesh value kindness and affection. Mead notes that their whole culture is oriented toward making things grow, plants and people. Both men and women are affectionate and cherishing and there is little sex-role differentiation. Little boys help to feed and care for their young betrothed wives. Both Arapesh men and women observe the taboos that protect the newborn and are involved equally in child care. The man is given as big a role in conceiving a child as his wife, since many acts of intercourse are considered necessary to build up the baby, which the Arapesh believe is made of a man's semen and a woman's blood.

The Arapesh disapprove of aggressiveness and displays of anger among both sexes and their feelings about children are very much part of their whole life-style.

The neighboring Mundugumor of the Sepik River are quite different. A people who used to practice cannibalism and still practice infanticide, their culture is almost a reverse of Arapesh values. Both male and female Mundugumor are fierce and aggressive. Warm, loving people are not acceptable in the culture. A woman who might pity another's neglected infant enough to breast-feed it would not find another husband if she were widowed.

The Mundugumor, both men and women, dislike and reject children. When children are allowed to survive, those of the opposite sex are favored by adults. Babies of the "wrong" sex are put on a piece of bark and set adrift in the river still alive. The Mundugumor attitude toward children is as much a part of their total culture as the Arapesh attitude is of theirs.

The vulnerability of children is constantly and fiercely exploited by Mundugumor adults. For example, a boy of seven might have to resist his own father if the father wishes to trade a daughter for an extra wife for himself instead of keeping the daughter to exchange for a wife for his boy. Lovemaking among the Mundugumor is accompanied by a lot of scratching and biting, and when babies cry, they are hushed by scratching on their bark cradle.

Mead, who as a young woman lived among and studied both tribes, was struck by the relationship between the harsh cultural style of the Mundugumor and the harshness of individual acts.

American cultural attitudes toward children are much more complex. They derive from a mix of cultures: American black, Caribbean, Puerto Rican, European; from dominant American attitudes toward youth and vitality; from a European tradition that has over the last several hundred years gradually increased the dependency of youth; and finally, a two-class society that discriminates against children in general but still treats poor children far worse than children of the middle class.

In Europe, before the Middle Ages, childhood as a concept did not exist. Children were considered miniature adults. In fact, the idea of children as a special subgroup is a relatively modern invention. In *Centuries of Childhood: A Social History of Family Life*, Philippe Ariès documents the development of the modern concept of childhood as paralleling the development of the bourgeoisie and the nuclear family.[2]

The separation of children from adults began around the 1600s. The transition is evident in the gradual segregation of children from adults and from other children of different ages, and in the gradual differentiation of children's clothing.

In the seventeenth century, girls went from swaddling clothes right into adult female dress. They did not go to school and at nine or ten they were supposed to act like little ladies. After puberty, and often as early as ten or twelve, they were married, usually to older men.

The class basis of childhood shows clearly in the costumes. Both girls and working-class boys were not differentiated by distinctive dress. As adults, lower-class males would still be servile to upper-class men. No initiation into freedom was necessary. For the same reason, girls did not have to go through costume changes. There was nothing to grow up to. Children were always children relative to the ruling class. While boys of the middle and upper classes temporarily shared the status of women and the working class, they gradually were elevated out. Women and boys stayed there. It's no coincidence that the effeminization of little-boys' dress was abolished at the beginning of this century, the same time that the feminists agitated for an end to oppressive women's clothes.

The class basis of the emerging concept of childhood was also clear in the system of childhood education that institutionalized it. At first only clerics and scholars went to school. Gradually school became the normal instrument of social initiation in the progress from childhood to manhood, as education for the middle class was redefined. Girls and working-class boys did not go to school for many centuries.

The priesthood, particularly the Jesuits and Jansenists, were the schoolteachers of the seventeenth century, and they emphasized discipline. Discipline thus became the keynote to modern schooling, much more important than imparting information; it was an instrument of moral and spiritual improvement. The schools adopted repression as a spiritual value and it remains so to this day.

The tendency in the new schooling was to effectively segre-

gate children from the adult world for longer and longer periods
of time, postponing the transition to adulthood and inevitably
underestimating the abilities of a child.

Strange as it seems when you first think about it, we expect
less from and for children today than people did in the Middle
Ages. Precocious children used to be fairly common. Now they
are a rare phenomenon. Today we can hardly believe in
Mozart's accomplishments, both as a writer and performer,
when he was a child. Yet many children, not only Mozart and
Haydn, played and wrote music seriously. Today we're likely to
give children the obligatory, routine, and watered-down music
and dancing lessons, about as superficial as the traditional
womanly accomplishments that were taught young girls in the
nineteenth century.

As an example of what was once expected from children, Ariès
quotes from the *Journal of the Childhood of Louis XIII*, kept
by the young Louis's doctor, Heroard.[3] The Dauphin, who was
born in 1601, was definitely not a superior child. He was, as a
matter of fact, of only average intelligence. Yet at the age of
seventeen months, he played the violin, mall, which was the
equivalent of golf, tennis, and he talked and played games of
military strategy. From three to four, he learned how to read
and write. At four and five he practiced archery, played cards,
and played chess at six. He was allowed to play with his dolls
until he was seven, when his education under male tutors began
and he started to wear adult male clothing.

After the eighteenth century, a rigid separation and distinction of ages took place in schools and children were no longer
able to learn from even older children. They were restricted in
most of their waking hours to chronological peer groups, with
little opportunity to learn from adults. It is no wonder the
child's development was retarded rather than enhanced by
modern schooling.

The development of the modern family meant the breakdown
of a large, integrated society into small, self-centered units. The
child now became important. It was the product of the unit and
the reason for its maintenance and continuance. It became

desirable to keep children at home as long as possible to bind them psychologically and emotionally to the family until they were ready to create a new one.

Adolescence, the "teens," are further ways of defining children as different not just in age but kind. Whole ideologies have developed around it, as well as special costumes and a ban on sexuality, which was once freely expressed.[4]

Within the family, the philosopher Engels observed, the husband is the bourgeois. The wife and children are the proletarians. In fact, the modern attributes of childhood are those of most degraded classes. Children are said to like to work with their hands, to be happy, carefree and good-natured, to be more in touch with their emotions and with reality, to be lucky to be spared the responsibilities of adulthood. The same qualities are attributed to women, to blacks, to whomever the society is interested in keeping down. Relations between them and the ruling class are usually marked by fear and frequently dishonesty, and certainly by inequality and a lesser legal status.

Like women, children have been increasingly romanticized, set apart by nonfunctional clothing, and kept strictly in their place. "Children should be seen and not heard" until recently reflected society's opinion of women as well.

Just as the pseudoemancipation of women in the Victorian era was sabotaged by consumerism, in America, particularly, the same thing has happened to children. Although some superficial distinctions like clothing have been eliminated, the myth of childhood still flourishes. Whole industries have been built on the manufacture of special toys and games, baby foods, books and comic books. Television and movies cater to them. There is a special literature for children and endless books instructing the lay mother in the fine art of child care. There are special doctors for children, as there are for women. There is a new psychology of the child. The development of children's products is like the development of the cosmetics industry, the women's magazines (heir to the nineteenth-century novel), women's TV programs, and now a whole psychology enumerating the ways in which women are different from men.

Advertisers encourage parents to give children those things that will make their childhood a golden age. Since all of us who are grown up have been children, we know that childhood is not a romantic time, yet the myth still persists.

America has inherited much of that European culture that, in the last several hundred years, has reinforced the natural physical inequality of children. In addition, in America, the child-welfare movement has reinforced the child's legal inequality. Children are minors, have no civil rights, and are the property of arbitrarily chosen parents. Yet when society moves in to protect them, it does not increase their freedom, but rather their bondage, by placing them in custodial situations where they are often worse off.

Our society treats all children like a lower class, but the differences among the lives of children of different economic classes is particularly striking. In the nineteenth century, middle- and upper-class children were safe in some dull schoolhouse studying Homer, while the children of the poor were laboring in the mills. Similarly, today middle-class children are suffocated with consumer goods and the newest in education while poor children are still exploited on a class basis—in migrant labor camps, in custodial institutions, in juvenile courts, in public schools, in most institutions that process or socialize children today.

Although there are as many cultural attitudes toward children in America as there are cultures, inevitably these attitudes become homogenized by institutions like the schools and by dominant cultural expectations as reflected in the media—movies, the press, and the ever present TV. Although immigrants or migrants have had different values that they have tried to preserve—like the Chinese with their tight families and communities, or like the American Indians before they drifted to the cities, or like any other number of different nationalities with fixed patterns of family relationship, child rearing, and cultural values—it has been hard to preserve them in the face of the dominant mores.

It used to be a commonplace that Chinese children were

never in trouble with the law due to the close discipline of the family. That is much less true today. The pride of many ethnic groups, along with their patterns of culture, tend to go down the American drain as they are infected with American ideals of success and consumerism and the desire to conform and be accepted by the majority.

The dominant American values, reflecting a combination of our Puritan and pioneer heritage, are a mixture of success, with an inordinate emphasis on winning. "Winning isn't everything," said America's hero, football coach Vince Lombardi, "it's the only thing." Vitality, strength, aggressiveness, productivity, self-reliance, individualism, and energy are also highly valued along with the traditional emphasis on hard work. We follow the Puritan ideal, "By your works shall ye know them." Also by their products. A man's wealth is a sign of God's grace, according to traditional Protestantism. If people are poor, so the American credo goes, it's their fault.

We worship energy, strength, good looks, potential, all of which we attribute to the young. In America it is a positive value to be young. The craze to keep in shape (the young shape), the recent popularity of cosmetic surgery among rich middle-aged women afraid to look their age, the imitation of youthful styles in dress and music are all part of the cult of youth.

In addition, the myth of America has always been the myth of the chance to do better. The European immigrant saw not only a golden land, where the streets were paved with gold, but a place where his children could have the success he never had. "My son, the doctor" is not only a Jewish badge of pride. A typical parental desire, particularly among middle-class children of immigrants, is to give their children all that they couldn't have.

At the same time, whatever respect for age minority cultures once had has evaporated in America, along with the inevitable dispersal of family clans. In a society where everything depends on what you can spend, and what you can spend depends on what you can bring in, the aged have no cash value.

The old in America are simply a maintenance problem. In a

society that manufactures obsolescence and where everyone wants the latest model, a machine that has stopped working has no inherent value. It is ready for the scrap heap. Everything is replaceable, people as well as parts. The things we want are new, young, shiny, and bright.

At the same time, perhaps because we have given them so much, and because aging is inevitable, we are jealous of our children's youth and of their inevitable tyranny over us. The youth revolution of the 1960s was a real watershed. The reaction of youth in the last decade was in part a rejection of their parents' middle-class values, a reexamination of America's domestic and foreign policy, and an attempt to integrate the values of other cultures into American life.

"Don't trust anyone over thirty," the kids said. They rejected the middle-class liberalism, the consumerism, the emphasis on rewards and success, the "nine-to-five-ism," the job syndrome, the straight, uptight suit and tie, skirt and stockings, heterosexuality, marriage, the family, the whole thing. And in peculiarly American fashion, they emphasized their disdain for age.

Part of their revolt was political, part cultural. For their political pains, we treated them as we were accustomed to treat native uprisings. In New York, Berkeley, Chicago, we gassed them, clubbed them, arrested them. Finally at Kent State we shot them.

Of course we had been treating black people and poor people in this country that way for a long time. A hippie, writing in an underground newspaper in 1967 about the way children are treated in this society, titled his article "Children Are Niggers," pointing up the class basis of the discrimination. Perhaps we discriminate against blacks and children for the same reasons: fear and envy, anger at their rejection of our generosity, denial of our negative feelings about them, envy of their open sexuality, weariness with the burden of past care.

Some people have explained the youth revolution of the 1960s as the first sign of a postindustrial society. Unlike the sixteenth, seventeenth, and eighteenth centuries when the labor of poor youth was used to build the beginnings of capitalist industry, in the sixties they had become a positive glut on a labor market that could not even find menial jobs for all its adults. We finally had a generation of youth who did not need to go to work, who rejected work, and for whom, in fact, there was no work anyway. The revolt of the sons is never accepted happily by the fathers. We did not accept our children's rebellion.

The youth revolt of the late 1960s was primarily a confrontation of white, middle-class youth with their society. Much of the movement's energy dissipated as the promise of a new permissiveness in life-style and political action—a reaction to this country's materialism and imperialistic policies—was replaced by the Nixonian seventies. By and large we've seen a return to the work ethic, to the patriotic and puritanical, although the Watergate debacle may have thrown all this in doubt. Watergate proved that the kids were right—the democratic product was not only falsely labeled and packaged, it was shoddy at the core. The phony patriotism, the rhetoric of law and order were just a cover for a group of men, headed by the President, whose lust for power led them to try to undermine the democratic system, flaunting in our faces all our constitutional safeguards, the President even enriching himself at the taxpayers' expense.

Worst of all, they reversed the whole direction of the society which had, under Kennedy and Johnson, been bending in the direction of America's other society: the poor and excluded. Much of the pressure to include poor people was part of another revolt in the 1960s, the civil-rights movement, whose half-gotten gains made a permanent impact on black youth.

Like the hippies, the civil-rights movement had questioned, publicly and openly, the legitimacy of a system that did not live up to its own professed ideals, that denied equal rights for black people, and that, by denying them dignified employment, kept them menial and poor. The black children of the sixties heard the lesson, and suddenly, after centuries of playing Uncle Tom, were told not to knuckle under, but to define their rights in a new way. One of the results has been the increasing willingness of blacks to take their chances outside the system. A combination of the civil-rights movement, the rhetoric of black power,

and the devastating effect in the big cities of black unemployment, broken homes, and kids adrift in the streets has been the
open, hostile, and violent rejection of so-called American values
by black youth. Black children have increasingly refused to be
"niggerized" by institutions that have been neglecting and
abusing them for so long. The result has been increasing
violence among children in our big cities, increasing at a greater
rate than violence among adults.[5]

Although politicians, social workers, the media, even congres-
sional committees are railing at parental abuse of children, in
fact it is our institutions—our schools, our legal system, our
welfare system, our unemployment system, even our child-
custodial system—that have most neglected and abused our
children.

It is hardly news that of all those failing American institutions, our schools lead all the rest. In large urban centers where
the public-school population is predominantly black and poor or
Puerto Rican and poor, the schools are consistently turning out
children who can't read.[6] In the long argument between nature
and nurture, those who find that the fault lies with the child's
family talk the loudest.

Among others, Kenneth Clark, educator and member of the
New York State Board of Regents, has long held that blaming
the schools' failure on the family is double-talk. According to
Clark, the fault lies with "teachers who don't teach, unions that
block reforms, and an educational establishment indifferent to
the fate of poor black and Hispanic children [who are] regarded
as sub-human and non-educable." [7]

The very fact that after decades of effort we still have not
found an effective way to teach poor children to read suggests
that it is not of very high priority. Is it possible that a society
that can mount the effort to develop an atom bomb or put a
man on the moon cannot teach its citizens to read, while Cuba
and China can?

The fact is that in cities like New York, a 35 percent truancy
rate in the public schools is not considered unusual. The fact is
that in times of budget cuts, the specialist is fired first. In the

1972–73 school year, while the school budget went up $200 million, virtually all the money went to mandated raises, pension and welfare costs. The *New York Post*'s education editor, Bernard Bard, has observed that "the school system operates to protect the economic self-interests of teachers and supervisors as a first priority." [8]

All big-city schools, faced with increasing numbers of black and Hispanic children, have similar problems. Figures for New York public schools tell a national story.

In March 1973, the New York City Board of Education figures showed that 66.3 percent of the city's elementary pupils and 71.3 percent of the junior-high- and intermediate-school pupils were reading below grade level. Not surprisingly, the situation was worse in schools with poor children; while schools in predominantly white neighborhoods, with pupils from middle-class and well-to-do families, were reading above grade level.

In the fall of 1973, the Fleischmann Commission, appointed by Governor Rockefeller to investigate New York State schools, reported that the city schools were a "dual system" in which white children learned to read above national norms and most black and Hispanic children came out virtually illiterate. The chances in New York State, according to the Fleischmann Commission, are four-to-one against a ninth-grader obtaining an academic diploma—the ticket to college and a decent job—and four-to-ten that they won't graduate high school with any diploma at all.

It appears to be no different in California, where the mother of a recent high-school graduate sued the state because after twelve years in California public schools, her son did not know how to read.

According to a 1974 study made by the New York State Office of Education, if Johnny can't read, it's because no one is trying to teach him, not because he is black, Spanish, and/or poor. [9] A study of two elementary schools with largely black and Hispanic enrollments showed that the more successful school had identified reading as a significant school problem, had adopted a plan to deal with it, and had implemented the plan throughout the school.

The director of the office, Daniel Klepak, told *The New York Times* that he hoped the findings would "shake up those people who keep pointing to non-school factors as a justification for the failure of inner city children to read." [10] Klepak noted that although nonschool factors like poverty and family structure had some relevance, the study found that school factors could be much more significant than generally acknowledged.

The "better" school in the New York study was 98 percent black and Hispanic in enrollment, with a median family income of $7,800, and 99 percent of the students eligible, because of poverty, for free lunch. The other school had a similar enrollment.

Poor children are not only "niggerized" in a two-class school system, they are also most likely to be punished physically. Surprisingly, although parents can be charged with child abuse for hitting their children, corporal punishment is more often than not condoned in our public schools. There are no accurate figures on how many states actually allow it. In the past thirteen years, however, eight states have passed laws allowing corporal punishment, and the practice is prevalent in many states where it is not necessarily legal. For instance, in Dallas, Texas, although it is a violation of school policy for a child to be struck without parental permission, they are, and often. *Time*, in an article on corporal punishment, quoted one Dallas school superintendent as saying he would not be school superintendent in a district where the principals were not allowed to punish children physically.[11]

According to *Time*, Dallas school officials said over 5,000 cases of corporal punishment were reported to them in 1972. In one case a black student came back after school for a drink of water, ignoring a teacher who tried to stop him. The boy was struck so hard he was knocked unconscious. Another black student was hit more than a dozen times by his coach for being late to gym class and failing to bring sneakers, among other misdemeanors. School officials estimated that the next year there might be 20,000 cases, "partly because of troubles stemming from the schools' newly achieved integration."

A lawsuit brought on behalf of the parents of the two students mentioned, plus others, tried merely to limit punishment to cases where parents give approval. It was lost in the circuit court.

The Boston School Board says it forbids corporal punishment, which is illegal in Massachusetts, but some people say the cruel and sadistic use of "rattaning"—hitting with a rattan cane—still continues.

According to Gallup polls, both parents and teachers in this country seem as a majority to favor corporal punishment. Many state laws not only permit the use of corporal punishment in the schools but prohibit local school boards from banning it. Gallup polls have showed that 62 percent of parents believe in "modest" use of corporal punishment and 65 percent of elementary teachers agree.[12]

It is hard to see how beating, caning, paddling, and rattaning teach anything but the idea that it's all right for adults to beat up people who are smaller and more defenseless.

It is important to look at corporal punishment in the schools for what it really is: first, an officially sanctioned use of violence against the young and defenseless; second, another way of institutionalizing class distinctions. Its purpose is to maintain the submissiveness and demonstrate the inferiority of the person punished. There are always exceptions for the upper class.

As E. L. Doctorow points out in *The Book of Daniel*, a novel about the Rosenberg case, all class distinctions are maintained by some kind of corporal punishment or the threat of physical intimidation. The authoritarian head of a society gets his power from the upper class or from a privileged bureaucracy that supports his government and divides its rewards. The support of the people is maintained only by constant physical intimidation or the threat of it. Societies that endure have complex systems of intimidation, either physical or economic. That is why Marx described the role of the working class under capitalism as slavery. Slavery defines the condition of absolute submissiveness to corporal punishment. When challenged, however, the ruling classes state their case for the right of corporal punishment in the name of law and order. The crime of a poor person is never against another human being but always against law and order.[13]

Our use of corporal punishment in the schools is just another example of culturally sanctioned violence. Our TV programs show it, our movies show it, our crime rate shows it, the fear of people rich and poor in our big cities shows it. Our violence is familial, racial, and generational. We have become casually accepting of it. And we have institutionalized it. The ease with which we pass from hard words to hard fists is extraordinary. And as crime statistics show, our children, who are exposed to it from infancy, have become increasingly violent. Violence, conquest, submission, exploitation are part of the history of America. It seems we believe in it. We just don't like it to get out of our hands.

Our legal system also discriminates against children, particularly poor children. Simply on the basis of its fee structure, the legal system has to discriminate against the poor. Even assuming that all other things were equal, there are simply not enough lawyers to go around. *The New York Times* noted that in most large cities in America, legal services for indigents are so inadequate that a person may have to wait years just for an appointment to see a lawyer about a divorce.[14]

The family court system, which has now replaced the old juvenile courts in most states, and to which go all matters regarding children in trouble with the law, family matters such as support, child abuse and neglect, is in most states in an incredible condition of disrepair. Although the family court will be dealt with in a separate chapter, as will the physical abuse of children in state custody, a few examples of the courts' harm to children may be mentioned here. To begin with, the family court's mandate is to help and rehabilitate, not to judge, the young—a function it is almost totally incapable of fulfilling. While there are of course bad people in the system, much of the time people are doing their best; but the system cannot help anyone. Mothers who do not understand the consequences may take children who are giving them trouble to court, hoping to get some help. As one middle-aged black woman told a family court social worker, "My son's going to do something terrible if he doesn't get some help." The accumulated evidence is that he will.

There is little, however, the courts have been able to do. Most people in the family court system acknowledge that court practices discriminate against the most seriously disturbed, deprived, and disorganized children, primarily black and Puerto Rican. In most cities services are not provided for children most in need, and racism—conscious or unconscious—pervades the child-care system. That in fact was the conclusion of a report on juvenile justice issued in 1973 by seven judges of the New York family court.[15]

A series of stories in The Washington Post in 1973 shows that things are much the same in Maryland. Headlined "JUVENILE FACILITIES FAIL TO REFORM LIVES," the Post noted that "nearly two out of every five children who are released from Maryland's juvenile institutions will be sent back by court order for more 'training and rehabilitation.' " The children, institutionalized under appalling conditions, had a 40 percent recidivism record. The article observed that they were among the most troubled, most disturbed, slowest, and most delinquent of the state's children, yet it also noted that state employees who spend the most time dealing with children and rehabilitating them are the least trained. The institutions in Maryland are so overcrowded that when new charges are sent there, they simply make room by releasing an equal number of inmates. Most children there have never even had a thorough psychiatric test, let alone treatment.[16]

According to Ronald J. Blake, an assistant director of Maryland's Department of Juvenile Services, while many of the children institutionalized have low IQs, most of the children who end up in institutions are the children of the poor, of families on welfare. In his opinion the scores often show a lack of incentive rather than ability. To prove his case, he pointed to one girl whom three psychologists had diagnosed as retarded. After she left the training school, she was found to have above-average intelligence, and she later went to college.[17]

It is almost universally acknowledged that what children need are families, not institutions, yet neither the states nor the federal government have any policy that would help families stay together.

The director of Colmar Manor, a group home for children, noted that in many instances a case could be made against the state for contributing to the delinquency of minors by keeping them in juvenile institutions. Many children whom the states remove from their homes for reasons ranging from parental neglect to juvenile delinquency are often placed in institutions where conditions are so injurious or inadequate that they violate the Eighth Amendment ban on cruel and unusual punishment. Moreover, despite the court's mandate to rehabilitate, the law nowhere makes it mandatory to treat children who are incarcerated in order to be helped. As one New York family court judge puts it, most of the American juvenile justice system does not "meet ordinary standards of human decency."

The law also discriminates against the young by allowing them fewer constitutional safeguards. Because juvenile law is supposed to ask whether a child is in need of rehabilitation, laws governing minors are more flexible. Thus children can be punished for offenses that would not be offenses for adults.

In addition, some family court social workers who have seen lawyers "get the kids off" complain that children are damned whatever happens: they will not be rehabilitated in a custodial institution, but their respect for the law, should they have any to begin with, disappears along with the lawyer's cavalier promise, "Don't worry, kid, we'll get you off."

One social worker quotes the mother of a very savvy fifteen-year-old who had been picked up for prostitution. "That lawyer don't have any respect for the law himself," the mother said. "He thinks he's helping her by sending her back to the street. I don't think he is, but I've lost control." The mother, says the social worker, was right: "The lawyer thinks if you just leave the kids to their own devices, they'll work it out. But most of them won't."

A child found guilty of a crime, no matter how petty, is adjudicated a juvenile delinquent, and may be committed to an institution for the remainder of his childhood and adolescent years. For example, in Connecticut, in a school dispute a couple of years ago, forty-five children and a number of adults were arrested for picketing a local public school. According to the law, the children could have gotten sentences from six to fourteen years. The maximum penalty for adults for the same "crime" was a $500 fine or six months in jail.[18]

What guides family courts in treating children is ostensibly their need for "protection" and special treatment, on the theory that kids who are in trouble are different from adult criminals. Family courts have tried to establish flexible standards by which judges and probation officers could act in the "best interests of the child," the supposed touchstone for child-welfare determinations. In practice, the sentiments of protectionism have resulted in a juvenile justice system that lacks special constitutional standards and has become arbitrary, impersonal, and punitive.

In the adjudicatory phase, children are treated much like adults. But what about afterward? Whereas adults are fined or given limited jail sentences, children are sentenced for "treatment or rehabilitation"—a euphemism for commitment to institutions that are at best custodial and at worst brutalizing. No law gives them the right to adequate response. There is no need to justify the incarceration of a neglected or troubled child.

In addition, girls, particularly adolescent girls, are treated to a special kind of discrimination. Under the guise of protection from a long list of evils, girls can be treated for longer than boys for acts that would not be considered criminal if committed by adults. For instance, in many states a "peace officer" may return to his parent any male under sixteen or female under eighteen who has run away. Young people in this age group who don't go to school or are "incorrigible, ungovernable, or habitually disobedient" [19] may wind up in family court and removed from their homes. With girls, the social misconduct is primarily sexual. Although more than half the girls referred to family court in 1965 were referred for conduct that would not be criminal if committed by adults, only one-fifth of the boys were so referred, yet there were more girls in institutions.[20]

One way of caring for children outside the home is to place them in foster care. Foster care, of course, is primarily utilized for the poor. And placement, frequently by voluntary agencies, is improperly supervised by city or state. Most people understand that moving small children about from one home to another is bad for them, making it harder for children to form attachments and develop a sense of trust. Yet a study of some 6,000 placements in foster care in Massachusetts showed that a fourth of the children had been in three or more homes, that only 25 percent were ever returned to their own homes, and that the agency had no plan for two-thirds of the children they placed other than continued placement.[21]

In Massachusetts and elsewhere, studies of foster care show that once a child is in care beyond one and a half years, his chances of being adopted or returned to his own home diminish radically. In Massachusetts, the department did not have the personnel to develop a tracking system to see if the child had contact with his parents, so the law could not release them for adoption. The Massachusetts study further showed that children were not freed for adoption because of bureaucratic reasons having nothing to do with the individual cases. The Massachusetts study speculated that if 16 percent had had preventive or other casework services, they could have remained in their own homes. Of those placed, probably three-fourths might have been adopted if the state had a subsidized adoption program. Caseworkers, however, were unable to rate foster-care homes in more than 10 percent of the cases because they never visited them. Worst of all, 40 percent of those children placed in foster care had been disabled in some way, in use of limbs, hearing, or speech, or were convulsives, and almost one-fifth of those had never been evaluated for treatment, much less treated.

The parents interviewed in the study said they placed children in foster care because options like homemakers and day care were not available. More than one-fourth did not see their child while in placement and almost 20 percent said they were prohibited from seeing the child by the social worker. Of the eighty-four children who were handicapped, only one-fourth of their foster parents knew about the handicap in advance.

The foster-care system in other states is not substantially better and is often worse. Most public agencies lack the personnel to do their job properly. A state that removes children from their own homes, warehouses them in institutions or in foster care, and then forgets them is both abusing and neglecting them. Despite what poverty agencies may plead, it is hard to avoid the conclusion that the children have no priority. They are neglected as a matter of social policy, even if that policy is due to lack of resources.

It is clear that children who are discriminated against this way are not going to grow up to be happy, healthy, creative individuals. At best they may make it through life giving little trouble or joy to themselves and others. At the worst, they will be unloved children growing up to be unloved and unloving parents. Those who have been labeled by society as "bad" will no doubt continue to prove themselves so. Most studies give that indication. In this violent age, they may even turn to violence as did the children in Chapter 9, doing damage to both themselves and society.

The saddest thing about many of these children is that they have never had a chance and probably never will. The New York State Assembly Committee on Child Abuse, which in 1973 passed a law setting up a central registry for abuse and neglect, has recently completed a proposal on the "feasibility of studying the relationship between child abuse and later socially deviant behavior." There is every expectation that the connection can be proved. To label abused children as potential deviants and then follow them to see if they turn out bad seems the grossest kind of social injustice.

Many if not most of the children described in this chapter who have been discriminated against and maltreated by society have done nothing wrong. They merely suffer the bad fortune of having been born to poor parents who will not treat them by the same standards middle-class parents deem correct. In addition, because they are poor, they will be discriminated against in most of our democratic institutions. From the 1800s on, we have been taking children away from "deprived" and "depraved" homes on the grounds that we are helping them, and then throwing them in the social wastebin.

The early colonists had mixed feelings about the orphaned poor, feelings of obligation that took second place to a stronger wish to spare themselves the costs. Orphans were often auctioned to the lowest bidder—whomever would care for the child at least expense to the town treasury. Children were chattel in America as they have been throughout history.

Americans have placed a special value on children, though, glorifying youth as a personification of the country, condemning them when they have rebelled and shown ingratitude. Reacting against some of our most cherished values, it was the children of the middle class who turned to violence in the 1960s, followed increasingly by the poor and the black.

3

Relief and Rehabilitation

Tom Annunzia is a social worker, dark-haired, thin, chain-smoking, intense. We are sitting in the office of the shelter he runs for abused children and their mothers, a shelter connected with a large Catholic hospital in a large midwestern city. On his desk are several gold-framed pictures of his children, studio portrait poses, and a picture of his wife. There is nothing else to look at in his office and he frequently turns around to look out the window at a neighboring housing project and a slum.

"All our patients are referred through protective services usually via juvenile court.* I would say it's 'voluntary' if you put the 'voluntary' in quotes. Many people don't realize what it's all about and are very upset when they get here. It's part a treatment program, part protective. The mother may not really know that. In some cases we work with the mother for placement.

"Mothers must be on welfare and they must be sixteen or over with only one child, though most are young, I'd say under eighteen. They have to be reported as an abusing or neglecting mother. They can't be addicts but they can be ex-addicts if they're enrolled in a drug program. They can't be psychotic.

"We keep them here three months to do a nine-month follow-up. Outpatients have to come in here twice a week. Their social worker visits them three times a week. We have eleven outpatients now.

"We've been bombarded with requests and we have a long

---

* The juvenile court was reorganized and in some states renamed family court.

waiting list, but we try to be very selective about which people we take. For instance, we don't take people whose problems are mainly ones of housing. Unfortunately, seventy-five percent of the people referred to us—people we have to turn down—have housing problems. In fact, most of the mothers we accept have housing problems, too. The problem is lousy housing. Run-down, rats, lousy wiring, lousy plumbing. We feel it's important to relocate them. But let's face it, it's difficult. They don't have much choice.

"Essentially our program is based on the Denver model. The idea is to provide abusing mothers with a strong mothering figure. They call them surrogate mothers, someone to provide lots of support, counseling, and help.

"But our people are quite different from the people they see in Denver. They are not dealing with people from the ghetto. We are. And the people who make up our population are not families, most of them. They're mothers and kids.

"We take eight mothers at a time as inpatients and keep two units open for emergencies. The mothers live here three months. They get intensive psychotherapy, both group and individual, and social services. We use paraprofessionals a lot to help them with employment, day care, finding new apartments. Most of all we have to teach them how to take care of babies. In fact, we have to teach them everything. We give them a course in consumer education. That's a fancy term for showing them how to make out a food budget. Initially it's a big problem. Someone goes to the supermarket with them to teach them how to shop on a welfare budget.

"We really prefer the resident program for treatment. With an outpatient, you can't see what's going on. Does she get mad when the baby cries? How does she hold the baby?

"The effectiveness of our program depends a lot on the trust the girls have established with the social worker and whether or not they'll contact her later, after they leave here. We look at whether or not they've learned how to take care of the baby. Do they make supper? Do they seek help when they're uptight? Do they try to get control of their impulses?

"A lot of girls deny there's been abuse. We insist on their recognizing it. Often it's the father who's the abuser. If the mother goes along with it, we feel there's a real problem. We had one case where the girl's husband, who was not the father, beat up the kid. The goal was to make her see it, then do something.

"There are girls here, young ones, whose children were fathered by different men, or they're living with a man who's not the child's father. That can cause problems.

"The program costs about eight thousand dollars per mother and child per year. But with the right kind of preventive action many things could be done cheaply before people get to this stage. For instance, we see a lot of malnutrition in kids, and much of it is caused by ignorance. This could be avoided if women could get help with family planning, if they could have a visiting nurse, if someone could teach them cooking. But no one really wants to take on the population we deal with.

"Some of these girls live in the most incredible housing and they stay in the house all day. We say, 'Why don't you go out?' And they say, 'Are you kidding? In that neighborhood?' "

Annunzia has been in social work for a long time. His last job was with a foster-care agency in the suburbs. He is, he says, very disappointed with foster care. "So many kids move from one family to another. When they reach preadolescence, they may be difficult. People have trouble dealing with their own preadolescents. They feel, 'Why deal with someone else's?'

"Also, in my experience, many people become foster parents because they've moved to the suburbs and gotten in over their heads; then they find foster care the way out. Not that foster parents shouldn't be paid. But if that's the only reason they become foster parents, it's a bad one. I'd prefer subsidized adoption.

"Of course, there is plenty of child abuse in the suburbs. I've seen women who have a lot of potential for trouble. They're alone all day. They're used to being in the city. They get 'cabin fever.' They get marital problems. Inevitably they take it out on the kids. The place to deal with local problems is locally."

Looking out the window again, Tom says, "There are lots of people out there who beat the hell out of their kids. No one knows about them. One thing that worries me is the history of abuse. Patterns of two or three generations would suggest it's on the upswing. We need more light on the problem; more programs. Henry Kempe who works with the Denver program has demonstrated things can be done. People are beginning to panic. Society has begun to realize it must do something. The old solution was to lock parents up.

"Income maintenance? I don't know if that's a solution. Isn't that socialism?"

CHILDREN are the most fragile members of a culture, the ones most affected by troubles in the family or upheavals in society. Americans today are experiencing a period of rapidly accelerating social disorganization caused by the breakdown in the family and the deterioration of our cities, but especially by economic fluctuations that have put large numbers of people out of work and on relief. And the children are showing it. For example, national figures show Aid to Families with Dependent Children, which rose by 17 percent or 110,000 families during the 1950s, skyrocketed by 107 percent or 800,000 families from December 1960 to February 1969.[1]

In the five biggest cities, the percent of increase was even greater. In New York, Philadelphia, Chicago, Detroit, and Los Angeles the rise was 217 percent, although the number of people on relief was increasing everywhere.

Unemployed parents have a hard time caring for their families. Figures vary from state to state, but in 1969 the average relief payment per month for a family of four was $60. In New Jersey it was $347.[2] Reflecting the influence of the English poor laws, relief is set at below-market wage levels in order to discourage the greedy and to lower wages generally.

In addition to the obvious hardship, like not having enough to eat and having to live in appalling housing, being out of work has certain emotional consequences. It infects the mood of the entire household. It leads to anger and despair. Frequently a father's unemployment causes the rapid breakdown of the marriage, a rupture in the relationship of parent and child, and the eventual dissolution of the family. When large numbers of people are involved, eventually the workings of society itself are affected. Inevitably, large numbers of children are left adrift, with parents unable or unwilling to care for them. Since the 1900s, increasing numbers of social workers, parole officers, juvenile courts, and penal institutions have been trying to deal with the consequences. Year by year, the growing numbers have overwhelmed the system. Assuming the system could function, there are not enough people to pick up all the pieces.

It's not just poor people whose families are falling apart. Divorce rates everywhere are soaring. Today four out of every ten marriages will end in divorce, on the average after seven years of marriage.[3]

Between 1960 and 1970, the number of female-headed families increased by 24 percent. Today one in nine families is headed by a woman and one out of every six children in the United States or one out of every five under eighteen lives with only one parent. But the number of single-parent families has increased disproportionately among the poor and black where their negative effects are greatest. In 1973, 10 percent of white families were headed by women, but among black families the figure was 35 percent.[4]

Even in good years, employment has become harder to find for blacks. Take 1963, which was a good year for most Americans. Despite that, 29.2 percent of all black males in the labor force were out of work at some time during that year.[5] The effects on the black family are inescapable. As sociologists have pointed out, men who are chronically unemployed or who work for very low wages will mate like other men but they are not so likely to either marry or sustain a stable relationship with women and children. Largely because of this, the proportion of black, female-headed families grew from 19 percent in 1949 to 27 percent in 1968 to 35 percent in 1973.[6]

Many of these women have a desperate time keeping their families together. Despite the women's-rights movement and equal-employment legislation, a working woman with a high-school education earns approximately 56 percent of the salary earned by a man with the same qualifications.[7] If she's black, she not only earns less than that, but she—and her children—must contend with the additional burdens of being black.

It is common knowledge, documented statistically and in ghettoes throughout the United States, that with unemployment go high crime rates, alcoholism, addiction, and family breakdown, as well as high rates of infant mortality, poor physical and mental health, malnutrition, bad schools, and eventually children in trouble with society and the law. It is therefore no surprise that the single most common factor among families reported for child abuse and for neglect is an unemployed father.

When the father is out of work and his family is living on relief, the result is unhappily predictable. And when there is no father and the mother is the head of a family on relief, it is often worse—as she is usually young, unskilled, unable to get job training for herself, unable to get a job once trained, unable to escape from the stressful conditions of her life. There may be plenty of wealthy and middle-class families who abuse and neglect their children, as the experts insist. And they undoubtedly need help as most families do today (see Chapter 11). But the abused and neglected children of wealthy and middle-class parents are not as badly off as the children whose family's economic situation has put them at the bottom of the social heap.

Dr. Arthur Green, a psychoanalyst who has worked with abused children and their families, acknowledges that the abused children of the poor suffer more. Examining the psychological effects of both neglect and abuse on children, Dr. Green says that "physical abuse occurring in the relative absence of neglect, poverty, and family disorganization would probably affect ego functions and behavior quite differently." One difference would be the degree of self-worth and self-esteem. With comfort, status, and employment—at least in this country —goes self-esteem.

The social and family disruption—with its effect on our
children—is much like the period of mass civil and economic
disturbance that erupted in Europe at the beginning of the
sixteenth century and lasted for several centuries during that
long and painful transition from feudalism to capitalism. As
Frances Fox Piven and Richard A. Cloward point out in their
book *Regulating the Poor*, Western relief systems originated in
the sixteenth century in government's attempt to deal with
disorder. The disorder was caused by declining death rates,
increasing population, the growth of industrialism, and the
beginning of land foreclosure, all of which threw large numbers
of people out of work. Describing the effect of mass unemployment, Piven and Cloward say:

> The regulation of civil behavior in all societies is intimately
> dependent on stable occupational arrangements. So long as
> people are fixed in their work roles, their activities and
> outlooks are also fixed. . . . But mass unemployment breaks
> that bond, loosening people from the main institution by
> which they are regulated and controlled.
>
> Moreover, mass unemployment that persists for any length
> of time diminishes the capacity of other institutions to bind
> and constrain people. Occupational behaviors and outlooks
> underpin a way of life and determine familial, cultural
> patterns. When large numbers of people are suddenly barred
> from their traditional occupations, the entire structure of
> social control is weakened and may even collapse . . . without
> work, people cannot conform to familial and communal roles;
> and if the dislocation is widespread, the legitimacy of the
> social order itself may come to be questioned. . . . To restore
> order, the society must create the means to reassert its
> authority.[8]

Children were eventually the most victimized by the series of
events beginning around 1500, which threw people out of jobs
and led to riots, large-scale vagrancy and begging, looting, and
bands of child robbers—what today we would call "crime in the
streets." The principal punishment, euphemistically named

"work relief," forced pauper children on relief to labor first at home, then in the public workhouses, and finally in the 1800s under conditions of semislavery in the English textile mills. Their counterparts in the United States today are the children, grandchildren, and great-grandchildren of people who came here—some brought in chains and slavery, some migrating here from other countries—all looking for or made to work. Later they moved from the country to the city or from other poorer countries, many unskilled, all wanting jobs. And for a variety of reasons—changes in the marketplace, the end of slavery, the shift from an agrarian to an industrial society, the Great Depression, World War II with its aftermath of recession and inflation—they now find themselves out of work, out of luck, out of family.

The English householder suffered badly, as the growing wool industry threw large numbers of peasants off the land toward the end of the fifteenth century. Contemporary accounts describe the plight of families thrown out of their homes, wandering about the countryside with all their household goods, with no money and no place to go. Their choices were to sell their goods for a pittance; to steal, for which they would be hanged; or to beg, and go to jail for being vagabonds.

Until the sixteenth century, charity—that is, the feeding of the poor—had been a private matter. But it became unsatisfactory to the state authorities for several reasons. The more prosperous citizens and the nobility customarily gave alms to buy their own salvation. When the numbers of the begging poor increased drastically, private charity was insufficient to contain it. Also it was difficult for a town to discourage begging if rewarding beggars had a religious aim.

As the governments in England and all over the continent began to replace local parishes with countrywide arrangements for relief early in the sixteenth century, almsgiving was outlawed and begging forbidden. The poor were registered and anyone else found trying to collect relief was punished severely. In England the penalty for begging was whipping until the blood ran.

The solution was a form of welfare that incorporated many of the features of modern relief. These included eligibility, or criteria to separate the worthy from the unworthy poor; an allowance small enough to discourage the habit; some kind of work to discourage idleness; and surveillance to discourage immorality. For the young especially, the rationalization was that this was the right way to bring up children.

In England, a 1572 statute that determined that poor relief would be paid for by taxes also directed overseers to put vagrants to work. A later statute spelled it out. Overseers were to obtain and then deliver to the poor a supply of raw goods—wool, hemp, iron—which they were to process at home for wages fixed according to "the desert of the work." The purpose was:

> . . . to the intent youth may be accustomed and brought up in labor and work, and then not like to grow to be idle rogues, and to the intent also that such as be already grown up in idleness and so rogues at this present, may not have any just excuse in saying that they cannot get any service or work.[9]

The fact that these were children did not seem to bother the citizens of the town, who were more concerned that they not be public charges.

In France, Lyons was one of the first cities to establish work relief. Although Lyons was a prosperous commercial and manufacturing center, attracting laborers from all over Europe, the seasonal nature of some trades plus foreign competition periodically threw large numbers of people out of work.

In 1529, 1530, and 1531 the town was plagued by food riots, by artisans and journeymen marching through the streets, by the looting of granaries and the homes of the rich. The Lyons town fathers consequently outlawed begging, and set up a system to identify and register those who were eligible to receive relief. Those certified were placed under supervision. They were forbidden to spend money at the tavern or at cards, and surprise visits were made to their homes to look for evidence of immorality. In order to insure that pauper children would be controlled, the town even subsidized new business if it guaranteed to train pauper children and teach them to read and write. Anyone considered employable who turned to begging was chained and given work digging sewers and ditches.[10]

The same thing was happening all over Europe. Sidney and Beatrice Webb, commenting on the new "statecraft relative to destitution," which had begun to emerge in Germany, the Netherlands, Switzerland, and England, and to a lesser extent in France and Scotland, noted that governments were realizing that "no policy of mere repression" was enough to stop either begging or vagrancy and that some organ of government had to provide for those in need of the means of existence, whatever the cause.[11]

The relief system was reactivated again toward the end of the eighteenth century when the English proletariat, by then landless, lost its final prerogative, the right to graze and grow crops on common land. As wool became more profitable, the last of the common lands were bought up and the tenants thrown off. In addition, changes in the economy had already altered the old master-servant relationship of farmer-tenant to employer and hired hand. One who was hired could be turned out when he was no longer needed. And he was.

Working for relief at home or in the public workhouse gave way in England in the late 1770s and early 1780s to factory labor. The rapid expansion of textile manufacturing had produced a great need for factory workers. Men who had been farmers and craftsmen resisted the whole concept of factory work. The textile industry solved its labor problems by using women and children.

The employment and apprenticing of children to work in factories led to new kinds of abuse, and often approached the conditions of slavery. When English parents, rebelling against the inhumane treatment of factory owners and supervisors, refused to send children to work, young paupers from the workhouse, children without parents to protect them, some as young as four and five years old, were sent instead.

Manufacturers bargained regularly with parish authorities for lots of fifty or more children from the poorhouses. In one

instance, cited by Piven and Cloward, a Lancashire manufac-
turer agreed to take one idiot for every twenty children that
were sound. In addition, "In order to make the children more
submissive, they were told they would live like ladies and
gentlemen on roast beef and plum pudding." [12]

Children from five up often worked sixteen hours a day,
sometimes in leg irons to prevent their escape. They were
starved and beaten; many died from occupational diseases; and
some committed suicide. Few who worked in that environment
lived very long.

Parish children were an ideal source of labor. They could be
shipped to remote factories that were located near sources of
water power. As the source of power shifted to steam, factories
were more likely to locate in towns where they could employ
local children. Children were preferred because they were more
docile and had a lighter touch at the loom. Moreover, pauper
children could be employed for food and lodging and since their
indentures usually bound them until the age of twenty-one, they
provided a stable labor supply.

The child-labor reform movement started in England by
Robert Owen was responsible for Parliament's passage of the
First Factory Act in 1802, breaking up the pauper apprentice
system. Since the act did not interfere with traditional parental
rights, however, it did not apply to children whose parents were
living. Those children whose parents allowed them or sent them
to work in the mills still worked long hours, were beaten—often
brutally—and sometimes dipped headfirst into barrels of cold
water to keep them awake.

Owen was considered humane when he insisted that the
children in his workshops should not work more than thirteen
hours and be allowed at least one exercise period a day.

During the same period, poor city children in England were
often bound out as chimney sweepers, a job that some historians
consider the most awful work ever demanded of children.
Chimney sweeps worked night and day and, exposed to all kinds
of brutality, deteriorated quickly both mentally and physically.
They frequently died early from cancer of the scrotum and from
pulmonary consumption, which was so common it became

known as the "chimney sweep's disease." Using children as chimney sweeps was finally outlawed in the nineteenth century.

In the United States child labor and the abuse of children in industry became a common theme of the muckraking journalists. Eventually it led to legislation ending child labor. But until then, in America as in Europe, most citizens turned their eyes from the sweatshops where children worked. In fact, in 1918, the U.S. Supreme Court upheld the right of manufacturers to transport the products of child labor in interstate commerce, thus in effect permitting child labor.[13]

But reform was in the air. Concern for the plight of a badly abused young girl in the 1890s led to the formation of the New York Society for the Prevention of Cruelty to Children. At about the same time, the impulses behind the child-welfare movement and the juvenile court system were quickening in the hearts of the nineteenth-century reformers. Both their motives and methods are important historically. Their analysis that social evils could be corrected by treating the victim and, in particular, their treatment of abused and neglected children by "rehabilitating" them in prisonlike institutions have affected the way we look at abuse and neglect today.

In the early 1800s, some states were already dealing with children who were "destitute" or who "lacked proper parental care or guardianship." These children became the concern of a group of reformers who, along with professional penologists, helped to create special judicial and correctional institutions for labeling, processing, and managing "troublesome and destitute" youth: the state industrial schools and reform schools and the juvenile court system.

Their theory was that neglected and destitute children, children whose parents brought them up improperly, were bound for lives of crime unless caught early enough and saved. The industrial schools would save them from a life of deviancy by catching and preventing criminal tendencies before they could take hold. Meanwhile the new juvenile courts were established to "rehabilitate" predelinquents and delinquents.

The "child savers," as Anthony Platt calls them in his book on

the child-welfare movement, viewed themselves as humanitari-
ans and altruists concerned with rescuing those less fortunately
placed in the social order. They believed in the rhetoric of
established religion, in the values of home, work, and family, in
the salvation of the innocent—much as social workers today
believe in the preservation of the family, the rehabilitation of
young offenders, the prevention of delinquency, and the proper
protection and guidance of the young.[14]

As Platt points out, despite the reformers' zeal, the programs
they enthusiastically supported diminished the civil liberties and
privacy of youth. Although the child savers were rhetorically
concerned with protecting children from the physical and moral
dangers of increasingly industrialized and urban society, their
remedies seemed to aggravate the problem.

The child savers, by and large middle-class or wealthy leisured
women, were typified by Jane Addams and Louise de Koven
Bowen. Their cause filled the void in their lives created by the
decline of traditional religion, the increase in leisure, the rise in
public education, and in particular, the problem of time on their
hands. Middle-class women at the turn of the century were
excluded from real work. Social decorum required that they lead
lives of leisure to enhance the status of their husbands. The
background of those people who were active in the child-saving
movement was remarkably similar. They were rich, well educated, and well traveled, and they all had little to do. If you
examine the boards of directors of our philanthropic child-saving
institutions today, you will find many women and men like
them, perpetuating their principles, their analysis, and their
work.

Their background might not matter to those poor children in
the jails and reform schools of America whose lives these ladies
were busy saving. What did matter was the way they viewed the
problem: and they viewed it from the lofty standpoint of
Protestant morality. As Louise de Koven Bowen wrote: "Here
we are, Chicago, a great city sprawling over a vast territory,
peopled with many nationalities, calling ourselves the commerce
center of the world. Our great buildings are lifting their towers

toward heaven. Our parks and playgrounds lead the world. We are fast becoming the center of literature, art and music and medicine . . . but what is it going to profit us if our children lose their souls?" [15]

Bowen and the other reformers were horrified that the "road to destruction" was made so easy in Chicago. Brothels, comic books, alcohol, amusement parks, and other "commercialized vices" were seen as a ubiquitous threat to the fragility of youth. "Unless this condition is soon remedied," said Louise Bowen, "the children, in order to quench their thirst for joy will take deep draughts of the poisonous stuff which is everywhere offered to them, and which ultimately will end in their complete demoralization." [16]

Jane Addams, who was more sophisticated and tough-minded than Louise Bowen, nevertheless drew the same conclusions. She recognized the exploitation of labor by capital and of children by adults and that industry had created a new set of victims. But she could not really indict capitalism. She realized that city children were overwhelmed by what she called the "ideals of Puritanism," yet at Hull House, the country's first settlement house, which she founded, she insisted that single girls be strictly chaperoned, that liquor and "certain types of dancing" be forbidden. Her reforms were directed at consoling the unfortunate poor and helping them adapt to a way of life that she acknowledged was oppressive and unjust.

The child savers were interested in morality and protecting children from moral weakness. They raised the issue of child protection mainly to satisfy their own view of deviance.

Sociologists Erikson and Durkheim, who have examined the role of deviance in society, have pointed out that social groups may actually create a deviance by inventing the category. To make something a crime, you first need a rule whose infraction constitutes criminality. Likewise, by defining proper or "normal" behavior, you create a standard from which a variation may be deviance.

According to Durkheim, social groups create deviance in order to preserve the social stability, status, and prestige of the ruling class and to maintain their power over the rest of society. If we are going to examine deviancy, Durkheim says, we should look not at the deviant—i.e., the neglecting parent or neglected child, or the delinquent, a category the nineteenth-century reformers invented—but at the law and the people that label him so.[17]

The nineteenth-century reformers' philosophy was an amalgam of various traditional beliefs, a reaffirmation of ideal values like home and family, the agricultural community, Protestantism, parental discipline, women's domesticity, all values rapidly being eroded by the influx of immigrants and the move from country to city and farm to factory.

The reformers were also influenced by the growing liberal penology at that time. The new penology emphasized the possibilities of reform, despite pessimistic views about the moral defects of the lower class. It was necessary for those involved in social reform to push the gloomy ideas of the social Darwinist about imperfectibility to the back of their mind in order to legitimize their own professions.

The reform movement generated new social and professional roles, especially for women, legitimized by a rising class of correctional administrators. The same thing is happening today as increasing interest in child abuse and neglect gives status to a new branch of social work, "protective workers" (to protect children), and a new profession, child advocates, and creates a new industry to study or treat the neglected and abused. Today, as in the late nineteenth and early twentieth centuries, the social work industry has its most direct consequences on the children of the urban poor.

Rehabilitation of the predelinquent, detected in time, was the theory. Enoch Wines, a leading penologist, set the tone. In his book published in 1880, *The State of Prisons and Child-Saving Institutions in the Civilized World*, he proposed that state authorities should assume control of children under fourteen years of age who lacked proper care or guardianship, delegating their supervision to private citizens and charitable organizations that would be state subsidized.[18] The result was the reform or industrial-training school.

The reformers, like Wines, de Koven Bowen and Addams, while emphasizing the value of home and family as the basic institutions of American society, actually made it easier to remove children from homes that failed, according to their definition, to fulfill their proper function. They set such high standards of propriety that almost any parent could be accused of not coming up to snuff. In any case, it was only lower-class families that were evaluated anyway. The propriety of middle-class families was largely exempt from investigation then as it is today.

Looking at families that fell short of their mark, the reformers defined the problem of neglect as one of hygiene and morality rather than economic and political power. The 1880 report of the Illinois Board of State Commissioners of Public Charities noted:

> If the prevention of crime is more important than its punishment and if such prevention can only be secured by rescuing children from criminal surroundings before the criminal character and habits become firmly established, then it is evident that the state reform school can not accomplish all we desire, since it does not receive children at a sufficiently early age nor does it receive children who still occupy the debatable ground between criminality and innocence, who have not yet committed any criminal act, but who are in imminent danger at every moment of becoming criminals.[19]

In order to get children early enough, they invented new standards. For example, when an individual school for girls was established by act of the Illinois legislature, it allowed any "responsible" resident to petition the county court to examine the fitness of the parent of any dependent girl whose background they deemed questionable. If a jury of six decided the parent or guardian was not a fit person to have custody, the girl could be committed to the industrial school until she was eighteen.

Once they had custody of the children, their goal was to "rehabilitate" them, although the industrial-school regimen was hardly likely to promote rehabilitation.

Both boys and girls were punished physically. In the Illinois Industrial School for Girls, corporal punishment was allowed "such as a kind mother would inflict on a refractory child." [20] Girls who were disobedient were locked up.

In the State Home for Delinquent Boys at St. Charles, boys had to observe rules of military courtesy. Infractions were punished by whippings with a leather strap. Some boys were punished by being locked up in the "hole" for up to thirty days with no shoes or mattress. They slept on wooden boards nailed to the concrete floor and were sometimes kept handcuffed to iron pipes.[21]

Rehabilitation took a strange course. Children were not educated and they were not taught any trade or skills. They were allowed to work, however, at labor profitable to the state.

The Illinois State Reform School for Boys, established in 1871, was described by the Board of Public Charities as a "house of refuge" where juveniles were "treated with tender pity." It exploited the labor of its charges as did most other such institutions of the day. Although the trustees were forbidden by law to make inmates work more than six hours a day, the first warden immediately contracted with a Chicago shoe firm for the labor of fifty boys to be employed seven hours a day. The boys' labor was also contracted for by Clark and Hill and Co., a company which manufactured brushes, and by the Bloomington Manufacturing Company, maker of cane-seat chairs.

In their enthusiasm to intervene in the lives of neglected children and rehabilitate them for the state, the reformers found they were netting more than they could treat. Six years after it was opened, the reform school was seriously overcrowded. In twelve years its population had nearly doubled, and even that population, as in other such schools, was to continue to grow.

It is hard to ignore the authoritarian punitive impulse behind this benevolent theory of intervention and prevention, just as it is difficult to accept the rationale of the English poor laws in the 1560s that forced labor of poor children would help prevent them from growing up to be idle, lazy rogues.

Relief, prevention, and rehabilitation as explicit social policy have developed over the last few centuries as the way to deal with the victims of social injustice and forced unemployment in the modern, industrial society. It is a combination of religious hypocrisy and capitalist greed to describe the forced labor of children in the eighteenth century as the need to make work for idle hands, or their forced institutionalization in the nineteenth century and today as the desire to protect the innocent from a life of crime or to rehabilitate the delinquent.

If we are serious about doing the best for our children, we might ask how children can be saved from a life of neglect by placing them in institutions where they are most likely to be further neglected and abused.

4

The Felumero Case

Alice might be the most attractive person in the Brooklyn Family Court. A tall, black twenty-six-year-old with an Afro, she always wears long dresses and bright colors, reds, purples, yellow. She is friendly and articulate and her co-workers seem drawn to her. A conversation in her office is constantly interrupted by doctors, social workers, lawyers dropping in to discuss a problem case.

Alice directs the community workers in the court's Rapid Intervention Unit. RIP's original purpose, she explains, was to consider whether individual clients needed hospitalization. "Of course, most things are not that black and white. People may be crazy but not dangerous. Sometimes we are asked, 'Should we take the kid away?' Or 'What about visitation?' We may have to do some rapid counseling to convince an angry mother to let her husband see the children. I have my own group of community workers, six of them, who do referrals and home visits."

At first, Alice says, the disorganization of the big city overwhelmed her. Alice is from a fundamentalist family in the South. "I was brought up very strictly," she says. Her father and her husband are both ministers.

According to Alice, the family court reflects the society. "It's a disorganized, crazy system. My community workers have a lot of initiative, but the probation officers see them as a threat. The probation officers are overworked and inadequate. They've been around for years. Most of them have a B.A. in psychology. That's a nuthin' degree anyway. The rest have B.A.'s in music and English."

Alice selects and trains her own community workers. Over a

five-month period, they had seen some 700 to 1,000 families. "I get a lot of sexual abuse cases," she says. "I see the father. If the child is old enough, I see the child. Many adolescent girls come in and accuse their father. There's lots of yelling and screaming. After two or three visits and a lot of denials from the father, the girl often says, 'Well, I lied.'

"If the kid is younger than ten or eleven, she probably didn't lie. Now she's scared of her father. Last week I had a case where both the girl and the father denied it. Most sexual abuse is connected with alcohol. And it's very often a stepfather. The worst I've had was a seven-year-old who got VD from her father. Then there are some who abuse infants.

"There's a disproportionate number of people who are just dumb, retarded, don't even know when they were born. We get a skewed population. Very few are sane and competent. At best they're inadequate. Usually they're schizophrenic. What are our choices? We send the mother to the hospital and the kid to the commissioner of social services. We don't know what happens after that. Then the mother returns. If we've been in contact, we try to involve her.

"In the cases we see, neglect and abuse are different. Abuse usually involves very angry people. For example, we had a case last week, a neglect case, with a chronic paranoid schiz-zy mother, a very guarded person. She has seven or eight kids, and four of her kids are in placement. Two are grown, and the other two are with her. She won't let the kids go to school; she's afraid to let them go out. We get a lot of cases like that. We have to recommend the kids be taken away. Those children were so deprived they couldn't even describe food. Didn't know the word for 'corn.' Frequently, if the mother has strengths, when we take the kids away, she'll mobilize herself.

"This lady was on welfare. She lived in an abandoned building with excreta all over the place. We put the two kids with relatives while we looked for an apartment for her. And we found her one. But she was so grandiose she wanted a house. She thought if she had a house, all her kids could come back to live with her.

"She's probably a loving mother, but she couldn't marshal the

*necessary strengths. The community workers were against re-
turning the kids to the home, so they're with their aunt now. But
the mother doesn't want her sister to have the kids. I don't know
what's going to happen. We're not supposed to follow up.*

"*We had another case, a mother with ten kids by seven
different men. Four of the children are grown, three are at
home, two are married, and one is with a grandmother. She's a
loving mother and relatively competent, but can't impose any
controls on her kids. Her paramour got in a fight with the three
at home. He said she lets them do whatever they want and he
tried to impose some discipline. He hurt two of the kids so badly
they had to be hospitalized. He beat them. It's a chaotic house,
but there's love. The problem is that the controls and order that
make for a stable individual and a stable family are not there.*

"*Our main focus is the kids. If it means helping the mother or
the kids, we come out for the kids. I suspect most often the kids
are just taken away. One mother said to me, 'Every time they
come out of me they take them away.'*

"*The parents are very resistant to treatment. A parent may
say, 'I can't go to the doctor. I don't have a clean shirt.'*

"*We'll say, 'Why don't you wash it?' The next step seems
impossible. We're called Rapid Intervention. To me, interven-
ing means we may have to tear down and start over. The judges
aren't trained. I don't think the family court should be a social
agency. But the court is necessary because of its power.*"

*Just then Dr. Silver, a court psychiatrist, walks in. She has
been interviewing a thirteen-year-old girl whose mother beats
her up. The mother is in the hospital, and they don't know
where to put the girl, since nonsecure detention facilities will
not accept neglect and abuse cases. The girl's mother has been
telling her she's a boy. The girl was in the Juvenile Center and
got into a fight, so they don't want her back. She says she will
walk out of a foster home.*

"*She's a difficult kid,*" *Dr. Silver says,* "*but she has tremendous
potential. She's really smart. She needs a positive role model.*"

"*But she's a problem,*" *says Alice,* "*and agencies want
motivated lost sheep. That's the rub. There's no place for*

difficult kids, and let's face it, most of the kids we get here are difficult."

"What about Geller House?" asks the doctor.

"They only take Jews," says Alice. "Catholic agencies only take Catholics."

"Well," says the doctor, "she's very bright."

"I don't think that will do," says Alice.

ON MARCH 23, 1969, the New York Daily News carried the following item, which subsequently became the scandal of the year:

> Police threw some 70 men into a search yesterday for 3-year-old Roxanne Felumero of 199 Avenue B who disappeared near her home at about 11 P.M. Friday. The girl weighs about 45 pounds, has short blond hair, and wore a green ski jacket with a hood, red corduroy pants and black patent leather shoes.

Three days later, according to the News:

> The body of Roxanne Felumero who was a bit over three feet tall . . . was recovered from the East River off 10th Street weighted with three cement slabs. The cement was believed by police to have come from a sidewalk in front of her home. . . . Her stepfather was charged with killing her with his fists and her mother was held as a material witness.

Roxanne's story is a prize example of the media exposé, the sensational media scandal, which at the same time unmasks the culprits and obscures the underlying problems. Roxanne was presented to the public as the perfect martyr to the child-abuse cause. She was in fact the pitiful victim of an addict mother, a brutal stepfather, a sloppy welfare department, a neglectful foundling home, and the bureaucratic bungling of the family court. If together they were the cause of her death, her death in turn resulted in the destruction of at least one family court judge, inspired numerous legislative investigations, and allowed a handful of politicians to make indignant statements and get their share of press. It briefly spurred reforms in New York State's reporting system.

Roxanne's death, as reported in the *Daily News*, helped sell millions of papers for almost a year. It helped pass a law lumping together abuse and neglect. It elicited, most of all, a great outpouring of public indignation and sloppy Christian moralizing, including calls for the dismissal of the judge and the death penalty for the stepfather. The press made plenty of mistakes on the facts, and did very little to change the problem. Although it did call attention to child abuse, its oversimplification probably did more harm than good. Here then is the sad story of Roxanne Felumero.

Roxanne's picture first appeared in the *News* on the cold March day that police retrieved her body from the river. The picture showed a pretty little girl with big eyes and short hair. She looked like a very appealing child. The head and shoulders shot of Roxanne was to appear perhaps twenty or thirty times in the *News* during that year.

There were plenty of other pictures as the tragedy unspun, mostly of Judge Sylvia Liese, always shown grinning. One of four family court judges who heard the case, Judge Liese's health and reputation were destroyed by the exposé. Other pictures were of Judge Florence Kelley, the New York City Family Court Administrative Judge; the child's stepfather, George Poplis; and Dr. Vincent Fontana, frequently described by the *News* as a leading foe of child abuse. William Federici wrote most of the *News* stories.

There were also inconsistencies. Poplis was alternately described by the *News* as thirty-two and forty years of age, sometimes as a waiter, sometimes as a housewrecker. The "cement slabs" mentioned in the March 26 story as weighting Roxanne's body were later changed to rocks and pieces of cement. Those were minor, however, compared to who got the blame.

The March 26 story noted that the stepfather was booked and that the mother, Marie Poplis, had told police the previous Friday that Roxanne disappeared after being left alone just a few minutes. It said the police were told her body had been "tossed" into the river sometime before Roxanne's mother reported her missing.

On March 28, a quarter-page story with a small picture of Judge Kelley headlined "CHILD SLAIN AFTER COURT TOOK HER FROM GOOD HOME" mentioned for the first time that Roxanne had been badly beaten and drew the battle lines:

> The 3-year-old blond girl whose badly beaten body was recovered Tuesday from the East River had been taken from a pleasant Long Island suburban home on order of Family Court and returned to her mother over the strenuous protests of her former foster parents, it was charged yesterday.

We now have the villain, the family court, and a picture of Administrative Judge Florence Kelley, who is quoted as refusing to discuss the case. The child's disappearance is summarized, her mother's age is given as twenty-four, her stepfather, George Poplis, age forty, is described as a waiter. The child's body is described as weighted down with "three cement slabs" and Assistant Chief Medical Examiner Elliot Gross is reported as having said that the child had been beaten to death, " 'suffering extensive fresh and recent contusions of the scalp and face and multiple contusions of the lower extremities.' "

At the age of ten months, according to the paper, Roxanne was placed with foster parents, Mr. and Mrs. Michael Boccio of Long Island, through New York's Foundling Hospital. Mr. Boccio, a cab driver, and his wife had protested when Roxanne was returned to her mother three months previously, a week before Christmas, "on order of Family Court."

While visiting the Boccios afterward, Roxanne was discovered by Mrs. Boccio to have welts all over her body. On February 27, the Boccios on subpoena took Marie Poplis into court with Roxanne and, according to the *News,*

> showed the Judge welts on the child's body, assertedly caused by beatings. The Boccios pleaded with the court that if Roxanne could not be returned to them, she should be put in protective custody. The Judge refused.

On a second visit to her former foster parents, Roxanne appeared to have been beaten again. The Boccios again got a subpoena to take Roxanne into court with Mrs. Poplis the next Monday, which would have been March 31.

Detectives told the *News* that neighbors in Roxanne's building said she was beaten frequently for bed-wetting. One neighbor claimed to have given Mrs. Poplis ten dollars to take Roxanne to a doctor because the child seemed ill. Mrs. Poplis said her husband told her to get penicillin tablets for the child and she had given Roxanne nine adult-sized tablets. The first and only mention was made of Roxanne's natural father, who told the *News* he had previously requested but been refused custody of Roxanne, though the court assured him his former wife would never get her. Roxanne's body, the story said, was unclaimed in the city morgue until the Boccios arranged for funeral services.

The New York Times and the *New York Post* did relatively little on the case, which quickly became a *Daily News* feature. The *Times* did note in its story that Mrs. Poplis and her husband had two other children living with them, a five-year-old who was Mrs. Poplis's child from a previous marriage and an eighteen-month-old daughter of their own.

On March 29, Dr. Vincent Fontana entered the story. The *News* and the *Times* both reported that Fontana, chairman of Mayor Lindsay's Task Force on Child Abuse and medical director of the New York Foundling Hospital, the hospital that had placed Roxanne with her foster parents, accused a family court judge of responsibility for Roxanne's death. The *Times* story was headlined "FAMILY COURT SCORED IN CHILD'S SLAYING."

> As a slain 3-year-old girl was buried yesterday by her foster parents, the Chairman of the Mayor's Task Force on Child Abuse charged that she might still be alive but for the order of a Family Court Judge.

Fontana claimed the incident was " 'a glaring example of the need for a special panel of judges to deal with cases of child abuse.' " He said that on January 2, when the child was examined at the Foundling Hospital, she was found to have " '20 black and blue marks in the small of the back and a swollen eye.' " This was about three weeks after Roxanne had been transferred by court order to the custody of her mother.

The *Times* said Fontana did not name the guilty judge. The *Times* did not name her either. However, it quoted Fontana as saying, " 'We opposed that transfer and we strongly objected again in January to leaving the child in her mother's home. The Judge was shown the bruises. But she gave the child to that mother.' "

Neither the Boccios' lawyer nor Administrative Judge Florence Kelley would comment on the case. Dr. Fontana however was reportedly "incensed." " 'We study and study and recommend and recommend and the Judges seem to have a blind spot. . . .' " He said there were two other children in the hospital, one slashed by a razor, the other so starved he looked like a Biafran, whose mothers wanted them back. " 'I suppose the courts will see that they get them,' " he told the *News*.

The story added that Roxanne originally came to the attention of the Foundling Hospital because of a complaint by the Society for the Prevention of Cruelty to Children.

The *News* not only named the judge, Sylvia J. Liese, but in a story headlined "COURT UNDER FIRE IN CHILD'S DEATH," ran a two-column picture of the judge smiling, with the caption, "Presided over the Case." The story read: "Family Court overrode urgent recommendations from the New York Foundling Hospital . . . Dr. Vincent J. Fontana, Medical Director of the Hospital, charged. . . . Judge Sylvia Jafflin Liese rendered her decision January 8 and on Tuesday Roxanne's badly beaten body was recovered from the East River. . . ."

Fontana accused the judges of being naïve, uninformed, and unaware of child abuse and neglect, thus again coupling the two, although neglect was not an issue in the case. He charged the court with " 'sacrificing' " Roxanne and said the judge left the child with her mother " 'despite strong and urgent recommendations by doctors and social workers' " that by returning Roxanne to her mother they were endangering her life.

Most of Fontana's charges subsequently proved untrue, though he was never publicly confronted with the discrepancies. In fact, the story contradicted itself, ending, "A report from the Foundling Hospital . . . approved . . . the child's return to her mother in December." If that was so, why didn't that appear in the lead? Did Dr. Fontana know his own hospital had recommended her return when he told the press they urged against it? Didn't the News check its own copy?

A News editorial called Roxanne's death "horrifying" and "heart-rending," reviewed the court proceedings, and rebuked Judge Liese for ignoring the "mass of welts on the poor thing's body." The News never understates. It asked the district attorney to "blast the case open," to question the family court's investigation, and called on the legislature to set up a watchdog agency over the court.

On March 30, the Times noted that the district attorney's office had subpoenaed family court records and repeated Fontana's charge that the Foundling Hospital had "strongly opposed" the child's removal from her foster parents.

The same day, the News took a half-page for a picture of Roxanne and another of the Boccios looking at a picture of her. The News lead was:

> With indignation raging over the circumstances surrounding the death of 3-year-old Roxanne Felumero—battered to death and thrown into the East River—a Supreme Court Justice yesterday subpoenaed all Family Court proceedings.

According to the March 30 News, Fontana claimed there was a "'mountain of evidence'" before the court prior to its decision to return Roxanne. Fontana's "mountain" was a report he claimed the court had received from Bellevue Hospital that described the mother as "'unorganized, of borderline intelligence, primitive . . . schizophrenic with depressive features and having self-destructive impulses.'" Fontana said the mother had been a patient at Creedmoor and "'other state mental institutions.'"

The News reported that Mr. Boccio, the foster parent, said

that during the January 3 hearing, Judge Liese had told them she was going on vacation and wanted to turn the case over to another judge, despite the fact that Liese "knew all about Marie and her entire history. . . . Boccio, a New York City cab driver, wiped a tear from his cheek. . . ." It turned out two other judges before Liese had also been involved in the case.

On March 31, with a picture of Roxanne captioned "Her body found in River," and headlined "REVEAL ROXANNE'S COURT FAILED TO INVESTIGATE," the News exposed a new wrinkle. Although the Poplises had been on welfare since 1967, the court had never contacted the Welfare Department to examine their records on the case. In addition, Poplis told a welfare investigator on December 19 that he had lied to Judge Liese a week earlier when he said he could support his family of four because he was regularly employed as a housewrecker. He claimed he had lied to the judge because his wife wanted Roxanne back.

According to the News, Poplis was in fact unemployed and had deserted Marie and his own child by her in August 1968. Marie was getting full support from welfare and had told an investigator in August that Poplis had left her. Yet the Welfare Department did not know that Roxanne had been returned to her mother until they received a notification from the Foundling Hospital on January 4, 1969. Marie later told the investigator that she hadn't asked for more money for the child because she was afraid Roxanne would be taken away.

The Welfare Department evidently reported this to the Foundling Hospital and also noted, according to the March 31 News, that on December 17 Roxanne had appeared to be nervous, quiet, and "looked as if she had been beaten." A Mr. Labatte, the Foundling Hospital supervisor, told welfare that they were trying to get a new hearing which would remove Roxanne from her home.

Apparently, the News noted, none of this information was ever requested by the family court. Because the News at this point was attacking the court it did not emphasize the rather shocking revelation that a welfare investigator thought a three-year-old child had been beaten and did not follow it up with an investigation. Nor did the Foundling Hospital, the original agency in the case to whom the beating was reported. The hospital also never passed this information on to Judge Liese.

On April 1, a News story headlined "FOE OF CHILD ABUSE CALLS FOR TOUGH NEW LAWS," described Fontana as "incensed by continuing revelations of child abuse and neglect [again abuse and neglect] including infanticide by parents." Fontana demanded laws to protect children from ill-treatment by relatives and inefficiency of the courts. He did not mention the bungling of his own agency.

Described as "angered" and "incensed," Fontana now called for an emergency meeting of the Task Force to deal with the inadequacies of the laws. The picture of Fontana was captioned "Calls Emergency Meeting"; Roxanne's, "Her Death Leads to Action," the action apparently being Fontana's demand for new laws. In case anyone had forgotten, the article ended: "The decision to return Roxanne to her mother was made by Family Court Judge Sylvia J. Liese."

On April 2 both the Times and the News carried stories on the Appellate Division's investigation of the case. The News also had an editorial, a picture of Judge Harold Stevens, presiding judge of the Appellate Court, and a statement from Mayor John Lindsay—" 'I am shocked and grieved. . . .' "—and said that Lindsay was setting the stage to enter "the gathering crusade against child abuse." There was no picture of Lindsay, never a News favorite. The News noted that as a result of its editorial asking for a watchdog agency, the Assembly Judiciary Committee was now drafting such legislation.

The News story contained a few inconsistencies. Although the end of the third paragraph said that the New York Foundling Hospital had "vigorously" opposed Roxanne's return to her mother, a later paragraph noted, "An original report by the Foundling authorities had persuaded Family Court to return Roxanne to her mother." Fontana was prominently mentioned in the article as submitting recommendations to the mayor and Judge Liese was given another shellacking.

An April 2 News editorial called for tougher child-abuse laws.

There was no story on April 3, for the first time in a week. But on April 4, a page-three *News* story running the width of the paper and featuring pictures of both Judge Stevens and Roxanne was headlined "JUDICIAL UNIT PROBES HANDLING OF ROXANNE CASE." The story reported that Judge Stevens had referred the investigation to the Judicial Relations Committee.

The real news was that Mrs. Poplis had just been arrested on a charge of child abuse with the hearing set for April 11. (Heretofore she had been held as a material witness to her husband's manslaughter charge.) Then Assemblyman (later Bronx Borough President) Robert Abrams got some free press for suggesting that photographs of abused children be taken at the time of treatment because injuries may have healed by the time a child gets to court, a useful idea that many hospitals now follow. The paper noted that Judge Liese saw Roxanne's welts, "according to [unnamed] Foundling Hospital officials."

Abrams took a free swipe at Mayor Lindsay, accusing him of playing politics with the lives of children by leaving five vacancies in family court, "when delays in the court calendar are what often lead to tragedy." A Lindsay aide called the assemblyman's charges "partisan political comment" but admitted to the delay in filling vacancies; one had been vacant for nearly eight months.

Poplis's indictment for murder got a front-page *News* headline just above Mamie Eisenhower's picture at President Eisenhower's funeral services. Evidently the *News* knew that to many New Yorkers, the indictment for murder of a thirty-two- or forty-year-old unemployed waiter or housewrecker was just as newsworthy as the funeral of a former U.S. President.

There were then three separate, concurrent investigations of the Felumero case: 1) the grand jury investigation and indictment of Poplis; 2) the grand jury investigation of the case's prior handling, and 3) a closed hearing by a subcommittee of the Mayor's Task Force, headed by Dr. Fontana.

In addition, the Appellate Division was investigating the family court's handling of the case. The *News* noted that State Senator Roy Goodman, "himself the father of three children," reported he would sponsor legislation on abuse and neglect.

Everyone claimed their investigation would insure more careful review by agencies in the future, improve the reporting apparatus, and reform family court procedures to insure better protection for children.

On April 7, the *News* ran a page-three story with a picture of Fontana ("Pushes for Changes") and the headline, "MAYOR'S PANEL CALLS FOR A CURB ON CHILD ABUSE." A rehash of the case followed. The charges called for by the mayor's panel were a watchdog committee over the children's part of family court, a panel of judges expert in child welfare to make decisions, and recruitment of more experienced social workers.

Fontana claimed, according to the article, that one or two children a day were killed by their parents, and that 10,000 or more were being abused. He pointed out that battered and abused children grow up and strike out at society. " 'As you go into the history of the Oswalds . . . and the Dillingers and the criminals, I think that perhaps these are the people that have had the type of life we are talking about.' "

On April 10, a page-two story in the *News*, with pictures of Poplis, New York State Assembly Speaker Perry Duryea, Roxanne, and Judge Liese, noted that Duryea, "outraged by the fatal beating of 3-year-old Roxanne Felumero [had] . . . prepared what is believed to be the nation's first Bill of Rights for abused children." The article stated that a member of Duryea's committee had singled out Judge Liese's handling of the case. The committee's recommendation included creation of a special child-neglect part of family court to handle abuse and neglect; legal representation for children; immediate forwarding of all official records—police, hospital, and others—to the court; a child-identification system using social security numbers and mandatory reporting of abuse by doctors, hospital personnel, welfare workers and schoolteachers. (Duryea was indicted in 1973 for election frauds and later acquitted because of the law's unconstitutionality.)

Next, a bombshell. On April 11, a *News* story, headlined "JUDGE PROTESTED SITUATION IN THE FAMILY COURT," featured pictures of Judge Liese and Judge Justine Wise Polier, a much-respected New York City Family Court judge, both grinning. The story read:

A month before her decision to leave 3-year-old Roxanne Felumero with her mother and stepfather despite evidence of beatings, Family Court Judge . . . Liese protested the deteriorating situation in the court in a letter to Administrative Judge Florence Kelley.

Judge Liese's letter complained about overcrowded dockets preventing judges from giving cases proper attention, about inadequate probation reports, and of frequent adjournments due to short staffing.

The *News* revealed that Judge Polier, who originally returned Roxanne to her mother in December (the first time we have heard that), "has written a letter to . . . Fontana" that was "highly critical" of his "hospital's role in the tragedy."

In her letter to Fontana, as quoted in the *News*, Judge Polier said the Foundling Hospital's social worker, Mrs. Carol Balet, had testified that she (Mrs. Balet) had worked three years with Roxanne's mother and because she was " 'in the process of leaving the hospital and . . . cleaning up her work' " had not seen Poplis at all. When asked by the family court in December for her recommendation, Balet recommended that Roxanne be returned to her mother and said she felt there was no need for supervision. Balet's supervisor, who was also in court that day, was asked if she had anything to add to the recommendation and answered no according to Judge Polier, as quoted in the *News*.

According to the *News*, in her letter to Fontana, Judge Polier accused the agency that had custody of Roxanne of failing to identify the problems and present them adequately to the court.

The judge also noted that Mrs. Poplis had a new apartment and had been asking for Roxanne's return for eight months, yet the social worker never visited her or Mr. Poplis, to whom she had been married for fifteen months. " 'One might ask what criteria are established under which a case worker and supervisor in a case where a mother seeks return of a child for well over eight months, fail to meet, and why they failed to request a further adjournment to study the home before approving the return,' " Judge Polier's letter continued. Furthermore, Judge Polier wrote, the Foundling Hospital had failed to produce the examining doctor in court or even tell Judge Liese that the report had been filed with the Department of Social Services.

Polier accused Fontana of failing to recognize the shortcomings of his own staff and then trying to place the whole burden of the tragedy on the family court. The *News* also ran a two-paragraph box with a story that "Representative Mario Biaggi [D–N.Y.], ex-cop hero" would propose national legislation to protect children from child abuse. Biaggi's bill would provide for the cutoff of federal welfare funds to parents found guilty of child abuse, an action that seems more punitive than protective and implies that all abusing parents are on welfare. Biaggi, a strong proponent of law enforcement, became a front-page story himself in 1972 when his chances for mayor of New York were reduced to zero because he lied about refusing to answer questions in a grand jury investigation of a rackets scandal.

The April 11 *New York Times* put Polier's case more bluntly. "FAMILY JUDGE REBUKES FONTANA IN GIRL'S SLAYING," the *Times* headline read, and the story ran:

> Judge Justine Wise Polier of Family Court has accused Dr. Vincent J. Fontana, a leading authority on child abuse and a vocal critic of the Court of evading his own responsibility in the murder of 3-year-old Roxanne Felumero. . . . Judge Polier in an indignant five page letter to Dr. Fontana said the hospital had at one time recommended the child's return, that despite contrary publicity, it had failed to advise the Court in time of suspected beatings, . . . failed to produce the doctor who had examined the beaten child, and had failed to submit a written report of the beating.

The *Times* story omitted the social worker's failure to investigate the home and her supervisor's failure to query her.

No one at any time then or later ever pointed out publicly that Fontana, as director of a hospital involved in the case and chairman of the Mayor's Task Force on Child Abuse, which was now investigating the case, might have a conflict of interest.

On April 11, the *News* ran a double-page spread with pictures of the Boccio home, and Roxanne in a highchair, headlined "ROXANNE—THE CHILD WHOM SOCIETY FAILED." Her happy life with the Boccios was described and her reported unhappiness at her real mother's periodic visits. For the first time in a story running almost daily for three weeks we are told that Roxanne was born out of wedlock and that she had been with other foster parents prior to the Boccios.

"JUDGE DEFENDS ROXANNE ACTION" was the next day's headline, with a story that "behind the closed doors" the Judiciary Committee of the Appellate Division heard Family Court Judge Liese "defend her conduct." We learn that a third judge, Michael Potoker, was involved in the original case.

More than a month passed until the next story. The New York State Legislature had by then passed a Bill of Rights for Abused Children, creating a separate part in family court to deal with abuse and neglect and stipulating that police lawyers represent children in court. It also appointed a watchdog committee to insure compliance.

A week or so later the *News* ran a story with Roxanne's picture, noting that the investigative agencies had still not reported "on the little girl whose death . . . is in danger of being forgotten."

This was followed by a *News* editorial the same day headlined "FORGET THE FELUMERO MURDER?" calling for the release of the reports on "this savage crime with its sinister judicial background" and promising the *News* would not let it be forgotten.

At the end of the month, the Judiciary Committee released its report.

Although the *Times* June 26 headline on the story was "COURT IS ASSAILED IN DEATH OF GIRL," the report itself blamed errors of judgment both inside and outside the family court for Roxanne Felumero's violent death. The report blamed all persons and agencies connected with the case for acting "ineptly, negligently, and ill advisedly," including Fontana's Foundling Hospital, the New York City Department of Social Services (which was responsible for supervising the hospital), and the court's warrant squad, law guardians, and probation department. It criticized the family court and the judges, although noting they were handicapped by inadequate information from other sources and by the Appellate Division's administrative weaknesses. It criticized Judge Polier for placing undue reliance on the Foundling Hospital's recommendation "in the light of the natural mother's unsavory background, much of which was reflected in the probation files before her." It criticized the Foundling Hospital for lack of information on stepfather George Poplis and for the fact that its information on the mother was more than two years old.

The Judiciary Committee report mentioned the "barrage of newspaper publicity," including "repeated statements accusing two Family Court Judges of mishandling the proceedings."

The committee's investigation actually focused on the manner in which the court system and related agencies functioned in the Felumero case, noting that, at the time, a neglect proceeding could be brought on behalf of a child whose parents were allegedly not providing adequate food, clothing, shelter, education, medical care, moral supervision, or guidance. Allegations of physical abuse of children were commonly determined in neglect proceedings. The New York law passed June 1, 1969, as a result, established a separate child-abuse part with jurisdiction over allegations of physical and mental abuse.

In New York City a neglect proceeding is originated by filing a petition of neglect. The court's probation department then conducts a preliminary investigation. Next, a fact-finding hearing determines "whether [the] allegations of a petition . . . are supported by a fair preponderance of the evidence." [1] At this hearing "only competent, material and relevant evidence may be admitted." [2] The presiding judge is not allowed to read probation reports or other background data. However, the court may order the temporary removal of a child if there is a "substantial probability" of a neglect finding, if it is "necessary to avoid imminent risk to the child's life or health" or if there is a substantial probability that the child will ultimately be taken from his home and placed elsewhere.

If the allegations are not established at the hearing, the court can dismiss the case. If they are, the court has several options. It can suspend judgment, discharge the child to the custody of parent or other guardian, or place the child elsewhere. Conditions, such as probation, may accompany the child's discharge.

A neglected child may be placed with a relative, the commissioner of public welfare (Department of Social Services), an authorized agency (like the Foundling Hospital), or a suitable institution. The maximum placement period is eighteen months, with successive extensions possible. In New York City, if the commissioner gets custody and the department places the child with a private agency, as happened in the case of Roxanne, the department is supposed to maintain supervisory control. On applications for discharge or extension of placement, the Bureau of Child Welfare (part of the Department of Social Services) is responsible for reviewing the matter with the agency and making appropriate recommendations to the court.

The Judiciary Committee's report noted that with thirty or forty cases per judge a day, the court cannot give enough time to very complex problems. It described auxiliary services as inadequate and underfinanced and said suitable treatment programs were unavailable. For those reasons, the report said, the court might feel that leaving a child at home is preferable to placing him either in overcrowded institutions or in a series of foster homes.

When a child is removed, the report said, "every effort is supposed to be made to rehabilitate the family for the child's return."

The committee report then reviewed the facts in the Felumero case, adding some that had not been reported by the press. In 1966, shortly after she was born, because of a neglect petition brought by the Society for the Prevention of Cruelty to

Children (SPCC), Roxanne was placed with the New York Foundling Hospital. They in turn placed her in a series of foster homes. The Boccios' was the last. No reason was given for the number of foster homes. In November 1968, Marie Poplis tried to regain the child's custody. However, on November 26, 1968, the first judge in the case, Judge Michael Potoker, granted the Foundling Hospital's request for an extension until December 12 for a hearing on Marie's application. He requested the hospital to appear at that hearing.

On that date at a hearing before Judge Polier (Judge Number 2), the Foundling Hospital social worker who had seen neither the child nor her parents—including the new stepfather—because she was, according to her testimony in court, "cleaning up her work" before leaving the hospital, recommended the child be returned to her mother. When asked if the hospital recommended probationary custody, they said no. Judge Polier then awarded Roxanne's custody to her natural mother.

Three weeks later, on January 3, 1969, the report continued, the Boccios brought a neglect petition before Judge Liese (Judge Number 3). Mrs. Poplis, Mrs. Boccio, a court probation officer, a Foundling Hospital representative, and a Legal Aid attorney charged with representing Roxanne's interests were present. Roxanne was found to have bruises on her lower back and a discoloration above her left eye. No medical report was produced, though one was mentioned. Mrs. Poplis told Judge Liese that Roxanne was injured when she fell from a swing and again when she hit her face on a bicycle. Mrs. Boccio testified that Roxanne told her "George did it." Roxanne told the judge she "fell." "I drop on the rocking chair and fall down, fell on my head and my eye," is what the court record claims Roxanne said. She also told the lawyer she "fell." When asked if her mother spanked her, she said no. When asked if her stepfather spanked her, she said "sometimes." When asked if she liked her stepfather, she said no.

Although Judge Liese said for the record that she didn't believe the child received "all those bruises just from falling" and that they did not look like bruises caused by a fall, she adjourned the matter for three weeks until January 27, and directed Catholic Charities to provide the mother with counseling.

On January 27 neither Roxanne nor her mother appeared in court. The court reporting officer said the mother claimed to be too "ill" to appear. Judge Liese directed the Catholic Charities representative, who had failed to carry out the judge's previous order, to make two home visits to the Poplises the next week and to continue to follow the case for four weeks, up to the time the mother was directed to appear for a hearing. Judge Liese's assignment was up at that point and she was about to leave the city for reasons of health.

When Mrs. Poplis did not appear in court on February 24, Judge Jane Molin (Judge Number 4) issued a warrant for the mother's arrest and the production of Roxanne in court. The warrant squad mailed Marie Poplis a letter to that effect but got no answer. On March 12, at 7:30 A.M., two police officers, who constituted the New York family court's entire warrant squad, knocked on Marie Poplis's door because, according to the report, they had other business in the neighborhood. There was no answer. They made no attempt to execute the warrant. On March 21 Roxanne's disappearance was reported and four days later she was found dead in the river.

The committee report noted that Dr. Fontana was quoted in the press as saying the Foundling Hospital opposed the return of Roxanne in December and again in January. He was also quoted as saying the court ignored evidence of a severe beating plus Roxanne's testimony that she had been beaten.

The committee said Dr. Fontana denied making such statements and noted that court transcripts showed his quotations, whether he really made them or not, at variance with the facts.

The committee was "disturbed" that the press would "excoriate" family court judges on the basis of statements that proved incorrect.

The committee report said that Judge Polier had placed "undue reliance" upon the hospital's recommendation in returning Roxanne. It added that while Judge Liese thought the

Foundling Hospital had acted too quickly in urging the child's original return, that issue was not before the court. The judge was merely obligated to determine if the mother had been neglectful from the time she obtained custody.

The Foundling Hospital's representative told the committee that since she did not think Roxanne was an abused child, she had not made any recommendation for supervision.

The committee concluded that Judge Liese should have granted "but a brief adjournment" on January 3 so that both the medical reports and George Poplis could be produced, meanwhile providing supervision or protection for the child. When the mother failed to appear in court on January 27, a warrant for her arrest with instructions for immediate execution should have been issued and Judge Liese should have retained jurisdiction.

The court noted that the social agencies had made no attempt to get any information about living conditions in the Poplises' home, and therefore, it was unavailable to Judge Leise.

The law guardian, Roxanne's court-appointed lawyer, was criticized for not taking a series of available legal steps to protect her, and particularly for not revealing to the court information in his files about Marie's background. However, to represent the best interests of the child, the committee said the lawyer needed better investigative services.

The Foundling Hospital was criticized for its "not warranted" and "not carefully considered" recommendation that the child be returned to her mother. The committee said "the calibre of the agency investigation was revealed" when it admitted for one and a half years not having met with George Poplis.

Foundling Hospital files indicated Marie Poplis was an addict and a prostitute, with a criminal assault conviction and a history of mental instability that included several suicide attempts. Despite that the caseworker who had intended to recommend probationary custody changed her mind shortly before the hearing when she met Poplis for the first time in court.

Furthermore, although obligated by law to notify the Bureau of Child Welfare by phone after a Foundling Hospital doctor found suspicious injuries on Marie, through a service available twenty-four hours a day, any day, the hospital did not notify them. Instead, it mailed, on January 9, a written notice prepared January 2. By that time, the matter was already in court. The Bureau of Child Welfare does not investigate matters before the court, although its mandate for investigative responsibility contains no such exception. The Bureau of Child Welfare received the information January 9, more than two months before Roxanne died. Had it investigated, it could have helped the court on January 27 in deciding what to do with Roxanne temporarily, how long to adjourn the case, and whether to issue a warrant for immediate execution. The bureau also failed in its responsibility to offer "protective social services to prevent injury to the child [and] safeguard [her] . . . welfare." Perhaps the most incredible euphemism in the committee's finding was the following statement: "The Committee has been advised that because of a shortage in personnel in the Bureau of Child Welfare, delays in undertaking the prescribed investigations and protective services sometimes occur."

Because of its gentle scolding tone, when it should have blasted—the family court, the Foundling Hospital, the bureau, and Dr. Fontana—the committee report, despite all its evidence, amounted to a whitewash. Like all other parties involved, it did not fulfill its responsibilities.

Two bureaus within the Department of Social Services had had relevant information they shared neither with each other nor any other agency. The Department of Social Services was told by Marie that her husband lied in court on December 12 and welfare records showed he didn't live with her. There was also the aforementioned Bureau of Child Welfare medical reports of suspected child abuse.

Furthermore, although the Foundling Hospital gets more than 90 percent of its authorized cost of child care from the city, there was no public review of the private agency's required casework.

Other details were noted critically, like the probation officer's limited court function, which only permitted him to hand over files, not to inform the judge of their contents; the court's reliance on other agencies, like Catholic Charities, which failed to follow the case; and the existence of a two-man warrant squad to execute 3,500 arrests.

The committee criticized the rotation system of judges, the improper drawing of the neglect petition (which should have named George Poplis as well as Marie), and concluded that although the press attributed Roxanne's death solely to the mishandling of the judges, the committee believed the real fault lay with the lack of resources within the court and the lack of coordination between the court and other agencies.

The state legislature meanwhile established, along with its watchdog committee, of which we will hear more later, a "child-abuse part" with exclusive jurisdiction over all proceedings for the protection of abused children, and changed the law to permit the judge at the fact-finding hearing to study relevant background data.

"AT LAST, A FELUMERO REPORT" was the headline of a *News* editorial on June 27, 1969, accusing the committee of diluting the blame attached to the judges. Noting the committee's expressed annoyance with the press, "notably the *News* which gave ample publicity to this heart-rending tragedy," the editorial said, "The *News* is not apologizing for that to anybody."

On September 16, the *News* announced, "BIG SHAKEUP HITS FAMILY COURT." The article featured a large photo of Roxanne with the caption "The Late Roxanne Felumero—Taken From Foster Home By Court."

> Five and a half months after the savage slaying of 3-year-old Roxanne Felumero shocked the public conscience, the State Supreme Court announced yesterday a "required drastic correction and change"—in effect a complete overhaul of Family Court.

The story listed the changes and corrections, which hardly added up to an overhaul. The *News* said the report indicated that widespread publicity, including many articles in the *News*, had been a goad to the persons conducting the study.

On September 17 a *News* editorial with Roxanne's picture

headed "LITTLE ROXANNE'S LEGACY," claimed, probably justly, that the reforms were due to her death and their prodding.

Pretrial hearings in the Felumero case started November 10 in New York's criminal court and were covered exhaustively by the *News. News* reporter Don Flynn wrote most of the trial stories. Four days after Poplis and Marie had reported the girl missing, Poplis confessed. Detective Gerald Burke testified that Marie first told him she went inside to get a blanket for the baby and when she came out, Roxanne was gone. Burke said that when he told Poplis he didn't believe their story of the child's disappearance, Poplis told him, "I threw the kid in the water."

According to Burke, as quoted in the *News,* Poplis had been slapping Roxanne for several days, first on March 16, " 'five or six times' " on her face and head because " 'she was always wetting her bed.' " Although he noticed next day that her head was swollen, he slapped her around again on March 19. " 'I hit her lots of times; she was always wetting,' " he said.

On March 21 at bedtime, Poplis reportedly told Burke, Roxanne said she was hungry and didn't feel good. She threw up her dinner and fell on the floor. Poplis said her eyes were closed and she was cold. He told her mother he thought there was something wrong with her and when her mother said, "What are we going to do?" he answered, according to the detective, " 'I think I'll have to throw her in the river.' " He then walked down to the river, while the mother pushed their eighteen-month-old in a stroller, stopped twice to smoke a cigarette, weighted her body down with stones, and threw her in.

Poplis's lawyer tried to get a delay on the grounds that his client's confession was made public before the trial. The judge refused. It was said Poplis had been promised a lighter sentence for confessing.

Several days passed while the jury was chosen. The trial was as emotionally charged as anyone might expect it to be. The prosecutor, during jury selection, warned the thirty prospective jurors they might be horrified, sick to their stomachs, and unable to keep a dry eye. Mrs. Boccio, the first witness on the stand, wept when shown a picture of Roxanne at her third birthday party. She broke into "wracking sobs," the *News* said. She cried out, " 'I've lost her. I can't do it. I want to go home.' "

The judge recessed the court until Mrs. Boccio could collect herself while the defense counsel demanded a mistrial on the grounds that the prosecutor put her on the stand first to inflame the jury.

Mrs. Boccio claimed that during the two years Roxanne was with her, she always threw up when her mother came to visit. Then she told the story of Roxanne's bruises. On January 1, she said, she took Roxanne to Rockefeller Center. Roxanne was coming to spend the night, and when Mrs. Boccio bathed her, she saw bruises on the child's body. The next day she took her to the Foundling Hospital to have her examined.

In his opening statement, the prosecutor said the last months of Roxanne's life had been a horror. Beaten because she wet the bed, her face turned black and her head swelled to two or three times its normal size. He said her stepfather had hit her as hard as a man would hit another man. The last week of her life, the prosecutor told the court, the child was numb with beatings.

The defense counsel claimed others who were guilty were not being tried, and specifically mentioned Marie. He called her "a depraved narcotics addict" without any compassion. He claimed the prosecutor promised Poplis his wife would not be arrested if he confessed.

On December 3, the *News* carried the testimony of Donna, a twenty-one-year-old addict friend of Marie Poplis's. Donna said that she had visited the Poplises' apartment three times in the ten days before Roxanne was killed and found her each time in a more pitiable condition. When Donna went to use the bathroom she found Roxanne huddled near the toilet. Her eye was black and blue. Donna said she was black and blue " 'all the way down to her legs' " and her head was twice its normal size. Roxanne reportedly never left the bathroom during the two hours Donna was in the Poplises' apartment.

Several days later, Donna said, Roxanne looked worse, her mouth " 'busted open.' " She saw the child again, the last day of Roxanne's life, lying on the bed, covered up to her head, which was " 'enormous.' " When cross-examined, Donna admitted taking heroin before each visit.

The Foundling Hospital social worker who advised that Roxanne be returned to her mother testified at the trial that she knew the mother had suicidal tendencies, was a former mental patient and an addict, but said the mother didn't appear to be on drugs in 1968. She did not know the Poplises were on welfare, she said. She found that out in the newspaper.

On December 5, according to the *News*, six witnesses, all addicts who used the Poplis apartment for a shooting gallery " 'in exchange for giving George a shot' " said they saw Roxanne in a corner of the bathroom, her head swollen up like a balloon.

When Marie Poplis took the stand on December 8 she said that her husband punched the girl when her head was swollen to twice its normal size. A few days later, she said, Roxanne died. Then she said they walked down to the East River, put stones in Roxanne's snowsuit pants, and threw her in.

A "friend" testified that he saw George slap and punch the child. He saw George beat Marie, too.

The *News* picture of Marie showed a young, attractive, pleasant-looking woman, her hair pulled back from her face; she looked young and innocent. A picture of Poplis showed him looking shifty.

Marie told the court that the man she was living with when Roxanne was an infant threw her out of a fourth-floor window. Both of Marie's legs were broken. She was sent to Creedmoor State Hospital as a would-be suicide and Roxanne was taken away by the Bureau of Child Welfare. Marie insisted she was thrown out the window. She said she was taking drugs during the time she was fighting to get Roxanne back, that the hospital knew about it and gave the child to her anyway.

Poplis took the stand and said his wife beat the child. He claimed he had to beat Marie in order to stop her.

The medical examiner told the court he had never seen a child beaten as badly as Roxanne. He also described Roxanne as emaciated.

On December 16, the *News* announced, "George Poplis, 41-year-old admitted dope addict was found guilty last night of 'murder under depraved circumstances,' beating to death his 3-year-old stepdaughter."

The judge was quoted by the *News* as telling the jury, " 'In 18 years on the bench, I have never said this. I would have voted as you. I believe justice was done.' "

The *News* editorialized that although Poplis had not yet been sentenced, his attorney would presumably appeal the case. "If the verdict is reversed, Poplis will go free, in his early 40's; if the verdict is sustained, he will live off the taxpayers for a number of years. . . . Makes you yearn for full restoration of the death penalty . . . doesn't it?"

Poplis was sentenced to twenty years to life imprisonment. His case was subsequently appealed and the verdict upheld.

In June 1970, a year after the new child-abuse law was passed and seven months after it was put into effect, the *News* did a wrap-up on how effective the law had been. A major factor in Roxanne's death had been the failure to execute the court warrant, reportedly because of inadequate personnel. A year after the law had been passed, not one more warrant officer had been added to the court's two-man squad.

The change in the court's setup, the abolition of specialized parts to all-purpose terms to handle all aspects of a family's difficulties also had not been accomplished, because, according to a court spokesman, the city hadn't yet come up with the money.

Charles Schinitsky, head of family court Legal Aid, told the *News* that the basic needs to solve the child-abuse problem were precourt techniques like child guidance and family counseling, services not available anywhere in needed amounts. When the problem gets to court, he said, it is insoluble.

Judge Nanette Dembitz, the first judge to preside over the new child-abuse part said the legislative watchdog committee "never set foot" in her courtroom, although she invited them personally several times.

"I kept sending . . . messages" to watchdog committee chairman, Alfred D. Lerner, "to come and sit," she said, "but no one ever arrived." According to Judge Dembitz, the committee had $50,000 to consider the state of child abuse, which they "considered in Paris, Rome, and London."

The *News* hailed the establishment of a state statute on child abuse and *News* reporter William Federici won two awards, the Brown Award for outstanding reporting and a Polk Award for metropolitan reporting.

What did it all add up to? The *News* reported some of the circumstances of a truly terrible, pitiable death with deserved outrage but with dangerous oversimplification. By focusing on the lurid details, it reinforced the idea that all child abusers are dope fiends and murderers, and that child abuse inevitably leads to a hideous death. It described the family court as sending children to that death, failing to note the problems and the culpability of the social agencies or examining the court's inability to deal in any real way with such problems. By depicting the foster parents as models of love and sentimentalizing their devotion, they created a false impression of foster care and provided no picture of the limited alternatives for abused children. By spotlighting Dr. Vincent Fontana as their child-abuse expert and publicizing his narrow view of the phenomenon, they further limited any real public understanding.

There are still some thirty to fifty cases of neglect and/or abuse before the New York City Family Court each day. Most people agree that a very small number result in real danger. And while it's easy to remove the child if the judge makes that determination, there's no place to put them. Institutions are overcrowded. "Temporary" foster care may mean the rest of the child's life. Foster homes are almost impossible to find for black and Puerto Rican children. And foster parents are seldom as loving as the Boccios seemed to be.

While administrative reforms are useful, as are more court resources, court reforms do not get to the heart of child abuse. The questions are: What makes people lash out at their children? How many incidents result in fatalities? What, if anything, can we do to prevent it?

Who's an abuser? And why?

5

Who's an Abuser?

Three young lawyers, two in blue jeans, one in a miniskirt, are sitting in the family court's Legal Aid office discussing child abuse.

"They're usually genuine cases," says Barbara, the skinny one in the miniskirt, "and the parents are usually beyond help. In the typical abuse case, the mother has four or five kids in placement already, voluntarily or through the court. She's schizophrenic. The father is brought in. He doesn't seem quite competent either. Who's going to care for the child that's still at home? The judges are reluctant to terminate the parents' rights. So the child is put in foster care for eighteen months. Then eighteen months later the petition is renewed again. The agencies don't have any facilities and no one knows what happens to the kids.

"Or here's another one," says Rita, one of the two in jeans. "The family consists of three children: a girl, twelve, psychotic, who's from the mother's first family; a boy, eleven—I'm not sure which is his parent; and a newborn, a child of both parents. They're both alcoholic, and the father is out of a job. They take their resentment out on the older girl. The girl goes to see her aunt and tells her she's sick. The aunt takes her to the hospital where the doctor says there are signs of physical abuse.

"We sent her to the Bureau of Child Welfare and they placed her. Her parents refused to visit her. The court could place the other two, but the need isn't so great."

"Here's another," says the third lawyer, going through her files. "This time the father brought the neglect petition. He had two children with this lady. Then they separated, and he wanted the kids. He said the mother wouldn't get out of bed, wouldn't cook, wouldn't take care of the children. It turns out that the mother had thrown the child from a previous lover out the window. The mother had abandoned the baby once before, but it was returned to her. She picked up the child at the agency, went home, and threw it out the window. The father's lawyer was a private lawyer so he wasn't concerned with getting the mother locked up. Just concerned with this man's kids."

While they are talking, a fourth lawyer, Steve, walks in. Steve was a teacher for several years, then went to law school. "It's so depressing," he says. "I have to stop thinking about it when I go home at night. Here I've got three kids in for truancy, ages six, seven, and eight. They just won't go to school. They've already been in on a neglect petition. Do you know how long it took the Board of Education to notify us? Fifty school days. That's about three months. Does a teacher suddenly realize that a kid hasn't been in school for three months?

"I have another truancy case of a seven-year-old who won't go to school and an eleven-year-old who's severely brain-damaged. He won't go either. The attendance teachers file a neglect petition. But here's what usually happens. The kid is hyperactive in kindergarten. So he's referred to the guidance counselors. Most of the guidance counselors I've seen are completely unqualified. So they don't give the kid or the teacher or the parents any help at all. The kid continues to be a problem, mostly because he can't read. By the time he's in the third grade you have to fight to get the Bureau of Child Welfare to evaluate him. A so-called psychiatrist says he's hyperactive and has reading problems. Of course, by the time the kid hits fourteen, forget it: he's really in trouble. If the parents did their job, this whole court could be done away with. Of course the schools don't do their job either."

IT WAS George Poplis, the stepfather, who was indicted, tried, and convicted of murder in the sad case of Roxanne Felumero. It is hard not to pass the harshest judgment on a grown man who could brutalize a child as he did. But what of the mother, Marie, who seemed so desperate for the return of her little girl, and then allowed her to be so terribly treated?

Marie Poplis would not seem to be anyone's choice for a mother. Roxanne was an illegitimate child, born while Marie was in her teens. It is not clear when Marie became a heroin addict. She claims it was after her child was taken away from her. She also claims that shortly after Roxanne's birth her boyfriend threw Marie out of the window, a fall that caused her to break her legs, and, indirectly, to lose custody of her child.

We cannot tell what kind of mother Marie would have been, left to her own devices. She apparently thought so little of herself that she chose to live with a series of men, including George Poplis, who could only make her life torture. The pattern of the passive parent who allows the partner to abuse their child is not uncommon. Certainly Marie was passive.

She allowed her husband to beat her three-year-old child for wetting the bed. She also allowed him to beat *her*. We do not know what she felt for Roxanne, only that, from the time Roxanne was taken away from her, she stubbornly pursued her child's return. We can only speculate idly what would have happened if Marie could have been helped. But we do have a few statistics to tell us whether or not she is typical.

Of all the soft information we have about child abuse and neglect, numbers are perhaps the most soft. In 1972, according to Senator Walter Mondale's Senate Committee on Child Abuse, some 60,000 cases of child neglect and abuse were reported to various registries, police, and departments of public welfare. That figure may be too high because it includes reports that are not investigated and others that are unsubstantiated. Or it may be too low, because doctors, especially private physicians, and others are reluctant to report cases. Whenever a lot of publicity has accompanied the establishment of a central registry, the number of reports has increased dramatically. However, upon investigation, up to 50 percent of those reports may turn out to be false (see Chapter 10).

Moreover, institutional abuse, that is, the punitive treatment of children in institutions, such as schools, reform schools, training schools, and institutional residences is not mandated by any state reporting system and could, at a minimum, increase the numbers by perhaps 100 percent.

The case of Roxanne Felumero was atypical in most respects. For one thing, and most important, a very small percentage of the victims of child abuse die, as a 1968 nationwide study conducted by sociologist David Gil revealed.[1] A 1973 pilot study of child abuse at Children's Hospital in Los Angeles showed that too much attention was given to reinjury and not enough to the long-range emotional effects of separating parent and child.

The Los Angeles study looked at 532 child-abuse victims over a six-month period and found that, in fact, most abuse victims experienced no injuries more serious than bruises or abrasions. Fifty-six percent had only bruises or cuts. The remainder was divided among burns, bone fractures, and subdural hematomas.

The study indicated that more children might be damaged in foster care. In four out of five reported abuse cases they studied, the child was sent to one or more foster homes for longer than three years. Thus, in two out of five cases, "temporary removal" was a misleading euphemism.

Other studies have reached similar conclusions. A 1959 study of 4,000 children in foster care predicted that "better than half" would spend "a major part of their childhood" in foster families and institutions.[2] Another study of children under twelve who were placed in foster care during 1966, showed 46 percent were still there three and a half years later.[3] A study of 772 children in foster care in San Francisco in 1973, approximately half the city's case load, found that 62 percent were expected to stay there until maturity. In the San Francisco study the average length of time in care for all children in the study was five years.[4]

These distinctions are critically important. A case like Roxanne Felumero's, with such a pitiable victim, has all the elements to allow the media to mislead and misinform the public in the service of sales and sensationalism. Most experts agree that 5 to 10 percent of reported child abusers are psychotic and outside the reach of treatment or services.

Because the Felumero case is so ugly it is harder to make the point that its most typical features are a parent or parents jobless and on welfare, a young and possibly addicted mother, and the inept management of publicly funded public and private agencies.

It is not, however, the ordinary lives of ordinary people who for months running make page one of the *Daily News*.

A more typical child case is the sad story of Lilly, whose partly lived life has now become a case history.[5]

Lilly was one of six children all alleged to have been neglected, whose mother came to New York City from Puerto Rico with her first child. She immediately went on welfare. Lilly's mother had one child after another until they added up to six. She had no friends, no family, no resources. She spent the usual life of such a woman, a victim of landlords and creditors, a producer of one after another unwanted child.

A neighbor reported Lilly's mother to the SPCC for neglecting her children. When the SPCC investigator found she was living in deteriorated housing with an older alcoholic man who regularly drank up her welfare check, the SPCC took her to court. The court ordered her to throw her friend out. She refused, the man stayed, and Lilly, along with two of her brothers, was removed from her mother's home. First the children were sent temporarily to a city shelter, then to a longer-term residential school. As far as the agency was concerned, Lilly had dropped out of sight.

To Lilly, the court-ordered separation from her mother and her later placement in an institution added up to overwhelming rejection by her mother. She could not accept any other view of it. "My mother put me away," she later told her social worker. She stayed put away for two years, from age ten to twelve. At twelve, when Lilly came home, she was no longer a child. She felt estranged from the people in her neighborhood, she felt that her classmates looked upon her with contempt. So she didn't go to school. She sat outside on the stoop of her building. A twelve-year-old who thought that no one wanted her, she was especially vulnerable.

Lilly realized that men liked her, in particular a sixteen-year-old named Carlos. So at fourteen, Lilly left home and went to live with Carlos. She had known him since she was a child. Carlos was born in Santo Domingo and raised by a foster family when his parents died. Possibly he too was neglected or abused during his early years. At any rate, like Lilly, he felt that his mother had abandoned him.

Carlos's childhood was not much happier than Lilly's. When he was little, Carlos's foster parents moved to New York. Both of them worked and he stayed home alone all day. He was terrified of staying alone but afraid to tell them for fear they might give him up, like his real parents. He wet his bed for years.

Carlos worked hard in school and got a good job when he graduated. Although girls frightened him he was not afraid of Lilly, perhaps because he had known her for a long time and sensed she needed him as much as he needed her. He was jealous of her, however, and did not want her to work or even leave the house without him.

His foster parents disapproved of Lilly, and Carlos disapproved of Lilly's mother, so gradually they saw less of their respective families. That meant there was no family to turn to with any problems. Lilly didn't know how to cook. They had bought furniture and were cheated by the credit company. They had no friends, not much money, and because of anger and resentment turned away from whatever family and support they had.

Carlos went to engineering school at night, but Lilly resented the time he was away. Then they had a child. Carlos saw the boy as a sign of his masculinity; at the same time, he was not sure the child was his. When he questioned Lilly about it, she made fun of him.

The baby cried a lot, spat up food, and became a foil for the conflict between the parents. Carlos hit him often. Once Lilly fixed a bottle that was too hot and gave it to Carlos for the baby. Carlos knew the bottle was too hot and fed it to the baby anyway.

A year later they had a second child. This child, a girl, did not cry, did not spit up, and was easier to manage. Becoming more and more anxious about her feelings toward Carlitos, Lilly first took the child to an emergency clinic, saying that he cried a lot, had diaper rash, and she couldn't handle him. She tried to get her mother to take the baby. Her mother refused. No one recognized how frightened Lilly was that she might hurt the child herself.

One afternoon, feeling low, Lilly took their rent money and bought clothes and curtains. When she failed to pay the rent, the landlord sent them a dispossess notice. Carlos's boss, who had already loaned Carlos money to pay for his college tuition, refused to loan him more. Carlos, jealous of Lilly, angry at his son, and desperately short of money, got furious, lost his temper, shouted at the boss, and nearly lost his job.

Two days later Lilly and Carlos brought Carlitos to the hospital. The child had a subdural hematoma, two rib fractures, and multiple contusions. Lilly said the baby fell while she was lifting him from the bath. The doctor did not believe the story and reported them for child abuse.

They were visited by a protective services caseworker from the Bureau of Child Welfare, a recent college graduate who had majored in literature. She told them she wanted to help. Lilly showed her the dispossess notice and asked where they might borrow money for the rent. She couldn't help with that. She asked Lilly and Carlos to place both children voluntarily. When they refused, her supervisor instructed her to take out a petition charging "child abuse and failure to cooperate with the Bureau of Child Welfare."

The children were taken away. Over the next fourteen months Lilly and Carlos were in family court eleven times trying to get them back.

Lilly was lucky in one respect. She found a social worker who understood how badly she needed help. Miriam Muravchik, at Mobilization for Youth's Legal Services office, knew of the work being done in Denver by Drs. Helfer, Kempe, and Steele on child abuse, and tried to apply their principles. She consulted with Helfer and with other child specialists in New York on how to help Lilly and Carlos. She spent time with them, allowing them to see her as a surrogate parent, encouraging them to talk about their problems of being parents. She also tried to get them help with practical problems, which they needed just as badly.

Mrs. Muravchik went with Lilly to visit her children, whom she was allowed to see only once a month. The children of course did not know her very well, and that upset Lilly even more. But they were important to her. She did not want to lose them. With help, she began to understand how she had taken her resentment of her mother out on her children. Her social worker felt she was doing well.

However, despite Muravchik's help and a psychiatrist's testimony that the baby should be returned and the parents should be allowed to visit Carlitos, now in foster care, more often than once a month to prepare for his return, the judge refused arbitrarily.

The probation officer, who had spent perhaps one hour with them, recommended long-term placement. She had found them "uncommunicative," she reported to her superiors. She was afraid to visit their home because it was in such a bad neighborhood. She knew that after the Felumero case, the judge would favor placement unless justification to return the children was overwhelming. The attorney for the Bureau of Child Welfare recommended continued temporary placement for the children, and psychiatric help for Carlos and Lilly. Not knowing them personally, he could not understand how ludicrous his recommendation was. Carlos and Lilly could not pay for psychiatric help and, since Carlos had a job, they were not poor enough to qualify for Medicaid. At any rate Carlos could not take time off from his job for therapy, and there were no clinics near them open at night.

With both children away, Lilly was now spending most of her time on the streets. Carlitos, who was fragile, had not done well in temporary foster care and had been placed in three successive homes. The baby was in an institution.

The children were eventually put in long-term foster care. The judge had a difficult choice. If the children were returned to their parents and injured it would look bad for him. If they were placed in an institution and starved emotionally, or went from one foster home to another, no one would hold him accountable.

Lilly and Carlos broke up after the judge put the children in long-term placement. Carlos went back to college and found another woman. Lilly became a junkie. A year or so later, a child of her junkie boyfriend was reported battered.

Miriam Muravchik spent a lot of time with Carlos and Lilly during these fourteen months and she felt she was helping them. But she couldn't beat the system. She could not get the court to allow the baby to come home on visits, or even to allow Lilly to visit Carlitos more often. This was despite the fact that the family court's stated aim is to help and rehabilitate the family and that every social work agency is charged with providing services to the family when a child is temporarily removed, in order to help change the present situation and prepare them for the child's return.

The agency of course did the opposite. It not only did not help, it was an obstruction to a mother who was reaching out to her children. It simply pushed her away. Under the circumstances, it was not likely that Lilly and Carlos would pull themselves and their marriage together.

Meanwhile Carlitos and the baby will spend the next several years, perhaps their entire childhood, in institutions. Once children are in "temporary" placement for over a year, their chances of adoption drop drastically, as few people will adopt an older or "difficult" child. The shifting, probably indifferent, care for Carlitos and his sister will cost $4,000 to $12,000 per year. Over the next twelve years, the two children may cost the city $96,000 to $300,000. They will be nobody's children, and they will in all likelihood repeat their parents' experiences. Lilly was nineteen when her children were taken away and she is likely to have more.

How are Marie and George Poplis or Lilly and Carlos typical?

One of the severe limitations in describing the characteristics of abusing and neglecting parents is the relatively little research on the subject. Most studies deal with reported cases, which almost exclusively involve poor people. Thus a study conducted in a big eastern city with a large black and Hispanic inner-city population will reveal that a large number of those reported are Spanish and black. In an area where the people at the bottom are poor whites, poor whites will predominate in the abusing class. The one common feature of such studies is that the largest percentage of people reported are the poorest in the area being studied. Even in New Zealand, a study of child abuse and neglect showed that the people most likely to be reported were the Maori and Polynesian, who are New Zealand's lower class.

Specialists in child abuse are always saying that child abuse and neglect cut across all income levels, that the Park Avenue mother, the Shaker Heights father, the Beverly Hills parent may be just as cruel and abusive as the black mother raising four out-of-wedlock children in a ghetto in Detroit. The experts often refer to the American Humane Society study in 1962 of 662 newspaper reports, demonstrating a wide range of socioeconomic levels,[6] and a Massachusetts SPCC study of 115 families with 180 children, which showed the majority of families were self-supporting.[7] There is the Brandeis University National Opinion Research Study, which described 40 percent of abusing parents as "comfortable" and 65 percent as self-supporting.[8] But that is not what most of the professional social work research literature says. And it is certainly not what the registers of reported child abusers say.

Who are reported abusers and neglecters? Overwhelmingly they are poor people, black people, Hispanic people, very young mothers. Mothers with illegitimate children. Parents with a lot of children. Alcoholics. Junkies. People on public assistance. People with no jobs. People with no friends. People with no resources. People with emotional problems, with medical problems, with poor physical health, with poor mental health. People with no wherewithal. People with no hope.

People reported for abusing and neglecting their children are more likely to live in cities, and in bad housing. They have inherited no family silver or heirlooms, rugs, books, or houses in the country. Some have inherited severe alcoholism, often going back three generations; some have inherited poor health, mental and physical. Instead of family traditions like the groaning Christmas board, their traditions are marginal employment and their family trees are many-stemmed from the divorces and remarriages and the temporary separations.

That is clearly the evidence as presented by social workers and sociologists in the existing literature on abuse and neglect. The book *Wednesday's Children*, by social worker Leontine Young, differentiates between what she calls severe neglect, which is primarily lack of feeding and moderate neglect that includes lack of cleanliness, lack of adequate clothing, and failure to provide medical care. Severe abuse according to Young is consistent beating that leaves visible results. Moderate abuse occurs when parents beat children under stress or when drunk. Young considers the severe category unable to be helped.

The abusing parents' hallmark is deliberate, calculated, consistent punishing without cause or purpose. In addition, Young characterizes both "severe" groups as socially isolated, belonging to no community, church, club, or group, a fact that allows people to hide severe pathology and probably even advances it.

According to Young, there is a close relationship between deviant behavior and social class. In general, she says, neglecting and abusing parents are "a group heavy with suffering and failure." They come from similar backgrounds. They were abused or neglected as children. Young also sees a high correlation between family disorganization and social class. She theorizes that because of the behavioral standards it enforces, social class permits or prohibits what a family will act out in view of the community. Lack of economic resources tends to make deviant behavior more visible. Public assistance invites investigation as does a child's delinquent behavior. In the absence of proof of abuse, economic status is protective. Young might have asked whether lack of economic resources causes deviant behavior.

Elizabeth Elmer's study, with her colleagues, of fifty abusing parents known to Children's Hospital in Pittsburgh, shows them to be passive, dependent, immature, hostile, aggressive, always angry, rigid, and cold.[9] The families in Elmer's study were predominantly white, Protestant, and low income. Elmer, an assistant professor of social work at the University of Pittsburgh, found that the mothers in her sample had negative feelings toward their children, suffered from depression, had frequent crying spells, had trouble eating, feared their husbands (many of whom drank), had poorly managed households, had few close friends, and had experienced many desertions and separations. In addition, the mother was often under twenty-one, the abused child was likely born out of wedlock, and there were three or more children with less than one year between their births.

Elmer also found that abused children with bone fractures also had a higher degree of mental retardation and speech difficulties, as well as more trouble expressing anger at a later stage.

All these studies suggested that many abusive parents had themselves been abused by their parents during childhood.

Dr. David Gil, whose book *Violence Against Children* reports the findings of the only systematic nationwide study of child abuse, has given us a picture of child abuse in America that is contrary to much popular opinion. Testifying in 1973 before the Senate Subcommittee on Children and Youth, Gil said his studies indicated that the "widespread acceptance in our culture of physical discipline of children is the underlying factor of physical child abuse" whether it was in private homes, in schools, or in various child-care institutions. Gil believes that while child abuse can and does exist at all levels of the population, its higher incidence among lower-income groups cannot be explained only by the argument that the poor are more likely to be reported. Child abuse is more likely to occur among low-income and minority groups, Gil believes, because, compared to other groups in the population, they live under conditions of much greater strain and frustration in their daily lives. The strain is reflected in a lower level of self-control and a greater inclination to take out angry feelings on children.[10]

Gil insists that there is no basis to the frequently made claim that the incidence of child abuse has increased in recent years.

As he points out, it is impossible to discuss increases and decreases when there have not been any accurate counts over a period of time. What has increased, he says, is the public's awareness, interest, and concern.

Gil studied all child-abuse incidents reported through legal channels in the United States in 1967–68, nearly 13,000 incidents.[11] He found that, in general, boys and girls were equally abused when it came to numbers, but differently with respect to age. Slightly more than half the children reported as abused were boys. Boys tended to outnumber girls in all age groups under twelve but teenage girls outnumbered teenage boys. Gil concludes that the change in sex distribution of the victims reflects cultural attitudes. As children, girls are considered more conforming than boys and therefore less physical force is used against them. When girls become adolescents, however, parents' worries about their dating and sexual behavior are more likely to cause arguments and lead to more use of force against them. With boys, force tends to be used more readily before adolescence and less as boys get older and are likely to be as strong as their parents.

Although other studies suggest that younger children are more likely to be abused, Gil's figures showed more than 75 percent of the victims to be over two years of age and nearly 50 percent over six. One-fifth were teenagers.

There were more nonwhite children reported. The rates were 21.0 per 100,000 for nonwhites and 6.7 for whites. Gil believes the overrepresentation of nonwhites may be due partly to reporting bias but mainly to the greater poverty, the higher rate of fatherless homes, and the larger families among nonwhites, all characteristics strongly associated with child abuse. In addition, Gil notes the possibility of real differences of child-rearing practices among different ethnic groups. Gil notes elsewhere that "some American Indians never use physical force in disciplining children, while the incidence rates of child abuse are relatively high among American blacks and Puerto Ricans." [12]

Some 29 percent of the abused children in Gil's study had problems in social interaction and general functioning the year preceding the abusive incident and nearly 14 percent had deviations in physical functioning. Over 13 percent of the school-aged children were in special classes for retarded children or in grades below their age level. Almost 3 percent of the school-aged children had never been to school. Ten percent had lived with foster families at some time and over 3 percent had lived in child-care or correctional institutions. Over 5 percent had been to juvenile court on other than traffic offenses. According to Gil, these items, taken together, suggest a higher level of deviance than would be found in any group of children selected from the population at large.

Over 60 percent of the children had a history of prior abuse, suggesting that physical abuse is not likely to be an isolated incident but a pattern of caretaker-child interaction.

Nearly 30 percent of the abused children lived in female-headed households. The child lived with his own father in 6 percent of the cases and a stepfather in nearly 20 percent. Over 2 percent lived in foster homes and .3 percent with adoptive parents. The child did not live with the mother in over 12 percent of the homes. Ten percent of the mothers were single, nearly 20 percent separated, divorced, or widowed, and over two-thirds living with a spouse. The homes of nonwhite children were less often intact. According to Gil the data on family structure suggests a definite link between child abuse and the normal family structure, and family structure seems especially weak for nonwhite abused children.

Although other studies show abusing parents are likely to be very young, Gil found a wide range of age among abusing parents.

A striking finding was that the proportion of families with four or more children was nearly twice as great among families of reported abused children than among families in the general population with children under eighteen. There was a much smaller proportion of small families among reported abusers. This reinforces Gil's conclusion that stressful living conditions contribute to child abuse. There were more nonwhites with larger families in the study than whites.

Levels of both occupation and education of parents were

much lower in the subject group than that of the general population, and the nonwhite parents tended to rank lower than the whites. Nearly half the fathers of abused children were unemployed throughout the year the study was done and about 12 percent were unemployed at the time of the abusive incident. Unemployment rates were higher for nonwhite fathers. The income of families of abused children was very low compared to all U.S. families and even lower for nonwhites. Over 37 percent of the families were receiving public assistance during the time of the abusive incident and nearly 60 percent had been on public assistance at some time.

The personal histories of the parents showed a level of deviance in psychosocial functioning higher than that of the population at large.

A mother or stepmother was the abuser in 50 percent of the incidents and the father or stepfather in about 40 percent. Others were caretakers, siblings, or unrelated perpetrators. However, since almost a third of the homes were headed by females, fathers had a higher involvement rate than mothers. Two-thirds of the incidents in homes where fathers or stepfathers were present were committed by the father or stepfather; while in homes with mothers or stepmothers, the mothers or stepmothers were perpetrators in less than half the incidents that took place. Over 70 percent of the children were hurt by a biological parent, 14 percent by a stepparent, less than 1 percent by an adoptive parent, 2 percent by foster parents, 1 percent by a sibling, 4 percent by other relatives, nearly 7 percent by unrelated caretakers.

Other findings showed almost two-thirds were members of minority groups, and well over half had problems in social and behavioral functioning during the year. There were also problems of physical illness, intellectual functioning, and mental illness.

What of the injuries? Gil's tabulation, based on medical verification in over 80 percent of the cases and therefore considered quite reliable, shows that 53.3 percent of the injuries were not considered serious. Less than 5 percent left permanent damage, and 3.4 percent were fatal. Ninety percent of the reported incidents were not expected to leave any lasting physical effects on the children. Thus Gil's findings are distinctly at odds with popular opinion. As Gil puts it, "Even if allowance is made for under-reporting, especially of fatal cases, one must question the view of many concerned professional and lay persons, according to which physical abuse of children constitutes a major cause of death and maiming of children throughout the nation."

The findings of a pilot study at Children's Hospital in Los Angeles agree with Gil's. This study looked at 532 child-abuse victims over a six-month period and found that contrary to popular opinion, most abuse victims experience no injuries more serious than bruises or abrasions. Fifty-six percent of the children had only bruises and cuts. The remainder divided into those with burns, bone fractures, and subdural hematomas.

Gil found injuries were more likely to be serious in children under three, a finding of most other studies, too, and among nonwhite children. They were about equal for boys and girls.

Nearly 60 percent in Gil's study did not require hospitalization and nearly 25 percent did not require medical treatment at all. Of those requiring hospitalization, over 41.7 percent were discharged in less than a week. Over one-fifth had to be hospitalized beyond a week.

Parents and perpetrators under the age of twenty-five were more likely to inflict serious injuries, and women, especially single women, were more likely to inflict serious injuries than men. This is somewhat surprising, and Gil does not suggest a reason. Perhaps young single women with the complete responsibility for child care are just more desperate.

Parents who had appeared before family courts, who had been in foster care themselves, and whose annual income was under $3,500, were also more likely to inflict serious injury.

Exploring the causes of child abuse, Gil's study found that discipline in association with uncontrolled anger and a general attitude of resentment and rejection toward a particular child were common. Another cause was anger directed at the hyperactive or otherwise annoying child.

Recent research by Dr. Anneliese Korner at Stanford University indicates that the personality of the young infant can be a factor in triggering abuse. For instance, unresponsive babies, sick babies, or babies who cry a lot are especially likely to evoke hostility from young, immature mothers, or mothers who for other reasons are feeling inadequate. The child's contribution to the mother-infant relationship has obvious implications for the study of child abuse.[13]

Another instance of child abuse, according to Gil, shows the child caught in a quarrel between caretakers, often with alcohol involved. Others were sexual abuse, excessively severe or sadistic disciplining, and mental or emotional problems on the part of the perpetrator. This was found in almost half the cases Gil studied and was strongly associated with stress. Abuse and neglect were found to occur together in about one-third of the cases. "Mounting stress in the life of the perpetrator" was evident in almost 60 percent of the cases. A typical instance, which precipitated abuse about 17 percent of the time, was an absent mother who had left the child with a boyfriend or male caretaker.

But probably the most important findings in Gil's research are the very low incomes of the families and the relatively small numbers of serious abuse.

Doctors Henry Kempe and Ray Helfer, who coined the term "battered child," as well as the concept "surrogate mother," have worked for many years on the problem.[14] They view the real patient as the battering parent. They believe that people who beat their children were beaten themselves, an idea that most psychiatrically oriented people would accept. Such people were never mothered themselves and consequently have never developed the "mothering instinct." By mothering instinct, Helfer and Kempe mean that protective love and sympathy that a person gives a dependent child, allowing him to grow and develop with confidence, self-love, and self-respect. People who grow to adulthood without parental love are likely to be emotionally isolated, Kempe says. They tend to be suspicious of others and shallow emotionally, unable when they have a child to provide him with mothering—instead, expecting the child to provide the gratification that their lack of internal development has denied them.

For people like this, who have never developed any controls or any inner strength, life is a constant, unbearable harassment. They cannot cope with anything. Everything is a source of frustration, anger, and anguish. In a family with many children, this parent is likely to select the most frustrating ones and single them out for his rage.

Having isolated the missing mothering, Helfer believes this can still be provided. In the Child Abuse Program at the University of Colorado Medical Center at Denver, he provides what he calls "surrogate mothers" who are available to a parent at all times for consultation, advice, and relief whenever the parent feels he cannot cope. A team that includes a lay therapist, a social worker, and a doctor, also works closely with the city's courts.

Dr. Arthur H. Green, a New York psychoanalyst who heads a research and treatment program in child abuse at Kings County Hospital, describes the abusing mother as one who had a poor relationship with her parents, lost her mother or maternal guardian by death or abandonment during childhood, and has difficulty with her husband or her current boyfriend, who frequently abuses her. Her mother was probably beaten by her husband or boyfriend, too. She is likely to have had an unplanned pregnancy, in addition to problems with drug addiction, alcoholism, and psychosis.

Green has studied the effects of neglect and abuse and has come to several tentative conclusions. The first is that most abused children that he has seen appear in the context of neglect; that repeated abuse in this context may lead children to actively perpetuate the abusing experience in order to get some, any attention; that neglected children have deep feelings of rejection and emotional deprivation and that physical abuse occurring in the relative absence of neglect, poverty, and family disorganization would probably have a different effect.

Green found that children who were subjected to painful, recurrent beatings within the first two years of life showed more self-destructive behavior in the form of self-hitting, self-biting, head-banging, hair-pulling, and other forms of self-mutilation. He sees these children as repeating the earlier painful experience, acting at the same time as aggressor and victim. Some displayed more covert forms of self-destructive behavior such as accident proneness and provocativeness. Because in most children Green saw, the abuse occurred in a matrix of rejection, neglect, and stimulus deprivation, he believes such a child values the painful interaction as an alternative to complete lack of contact and may even stimulate it. Neglected children appear to be more passive and apathetic and less interested in getting others to react.

Green shares the Kempe hypothesis of role reversal. The mother (and/or father) whose own parent was cruel or inadequate, rejecting or demanding, who was unloved as a child and feels herself to be a bad, unloved, unloving person, will likely select a partner who is sadistic, exploitative, and ungiving, who will confirm her bad or shifting feeling about herself. She herself, the theory goes, has dependency needs that have never been satisfied. When she has children she will find that she cannot gratify the child. The child's demands are a painful reminder of the bad child she was. The child's increased demand for care intensifies the mother's own feelings of dependency. She wants someone to take care of her, so she turns to the child for satisfaction, which the child, of course, cannot provide. Her inability to satisfy the child makes her unconsciously equate the child with her own critical and demanding mother. She reenacts with her child the rejection and humiliating experiences she herself had as a child.

As to the long-term effects on the child as he proceeds toward adulthood, Green wonders "if the abused child's defective impulse control might eventually lead to delinquency and assaultive violent behavior during adolescence and to child battering if he becomes a parent himself." [15]

A second study Dr. Green conducted showed a high degree of self-destructive impulses including suicide, as severely disciplined children reached adolescence, particularly among girls and

Puerto Rican boys. The histories of the latter revealed frequent abandonment and early separations from one or both parents, mothers often leaving children with relatives while they moved to America to look for jobs. According to Green, males who are severely punished as children are more able than girls to act out their aggressions, particularly as they approach adolescence.[16]

Whatever the studies, neglecting and abusing parents are most frequently described as being poor, out of work, on relief; badly educated; alcoholics or addicts; in poor physical and mental health; socially isolated; having a lot of unwanted, unplanned, frequently out-of-wedlock children; having an unstable family. Most of all they are described as living under conditions of great stress.

While there have been few substantial studies of abusing and neglecting parents, there has been even less research concerning the children. Green and others have described them as stubborn, negativistic, chronic criers, fearful, apathetic, unappealing, provocative, withdrawn, and passive.

The kind of labeling is important because it determines the treatment. If people are considered sick, they need a doctor. If the problem is poverty, perhaps the answer is money. If it is a combination of factors, what is the right way to treat the symptoms?

Putting aside for the moment the question of how we should treat so-called abusing and neglecting parents, let us look at how we do treat them. And while we do, we should keep in mind some other questions. How do people get labeled this way? Who makes up the categories? Who applies them? What is their interest in doing so? What, for instance, is the court's interest in labeling parents as "neglecting" and "abusing"? What institutions have an interest in applying such labels? And what is the effect of that process on human lives?

Over 36 percent of the abused children in Gil's study were removed from their families after the abusing incident. In 15.4 percent of the cases, not only the victims but their siblings were removed as well. In the case of both abused and neglected children, we can estimate that well over a third are removed from their homes.

The rationale for removing these children from their homes has not changed much since the nineteenth-century reformers convinced themselves that by detecting predelinquents at an early age, they could save and rehabilitate the children in institutions.

The family court is still operating on the same rationalizations, claiming to save children from the potential harm done to them by unfit parents. At the same time we have created and gradually expanded a relatively new service industry based on the labeling, servicing, storing, and rehabilitating of the poor and the deviant. All of these professions that live off poor people in trouble—social work, child welfare, protective services, institutional administration—have not only grown tremendously but have also increased their own professional status.

In the good old American way, we have, over the years, managed to create a new product whose development and management supports thousands of others in the society. Taking care of the unfit poor has in fact become a kind of government subsidy for a large part of our society. And, as befits a country where advertising has become an art form, we are continually changing the labeling and packaging of our products. "Juvenile delinquent" was one of the earlier labels; "abused and neglected" are the latest.

From the late 1800s to the 1960s, we have seen the gradual development of the child-welfare industry, expanding its umbrella over growing numbers of children whose parents were economically marginal members of the society. In the mid-1950s, another entity was discovered that enlarged the concerns of the child-welfare movement: child abuse.

Briefly, in the mid-1950s, the discovery of radiologic evidence of multiple fractures accompanied by subdural hematomas in small children led to the recognition that parents were actually inflicting these injuries. In the 1960s most states passed laws to identify children who had been physically mistreated and to prevent further harm. Mandatory reporting theoretically provided data for studies and also exposed the reported parents to legal process. On the state level, procedures were instituted in the juvenile or family courts to adjudicate abuse and to offer protective and rehabilitative services. Increasingly abuse and neglect have been linked as one entity.

Assuming that "rehabilitation" is possible, the necessary facilities for rehabilitative services are sadly lacking in most courts and social work agencies. The courts themselves are understaffed to deal with the problems. So are protective agencies. It is hard to recruit staff to deal with such unattractive people, particularly when salaries are low compared to salaries for teachers and nurses, and the training is more demanding. Therefore, what staff agencies manage to get is, usually, overworked and undertrained. It is important to keep that in mind when a particularly ugly incident of genuine child abuse stirs up a local outcry. The result, as in New York City after the Felumero case, is to put harsher laws on the books and enlarge the number and kinds of people who can or must report abuse and neglect to local registries. It is seldom explained that abuse that ends in fatality is statistically a small part of the problem. The real problem is the continued social neglect of all our children, particularly poor and minority children—their health, their subsistence, their housing, their schooling—and the deterioration of the family and the lack of constructive social, health, and welfare policies that could have a significant impact on child and parents.

Most reported cases do not result in criminal charges, but many result in the removal of the children. The law varies throughout the country. Some states include abuse and neglect in the same category. Some descriptions of unfit homes allow states to pass moral judgment on family behavior, which many people believe should not be the state's business.

California, for instance, defines a dependent child as one "not provided with a home or suitable place of abode, or whose home is an unfit place for him by reason of neglect, cruelty, or depravity."

In Pennsylvania, the code focuses on omissions of the parent.

A neglected child in Pennsylvania is one who "lacks proper parental care by reason [of the] fault or habits of his or her parent."

New York and other states have special statutory provisions dealing specifically with child abuse. In some states the definition of neglect encompasses morality. A Utah court, for example, found children neglected because their parents practiced and advocated plural marriage as part of their religion. The children were taken away.

In Maryland, a woman's children were removed because she had another illegitimate child. In Iowa five children were taken from their parents after one report from a social worker because the parents were considered to have an insufficient IQ. This case is now being challenged in the courts by the American Civil Liberties Union.

These are cases we know about because they have been appealed to higher courts. Most cases where children are taken away from their parents get no publicity.

Where parental conduct rather than its effect on the children leads to a neglect determination, it is hard to avoid the conclusion of harassment. We have always had a double standard of morality for the poor, but changing life-styles make its enforcement an ugly hypocrisy. Is it fair, for instance, that poor people are held to a stricter moral code than the middle class in an age where divorce is nearly as common as marriage? Is it just to take away a poor woman's child because she has a lover when middle-class mothers have boyfriends staying overnight? While the chic magazines herald liberation and freedom for the middle-class mama, the poor mother whose "liberation" is brought to the attention of the family court may pay for her freedom with her family.

The lady who goes off with her lover for the weekend, leaving her ten-year-old in the charge of her sixteen-year-old, is safe from the police if she lives in the fashionable part of town. If she stays out overnight in the ghetto she may be in real trouble.

Most states now have mandatory reporting laws. Physicians as well as others are now told to report instances of suspected abuse to the appropriate authority, which is usually the local bureau of child welfare. The theory is that these symptoms are susceptible to medical, psychiatric, or social treatment and should be referred there before reported to a law-enforcement agency. In many cases, however, referrals are made directly to the police.

There are literally thousands of cases across the country where children are removed from their parents on questionable legal grounds and put in institutions. In New York City many mothers who have been addicts have had their infant taken away before they left the hospital—illegally, if the mother has been enrolled in a rehabilitative program at the time of the baby's birth. This is just a statistic when you read about it. To the mother and the child, it can mean emotional life or death.

Once a case is reported, a social worker, usually employed by the child-protective agency, will investigate to determine if it is necessary to offer services or to take the case to court, as in Lilly's case. Many of these social workers are inadequately trained, afraid of neighborhoods they must visit, unable to establish contact with the parent. Furthermore, according to the final report of the New York City Mayor's Task Force on Child Abuse, the checklist of indicators of neglect may be unjust, amounting "to no more than accusations of poverty":

Many child protective petitions are not precisely drawn. For example, a neglect petition often contains allegations that cannot be substantiated by evidence. It is often the practice of city attorneys to include all and every allegation under the sun, hoping to legally prove one or two. The statute on neglect, and what constitutes neglect, is not only unclear— but so broad in scope that this practice should be avoided. Some of the charges alleged in neglect petitions are unjust as well. They include roach infestation, rodents in the building, poorly kept hallways, ill-kept apartments, children poorly clad, etc., etc. These allegations amount to no more than accusations of poverty. Since a high proportion of neglectful parents are currently receiving public assistance, these accusations may equally be made against a society that cannot provide the minimum requirements for a healthy life for all its citizens. Moreover, impressionistic data revealed by some Family Court judges imply that a great number of neglect cases (and some abuse as well) are directly aggravated by poor and inadequate housing. Shall we continue to accuse individuals (mainly Negroes and Puerto Ricans) for a neglect that is condoned by a society that cannot provide adequate and proper housing?[17]

Once the agency gets the report and evaluates it, it may try to maneuver out of court. It may ask for voluntary placement of the children, as it asked in the case of Lilly. It may refer parents for treatment. Unfortunately, the agency usually cannot follow up on the case. It has infrequent contacts with the family, as in Roxanne Felumero's case. It may put the children in foster care, as it did Carlos's and Lilly's baby, thus causing additional anguish for family and child and effecting no change in the parent.

While definitions of abuse and neglect raise many important issues, the question of removal constitutes the heart of the dilemma.

Often the children, like Lilly herself, are removed "temporarily." Temporary removal, as we have noted, is a misnomer. In most states, "temporary removal" is long-term; "short-term" removal is often more than ninety days.

There are conflicting legal opinions on the removal of a child. One Pittsburgh family court judge echoes the opinions of many others that sociological and psychiatric investigations are often inconclusive, that evidence is rarely clear-cut or objective, and that removal may be a drastic solution since children are often very attached to their parents, even neglected and mistreated children.

In New York City in 1968 and 1969, just under 30 percent out of a total of 5,822 neglect and abuse cases were ultimately removed from their homes, according to figures from New York City Family Court.

The Massachusetts study of some 6,000 children in foster care referred to earlier showed that 13.6 percent had been neglected or abused, 8.5 percent abandoned, 23 percent placed because of the mental illness of parents. Only a fourth of these children returned to their homes. Many children placed in foster care are doomed, like Carlitos and his sister, to a shadowy existence, shifted from one home to another, never belonging to anyone. Judges, lawyers, and social workers repeatedly complain that services that might allow parents to keep their children, like homemaker services, are seldom available.

There is a reasonable conflict over the effects of abuse and neglect and what should be done. The New York State Assembly Select Committee has found that the abuse of children, whether by parents or institutions, turns the abused child inward toward aggression, violence, and criminalization. It views the mistreatment of children as a major contributing factor to increasing violence and rising crime rates. One study has shown that seven out of thirty-nine abused children were in court as juvenile delinquents after being reported abused. Although he may say it too often, Dr. Vincent Fontana is right when he points out that abuse is a dynamic phenomenon, reflected in all our statistics on crime.

Leontine Young believes that children must be taken out of the home in most serious cases. A "democratic society depends on the voluntary and firm compliance of its citizens with certain standards of behavior. The confusions and weakness that result from a lack of self-discipline and self-respect can be quite as destructive as open defiance of social standards. The children grow up aimlessly. As adults they can be blown like weather in every direction and following none." [18]

Others, while not questioning removal of really serious cases, take a broader view. The Los Angeles, California, study cited earlier indicated their doctors were convinced that too much attention is given to reinjury and not enough to the long-range emotional effects of separating child from parent. Since what figures we do have show that most cases of abuse and neglect do not involve serious injury, why set up a system with a demonstrated capacity to hurt and harass many in order to protect a few?

6

Family Court: We Are Only Here to Help You

Harry Sherman has been working as a Legal Aid lawyer three years. Before that he went to a third-rate law school and then worked for an insurance company. Medium height, in his mid-twenties, Harry wears horn-rimmed glasses and his hair in a kind of Afro. The hairdo is not by design. Just sort of disheveled. His whole manner is distracted. Harry wants to talk.

On any average day, Harry handles fifteen to twenty cases. He estimates some 15 percent are abuse and neglect, which means one or two of his cases each day. Legal Aid represents the child in neglect and abuse cases. According to Harry, their role is very unclear.

"If the child is old enough—thirteen, fourteen—we ask him what he wants to do. A lot say they want to go home. In neglect cases the judge usually remands them to the commissioner of social services and the agency places them.

"In abuse cases, if it's the father who's the abuser, the kid usually wants to stay with the mother. If both are mistreating them, the child may want to stay with grandma. It's a problem when the kid is severely beaten. I had a recent case of an eight-year-old boy who wanted to go home, and I told the judge that, but I said I felt there might be danger. If he had been sent home, and something happened, it might have been sticky."

Harry adjusts his glasses. "Here's a good example. In January, the grandmother comes in with a boy. She says the mother is beating him. Then the mother comes in with the boy and a lawyer; she denies excessive punishment. The judge adjourns the case to February. They come back in February but there has been no psychiatric exam yet, so the case is adjourned to March. If there's a finding of abuse, the Corporation Counsel will try the case. We're supposed to stay neutral. There's a possibility of plea bargaining, but I don't think it will go to that. We'll bring in hospital reports and may put the boy on the stand. If there are unexplained bruises and welts, the mother has to go forward. If there is a finding, then the question is, Will the boy be paroled or remanded? He'll probably go to his mother's home, maybe his grandmother's. The judge will order a psychological on both. That will take a couple of months. Sometimes you can't get a psychological for three months. Then we'll have to wait another couple of weeks until it's typed. It's possible that a lot of people just aren't doing their job.

"Then we come back with the records. The purpose of the court is to unite the family, not separate it. We try to go on our own experience and what the kid wants.

"Many abuse cases are kids born with withdrawal symptoms. There's been a tremendous drop, though, in heroin. If the mother's in a program, we'll go along with probation. If there's a relative, we try to send the kid there for placement.

"I started here right after the Felumero case. Legal Aid was taken off child abuse at first, then put back on. Sometimes the charges are trumped up and it's in the child's best interest to go home.

"After Felumero, the judges were afraid to send kids home. They'd say right out, 'I'm not going to get my name in the Daily News. I'm remanding the kid,' putting them in placement.

"Our problem is we really can't do very much investigation. We have three investigators here for all our cases. Only two can go out at a time. The third has to be in the office. And every day there's a new case load. It's really not possible for us to do the kind of job we should.

"In a typical case there's a fight between the husband and wife and they use the kids. The wife refuses visitation rights. He withholds support. On the support petition, he frequently counters with a neglect charge.

"Then the agencies come in on it. Like Department of Social

Services. Maybe the home is dirty and the kids don't have enough clothes. Maybe there is some sort of neglect. They probably need supervision and the mother probably needs help. Usually on that kind of case the judge threatens the mother with removal of the kids.

"You figure you may occasionally save a life. But not often. As for rehabilitation, very little is done. The kid may stay in an institution indefinitely. The Department of Social Services meanwhile says it's still exploring placement. There's the psychological damage done to the kid by a poor institution. Worse yet by a bad one. And what about children dying psychologically? That can't be weighed.

"Most of the younger judges have forgotten Felumero. If there are any redeeming features in the home, the kids are returned or sent to a relative rather than placement. It's generally agreed that institutions are terrible. And the judges are jaded. The judge has heard the story a thousand times, too.

"Judges like to give the parents moral instruction. But the problems are so deep-rooted, what good could lecturing possibly do? And they've heard it all before. The judge lectures so he can say he's tried. If this court were closed down today, it wouldn't make much difference to the city.

"Everybody talks about more money, more resources. I'm not sure money is the answer. We don't know how to handle it. Judging from the whole country, social services are just not working. Take a kid from the ghetto. By the time he comes to court, I don't know if anything can be done—or undone. And in New York kids probably have more rights than elsewhere.

"I've heard a lot of talk about a guaranteed annual income. I don't know if that would help. But I do know one thing. People with money stay out of court. They can also get a better lawyer if they do go, although here I don't think that would make a difference. Even good lawyers are not used to the proceedings.

"Anyway, if the family were working, that is if things were O.K., they wouldn't be in court. They might have problems—a lot goes on in so-called decent homes—but they wouldn't be here.

"At first I was simply stunned at the amount of sexual abuse. There's a high rate of stepfathers having intercourse with stepdaughters. Maybe that's true in the upper and middle classes, too. I don't know. Usually by the time the kids come to the court, there have been many instances. Usually if it just happened once, they wouldn't get to court. I had one particularly ugly case where a father raped a retarded daughter and forced the mother and son to participate.

"One problem here is the judges are antirespondent. They're anxious to make a finding of neglect or delinquency. That may be the nature of judges, but in other cases, the respondent has the protection of the jury. Here the court wants to take jurisdiction.

"And they do love to lecture. I had a case where a kid was brought in on the charge of stealing a car. The judge couldn't hear the case because the complaining witness wasn't there. So he got the kid in front of him, and he says, 'I don't know if you did it, but keep out of trouble.' Before trial, that's the attitude.

"I don't know why I do it. I enjoy it, believe it or not. But it's futile."

JANUS, the two-faced god, is the proper symbol for the family court, which has been plagued from the start with the contradictions inherent in its dual role as social work agency and tribunal of justice. It performs neither role well. The child who comes before the court gets the "worst of both worlds," as Supreme Court Justice Abe Fortas noted some eight years ago, for "he gets neither the protections accorded adults nor the solicitous care and regenerative treatment postulated for children."

Neither solicitous care nor regenerative treatment are much in evidence at the Brooklyn Family Court. At 8:30 A.M., the lobby is already crowded with clients and petitioners, mostly black and Puerto Rican. "Sometimes I can't quite get used to it," says a young, white, blond social worker. "It's like a colonial situation. We're all white. They're all black. Sometimes I walk through the waiting rooms and I think, 'Here I am, here we are, handing out, what? Justice, referrals, IQ tests.' "

Downstairs, two guards sit at either door. No reporters are permitted because, unlike every other court in the land, the proceedings of the family court are confidential. To protect the family involved, the court says. To protect the judges involved, the press says. The one institution in this country that can literally change the course and circumstances of a child's life, that has the power to remove him from his parents forever, is subject to no public scrutiny. In fact, no one pays much attention to family court except on special occasions, when a child like Roxanne Felumero is killed and a newspaper like the *News* makes public review unavoidable.

Fortunately there is an information desk in the Brooklyn Family Court lobby, because the building itself is like a maze. Courts are in "parts" and "sections." Numbers of rooms are not consecutive. Elevators go to some floors but not others. Everyone seems tense. Hostility hangs in the air like stale breath. You would have to air out the society to get rid of it.

If you're there because your case is on that day, you may have to sit the whole day and wait. Obviously your time, and if you're lucky enough to have a job, your day's pay, is irrelevant to a court that deals only with poor people anyway.

The waiting room is dreary, too ordinary to be even ugly, and the brown benches are filled from 9:00 A.M. on with people waiting, clutching handbags, newspapers, coats, bundles, babies. The babies cry and the mothers scold them.

In the courtroom the absence of dignity, decorum, civility, humanity is appalling. If this were a people's court, by and for the people, perhaps the informality would be welcome, signaling equal status for all. This court, however, reeks of inequality.

In the courtroom the judge wears a robe to show his unassailability and the lawyers, many of them women, wear miniskirts or blue jeans, presumably to show their liberation. The men do wear jackets and ties. Most of the lawyers are young with several years' experience in the court, and most work for Legal Aid. An older, more conservatively dressed man or woman is likely to represent the city as the Corporation Counsel, which in recent years prosecutes neglect and abuse cases. A lawyer in a shiny suit is more likely to be a private lawyer.

These are not Wall Street lawyers, corporation lawyers. These are the people's lawyers. Some are caring, most are underpaid, all are overworked.

Off the waiting rooms are the courtrooms and behind them, the chambers. In one, a black judge talks about the court before starting for the day.

"When people come in here," he says, "we can only make them worse. Talk about child abuse. Sure, I see plenty of it. But all these kids are in a vacuum. They are mistreated and abused by society. What are we to do with them? There's no place to put them. There is no regulation of private social-service agencies that discriminate against the black and the poor, although some of the most important people in the country are on their boards and billions of dollars, including public dollars, are involved. Society uses the court as a club, like welfare. We want subservience from the recipients.

"Some judges are insensitive to the poor. They try to impose their personal morality. Blacks and Puerto Ricans get short shrift everywhere. People who have money avoid this court. The poor can only be hostile.

"What can you expect from people who have little training and nothing to work with? We are all conditioned by our backgrounds. The judges are successful or we wouldn't be here. The people we judge have had very little success or they wouldn't be here. In most situations we try to put our values on them. Don't quote me by name."

At ten o'clock the judge enters his courtroom, an ugly room with peeling paint and two chairs facing him, where all parties sit when the court addresses them. Case number one involves six children whose father drinks and beats them. He beats their mother, too. The father is sullen as he sits before the judge and looks at the floor. The children huddle around their mother, who is sitting next to him. The judge warns the father that if he drinks in the house, he'll send him to jail for six months. He tells the mother to call the police if that happens.

As they leave the courtroom, the judge says, "What can I do? Send the boys to a shelter where they'll be raped by the boys, and the girls to another where they'll be raped by the girls?

They're better off at home. As for the father, of course he'll drink."

CASE NUMBER TWO: Two black boys are brought into the courtroom by the police. They are clean and neatly dressed and small for their age. One is eleven and looks eight; the other is fourteen and looks eleven. They ran away from home. Their mother is in the court, too. She doesn't want them. The older boy has been arrested twice before for minor crimes, theft and robbery. The mother can't discipline them, she says. The judge puts them temporarily in a city shelter.

CASE NUMBER THREE: Rita, who is eleven, and her mother, who looks harassed and fifty, have brought Rita's father to court on an abuse petition. He beats Rita. In the course of questioning, the child's lawyer tells the judge that the father has abused the child sexually. The judge tells the father he must have a lawyer, sets a date for another hearing, and issues an Order of Protection against the father, which means the father must stay out of the house. "You better call us if he comes home," the judge tells the mother. "And if you do," he tells the father, "I'll put you in jail for six months."

CASE NUMBER FOUR: The wife, who is eighteen, says her husband beats her. The husband says he had a few drinks and got mad. The wife says he has beaten her before. "When he's been drunk?" asks the judge. "Yes," she says. The judge asks if she'd like help. She says yes. He orders them both to go for counseling and tells the husband if he doesn't go for counseling he'll go to jail for six months.

"You know," the judge says, "I don't even think sexual abuse is so bad anymore. It seems to be very common with poor people. The rich can afford prostitutes. A guy has a lousy job, comes home, drinks, and goes after the kid. Everyone else is protected by someone. Last month I had the case of a Jewish kid who set fire to a synagogue. Three times. He came in here protected by all the Jewish agencies. They said he's rebelling. If he were Catholic, he'd be protected by the Catholic agencies. The few Protestants that aren't black and Puerto Rican are protected by the Protestant agencies. It's all a joke."

As the day progressed, the judge was interrupted by two small near-riots in the waiting room and heard the following cases: a fourteen-year-old boy who threw a brick at his sister; a man who beat up his pregnant wife; a woman whose husband pulled a gun on her; two cases where the husbands are delinquent on child-support payments; one where a husband beat up his wife and put her out of the house with their five kids; a fifteen-year-old girl who had run away from home three times for fear of a neighborhood gang and an angry mother; a snappy-looking mother in a fur coat and her fifteen-year-old son in brim hat, flowered shirt, bell-bottom pants, and red shoes, brought in for robbery; a boy who stole a car; a murder case.

Another judge, one of the few Puerto Ricans on the bench, says, "This court just provides a rug for society to throw its problems under, and don't quote me by name. The system doesn't provide help. We deal with people in their formative stages. I'm supposed to be a father figure. What good am I as a father figure for a kid who is schizophrenic? Sure these kids are rebelling. They're rebelling against the inadequacies of their own families and what society does to them."

Another judge says simply, "Most of the people here have money problems. They're on welfare. We'd all be better off with a guaranteed income. Welfare takes away initiative and imposes phony criteria."

In another courtroom, a man is being questioned about his failure to keep up child-support payments. The man and his wife, separated since 1957, face each other grimly, seated side by side in front of the judge. She is nicely dressed and well spoken. His suit bags, his shoes are run-down, and he looks sick. They have nine children. For the last several years, only four were at home. Now just one is left.

The man, who is a cook, had been paying thirty dollars support per week for the four children until 1971 when he became disabled. Since then he has been paying seventeen dollars. There is only one child left at home, an eighteen-year-old who goes to school and works at night. The father has been working as a janitor at night in a day-care center but several weeks ago his arthritis became so bad he claims he can't work without great pain. He says his wife, who has a good job, is always going away on trips.

The judge compliments the wife on her raising nine children, two of whom are in college. The husband's lawyer says he should compliment the husband too.

The father says, "Judge, I'm sick. I used to pay thirty dollars for four kids. Why should I pay seventeen dollars for one."

The judge says, "When you can't work any longer, come in and we'll adjust it. I'm not very sympathetic. What you're paying is one-third the welfare budget."

Child abuse and neglect takes place in a climate of collective societal abuse. Dr. Brandt F. Steele, one of the founders with Helfer and Kempe of the Denver program, says that abuse is a pattern of interaction between caretaker and child, unusual because of the intensity of the expression. The pattern itself, he is convinced, is "quite prevalent in our culture. To be aware of this, one has only to look at the families of one's friends and neighbors, to look and listen to the parent-child interactions at the playground and the supermarket, or even to recall how one raised one's own children or how one was raised oneself. The amount of yelling, scolding, slapping, punching, hitting and yanking acted out by parents on very small children is almost shocking. . . . In dealing with the abused child we are not observing an isolated, unique phenomenon." [1] How can a court handle that?

As Sanford Katz, lawyer and author of *When Parents Fail: The Law's Response to Family Breakdown*, puts it in his book, "There is no way of knowing precisely how many parents neglect their children as long as society protects the privacy of large numbers of families, particularly those in the middle and upper classes. This does not mean that middle and upper-class parents do not neglect their children. Rather [that] . . . child neglect proceedings are primarily instituted against lower-class parents." Katz notes for example that "the community does not regard parents of children who ran away to Haight-Ashbury or use drugs as neglectful." Instead, they are described as "social problems." They are not considered problems of individual parental neglect. However, when a fifteen-year-old black child is caught with drugs, that is considered parental neglect, not a social problem.

Half of all major crimes reported in the United States are committed by people under eighteen. The judge who "tries" them—there is no jury in family court—will send some children to mental hospitals, some to state training schools, some home, some back to the streets. A very few receive the kind of care and treatment they desperately need, even if they are "sentenced" to it. Why? Because for the ones who most need it, there are no facilities. Because those facilities that are available rarely are equipped to treat anyone. Hospital and training schools alike are mainly custodial. They don't have the resources. And the few places that do, do not want the difficult kids.

There are some children who don't like home, who would prefer foster homes. But frequently there are no homes for them. The older and more difficult the child, the more they need help, the less likely they are to find it.

As the head of probation in a Philadelphia family court said, "Our problem is the number of people who need services badly, in areas where services don't exist. A mother may not need psychotherapy but she needs someone to talk to, and it's lacking. We have kids who ought to be out of their homes, and we don't have a place to put them. It's much worse today than it was ten years ago. The private agencies that have done traditional social work can't seem to adjust to the involuntary client. They want cooperation. They're not used to dealing with hostile people. They don't want people who won't make the grade."

A medical reporter in a large northeastern city said, "The fact is that there's really no place for kids who need help, rich or poor. I have some very good rich friends who have an autistic child. At least they thought he was autistic. Now it seems after years that he's schizophrenic. They have two other children at home. They would like to find a place where this child can be helped. Their child is not black and not poor. They can pay. But in the whole country they can't find a place to send him. So what kind of help do you think a poor child could get from a family court?"

José is a poor, fifteen-year-old Puerto Rican. His parents have brought him into court because he ran away from home. The boy tells the judge that he ran away because his father drinks all the time and when he drinks he beats up José's mother. José's parents say they can't control him. He has been in court before for running away. He has two brothers in a children's home and one in a state training school. His psychological report says he is starved for affection and recognition, none of which he gets at home. His school report says he is bright and comes to school regularly. His social worker says his home is below standard, his neighborhood full of addicts, his father an alcoholic. His mother, thirty years old, speaks no English and has no skills. She had her first child at sixteen.

The last time José ran away they put him in a detention center where he was afraid of the other children. He would like to live in a foster home. But there are no foster parents in this city who want a fifteen-year-old Puerto Rican boy who has run away from home twice. The judge knows the boy will run away from home again. She tells him she is sending him back to the children's center. He tells her he will run away again. The judge puts a note in José's record to the probation department to look for placement.

José's social worker comments, "Puerto Rican parents are harsh disciplinarians. In Puerto Rico, they remember that the local policeman could teach a disrespectful child how to behave. So they take their children to the courts, hoping for the same thing. Unfortunately, that's where the child becomes criminalized. He goes to jail, like José, and he sees worse things than he sees at home."

The judge adds, "Immature and authoritarian parents use the court as a threat. It's a way to evade their own obligation. José's parents are incapable of dealing with him so they threaten him. Children who can't make it at home should not be a court problem. They should be a community problem. So should the parents. I can't make the father stop drinking. I could refer him to an alcoholism program. But he probably wouldn't go. And what about the mother? She's had four kids and can't take care of any of them. I think she drinks, too. She needs help. The father takes the welfare money. Who's going to help her? The Department of Social Services? How can this mother, who has so little love and security in her own life, who lives in a crime-ridden, drug-ridden ghetto, whose husband is an alcoholic who beats her, who came here at fifteen and had the first of four babies the next year, how can we expect her to raise her children to be whole, loving people?"

In most American cities, it costs up to $24,000 a year to care for a child in a private institution. But there are too few of these and they take only the children who are easiest to help. Children who are difficult and disruptive, children with histories of suicide, drug use, assault, low IQs, children who run away, like José, or those who simply do not fall within the institution's religious and racial preferences will not be accepted. In many cities children with low IQs will not even be accepted in state training schools and end up, like José did, in juvenile jails called detention centers, waiting endlessly for placement.

Most judges, social workers, and probation officers say that children they see in family court today appear more disturbed than the children did ten years ago. They blame it on the accelerating breakdown of the old controls—like respect for one's parents and teacher, the greater permissiveness of the society, the increase in the use of drugs, the increase in violence in the whole society, and the greater sophistication of children.

A Washington, D.C., social worker reported an increase in the number of thirteen- and fourteen-year-old black girls who are pregnant and want to keep their babies. The D.C. health service won't give a girl under eighteen birth-control information, even with her parents' consent, unless she's had an abortion or a baby. When she's pregnant and her teacher reports her, she's declared "beyond control." The court puts her in a shelter. Often she decides she wants to have the baby. How is a thirteen-year-old girl going to take care of a baby? She hates living at home, so she is now living on the streets. What will happen to the child? What happens psychologically to a thirteen-year-old who has a baby? Or an abortion? Why couldn't she have gotten help before?

Although America is considered a child-centered culture, it allows millions of children to grow up under circumstances of severe social and economic deprivation. Columnist Sylvia Porter recently estimated that 40 percent of Americans living in poverty are children.[2] Millions of American adults are living in social and economic deprivation. They are going to have children. They may have fewer children because the birth rate is dropping for all colors and classes, but they will surely continue to give birth. Since this country has no policy for helping children or families with children, they will live in much the same circumstances as their parents and they will inevitably be neglected and deprived. Their mothers, if they are on welfare, will not be able to work because there are few day-care facilities, few places to leave the child—that is, if the mother has any skills or training that will allow her to get a job in the first place. How is that thirteen-year-old with a baby going to get training?

She will have to live in the slums because she will not be able to afford any other place to live and even if her welfare check could pay for it, most middle-class neighborhoods do not welcome welfare families. Her children may be malnourished, they may have health problems, they may have reading difficulties, and then they may have troubles in school. If they are truant, they will be reported to the family court, which will put them on probation, on condition they go to school. If they are truant a second time, they may be put in an institution.

Mary Selmen, now forty, as a child was a ward of the New Jersey Department of Welfare. Her records tell us nothing about her parents, but from the fifth grade on, she was in foster care, going from one home to another. At eighteen she came to New York. Living by herself, lonely and unhappy, Mary was afraid she might go crazy. She signed herself into a state hospital where she stayed for two years.

Mary had three children before she was thirty and gave them away at birth for adoption. She had managed to find herself a job as a clerk in a five-and-ten-cent store and knew she could not keep both the job as a clerk and the babies. Besides, she did not feel able to care for a child.

But at the age of thirty-three Mary had a baby she wanted to keep, even though that meant going on welfare. The apartment she was living in had only one room, and the Welfare Department said it wasn't big enough, so they found her another one. The apartment they moved her to had a crack that ran all the way through the wall, letting in cold air. It was so cold she had to use a lot of gas to keep it warm. Mary ran up a gas bill that was hard to pay on her welfare check. She got forty-six dollars every two weeks and was spending so much for heat that it frequently left her with nothing to eat.

Her son, Jimmy, was difficult but bright and she loved him and was proud of him. One day when Jimmy was seven, Mary took her pocketbook with literally her last dollar and went to the market to buy rice and chicken wings for dinner. When she got to the checkout counter, she discovered she had no money. When she got home she found Jimmy had taken it.

Mary took Jimmy's belt off and beat him with it. Jimmy screamed and the neighbors called the police. The police took Jimmy to the hospital where the doctor described his welts and bruises and made a note of the "battered-child syndrome." The hospital social worker called the Society for the Prevention of Cruelty to Children (SPCC) who picked up the case. The police arrested Mary.

When Mary's case came up, the court psychiatrist noted that she had been in Rockland State Hospital for two years and said she was schizophrenic with a history of mental illness, although her "history" was ancient, twenty years in the past, and she'd had no treatment since. Jimmy was still in the hospital and couldn't leave without a court order. At the hearing, the judge mentioned the mother's "history of mental illness" and refused to let the child go home, although she released Mary.

Jimmy stayed in the hospital for a month. His mother visited him every day, and as the nurses later reported, always brought him something, despite her very meager allowance. They said she appeared affectionate and caring.

When Mary's case came up for disposition, it was the twentieth case on the judge's calendar that day. The lawyer who represented Mary did not feel she was likely to repeat the incident. She told the judge that there was no evidence of Mary even hitting the child before.

According to Mary's lawyer, "I told him it was a human response, unfortunately overdone, that any of us might be guilty of." When the lawyer noted that Jimmy "was sent home by the hospital," the judge said he didn't think much of Harlem Hospital anyway.

The dispositional hearing was set for two months later. The social worker at the hospital wouldn't come to court to testify although she was for the mother because, she told Mary's lawyer, "The judge is a liberal and it's not necessary."

Meanwhile, according to the lawyer, Jimmy, a hyperactive child, was having problems in school.

The hospital social worker referred Mary to a clinic with a long waiting list in another part of town.

Jimmy had been in the hospital a month, away from his mother, and in court where he could see that his mother was being punished. "If he were white and middle class," said the lawyer, "we might expect him to have a little trouble adjusting at school. Anyway, they asked his mother to stay. Halfway through the day, the child had a temper tantrum and they sent them home."

The lawyer says Jimmy is lively and alert. "Obviously he could use help. He asks everyone for money. 'Gimme a nickel. Gimme a quarter.' The social worker thinks that's terrible. Yet everyone knows money is a major source of difficulty. Why shouldn't kids know? He's not a perfectly normal boy. She's not a perfectly normal mother.

"It disturbs me that the SPCC uses what they get from the mother against her in court when they are trying to take her child away. You can actually take a child away from a mother without a civil proceeding because there are no such protections in family court.

"As for the child, I should say if he comes to school every day and is manageable, that's great. But the guidance counselor says he's a problem because he's late and he spills milk in the lunchroom.

"His teacher says she feels she can work with him in a structured setting but lunch is not structured. That came to be the final mark against him, that he's late and spills milk in the lunchroom."

Finally, the school said they could not handle him. After much urging, the hospital put the child in a special class for problem children, provided his mother attend, too. One day she didn't show up. The hospital told the mother to put the child in foster care. Her lawyer wrote to her—Mary Selmen had no phone—and said, "Don't sign any papers without talking to me." But she went ahead.

The lawyer believes Mary was fooled by the hospital social worker. "I think the social worker told her she would get the child back. The mother was black and so was the social worker. I think she instinctively trusted her and felt more comfortable with her. In this case, she should have trusted me.

"What bothers me in this case is a whole orientation designed to separate children from parents. If they really had something to offer the child, you might possibly weigh things differently. Maybe she's not the best mother. Maybe if there were a place available. . . . He's a manipulative kid. He wraps her around his finger. He's difficult. But she loves him because she is his mother. I know difficult black children can't get foster placement. I know difficult black kids can't get good residential homes. If the child is difficult, the family says 'We don't want him.' That's why so many foster children have so many placements.

"And all the studies show the residential homes don't replace the mother. Only the most expensive institutions could compete. And we haven't got it. Certainly not for the poor.

"And let me tell you some of the other problems. I am paid to represent the woman. The maximum fee is three hundred dollars. In a really exceptional case I might get five hundred dollars. Who's going to be able to afford to put in the kind of work I did? If that were a private case, for the amount of work I did I could charge ten thousand dollars. I've been to the school, I've talked endlessly with the hospital, I've talked to the social worker. I tried to talk to the Welfare Department but they wouldn't talk to me. I asked the judge to investigate her home. She told me I should. Probation told me social workers are afraid to go to her neighborhood because they're afraid they'll be mugged. I finally got her an independent medical and psychiatric exam. You know how hard that is? I called twenty-five psychiatrists before I could get one. Twenty-five. It's a bother. They don't want to be involved. And the fee is less than they can charge privately.

"The judges and psychiatrists make prescriptions that can't be filled. Except in extreme cases, they do more harm. Someone has to separate those out. I think there's too much propaganda about the 'battered child.' What about the battered mother? And the battering society?

"Most of these cases involve welfare mothers. It's hard to live alone with children, even when you're reasonably well off. When you're poor, it's really hard.

"I've had a lot of cases like that. Where kids were removed with less reason. One woman had three kids under six. She was on welfare and had to go for surplus food. She knew that could mean waiting in line for an hour. I know what it's like if I take my one kid to the supermarket: he drives me crazy. She said, 'I'll just run down.' There was a long line. It took her an hour. One of the kids played with the electric iron and it started a fire because the wiring was faulty.

"I've learned that mothers in all walks of life do that. Women in expensive apartments run down to the laundry room and leave their kids. Or they may run out to get a pack of cigarettes. Or a quart of milk. But this mother's kid played with an iron and started a fire and one child died. She had, by the way, a baby-sitter who didn't come. So the court took the other children away.

"I had another case, a white mother with four children who left them alone one evening and went out with her black boyfriend. Her sister who lived in the building was jealous and reported her. It was an Italian neighborhood and she was afraid to get a white baby-sitter because her boyfriend was black. The mother obviously wasn't doing right by those kids, but she was affectionate. She could have used help. They took her kids away too. I make an important distinction between mothers who care and give you proof.

"The family court doesn't help. I haven't seen it help in any of the cases I've been involved in. The first thing that would help is more money. Then there should be education for parenthood. They have it in Sweden. There should be a parents' information service. There should be a visiting-nurse service. There should be a community center with crisis therapy, family therapy. Everyone knows they work. Why doesn't welfare have them? We have to get people sensitized to get help without punishing them."

Most criticism of the family courts has to do with bad management, lack of resources, and the judges' lack of alternatives. How can a judge choose between sending children back to a home where they may be hurt or to a jail or in placement where they are also likely to suffer? The reformers argue for better institutions, more money, more resources, trained probation officers, more protective workers, more psychiatrists, even more typists.

But would they help? The function of the court psychiatric services, for instance, are misunderstood. They are not a treatment service but a diagnostic service to help the judge make quick, informal decisions, so as not to have to commit people in the interim. Although most written comments on the court deal with the need for resources, it is amazing how many judges, social workers, even lawyers say privately if we could find another way to deal with the problems, we'd probably be better off without it.

It is doubtful that more resources would really help much. Rather, they would simply make a bad machine function better. The real problem with family court is that at its heart it operates on a fallacy of rehabilitation.

Ostensibly we are still operating on the same principles that led to the establishment in 1825 of the House of Refuge in New York and, almost three-quarters of a century later, the first juvenile court in Illinois; that is to feed, shelter, and educate destitute youth and to save juvenile offenders from adult prison.

The theoretical justification for subjecting predelinquents to court commitment was the doctrine of *parens patriae* (the state's responsibility to act as parent for children or others who do not have legal capacity), which made no distinction in the nineteenth century between neglected and delinquent children. The Illinois Juvenile Court Act in 1899, which became a model for other states, specified that child to be brought under the rehabilitating arm who "is destitute or homeless or abandoned; or dependent upon the public for support, or has not proper parental care or guardianship; or who habitually begs or receives alms; . . . or whose home, by reason of neglect, cruelty, or depravity on the part of its parents, guardian or other person in whose care it may be is an unfit place for such a child." The nineteenth-century reformers, as we noted in Chapter 3, saw it as the duty of the government to intervene in the lives of all children who might become a community crime problem.

The failure of the penal system was recognized in the early 1880s. Although the revolving-door analogy was clear then, it did not lead to a change in the system, but more to a shift in the blame. Poverty was blamed for criminality, or at least unsupervised poverty, with intemperance a leading cause. There was the old public fear dating back to the poor laws that public charity might be too attractive and institutions too comfortable.

The immigrant pauper was an important figure in the social mythology of the time. Many children on poor relief were the children of immigrants. So were many children in the House of Refuge. The "bad" immigrant was necessary in order to define, by contrast, the good American.

The early nineteenth century was a period of political and social upheaval. The immigrant was an asset to the society trying to work out a definition of morality. His deviance was un-American. It consisted of intemperance, poverty, criminality, immorality. These were considered characteristic of aliens. If aliens transgressed on current values or morality, they were simply called un-American. It is notable that starting with the Wobblies, many leftist groups that mainstream America considered a threat have been defined as harboring either large numbers of "dirty" foreigners or large numbers of "dirty commies."[3] The instinct is to label any threat or challenge "un-American." Today we have simply transferred the deviant qualities we used to attach to white immigrants to blacks and Hispanics. They are poor, they are intemperate, they are the majority of drug users, they fill the jails.

The hostility generated by immigrants was manifest even before the waves of immigration in the 1830s. In 1819 the Society for the Prevention of Pauperism reported that immigration was the foremost cause of poverty. It was noted in one of its reports: "This inlet of pauperism threatens us with overwhelming consequences. . . . Many . . . arrive here destitute of everything . . . clustering in our cities. . . . depending on charity or depredation, for subsistence." That was the other side of the Statue of Liberty's welcome to "the wretched refuse" of the European shore.

Although the House of Refuge employed corporal punishment and in general displayed a complex attitude of benevolence and hostility to its charges, it was accepted as a triumph in child welfare. Judicial opinion began increasingly to reflect the view that the state was justified in "instilling virtue" in children when their natural parents couldn't. The Illinois Juvenile Court Act of 1899 perpetuated all these ideas. Similar child-welfare organizations in New York sent neglected paupers, whom they viewed as predelinquent criminals, to foster placement in the western states, where they could learn the rural values. By 1870, 48,000 had been sent out of state.

In time the juvenile court became increasingly irrelevant as an institution to funnel law-violating children to private schools or agencies. In many states, the state government acquired a virtual monopoly in the care and treatment of these children. Private enterprise got a share of the business in the guise of religion, maintaining its own homes and placement agencies, and gradually racial discrimination became institutionalized. Likewise, the court's responsibility to place predelinquent children with families was changed by industrialization and urbanization, which, early in the twentieth century, made the whole business of deporting children from the city to the country an anachronism. In addition, the call for "family relations" within institutions washed out to wishful thinking.

The court's greatest loss has been the questioning of its role in preventing crime by catching the predelinquent. That concept depended on the belief that society could recognize childhood conditions that would make adult criminals, and that techniques were available (foster homes, probation, institutionalization, psychiatry) to prevent future crime.

That idea has come to be questioned seriously along with society's views of the relationship between poverty and crime. The Great Depression erased, for many, the idea that immorality is necessarily inherent in poverty and that the condition of poverty necessarily leads one to crime.

It did not erase it completely, however. Some professionals are now leaning toward the old ideas of a "predictive" behavior pattern expressed in a more sophisticated way.

What can we do about the courts? If they have lost their function in placing children, if they have never been successful in rehabilitating them, if they have such meager resources that their existence insures only that families brought before it undergo a bureaucratic, unsympathetic, often destructive experience with the law, what is the point of maintaining them?

The time for reform and redefinition in the family courts is long overdue. It is generally agreed that the courts are a revolving door, that they do not have the resources to help, that in putting children through the court process, they lose whatever little respect for law and order they might have originally had. Perhaps it is true of other courts as well, but certainly the family courts have become repressive institutions, colonial-like in administration, reinforcing a hypocritical middle-class morality at their clients' expense.

Our institutions don't get much respect from anyone, poor or otherwise, paupers or presidents, and the attitude toward law and order is just as critical among the middle-class children who rioted at Columbia, Harvard, and Berkeley as it is in the ghettoes. The difference is that they are not at odds with the system every day of their lives.

There are some 27,000 juvenile or family courts across the country. Every city does not have a family court, which may pose problems in itself for juveniles who are still being treated— and jailed—as adults. Also, one of the shortcomings in those places where family courts do exist is the failure to come to grips with really serious juvenile crimes, and there *are* serious crimes. That too is part of the history of family courts; its inability to deal seriously with real problems. But the history of the child-welfare movement shows that punishment doesn't punish, that incarceration doesn't rehabilitate, and that social work, at least the kind we practice, is a failure, too.

Perhaps worst of all, the courts help perpetuate the model of Freudian psychology, treating social problems as matters of individual adjustment.

The origin of the juvenile or family court was to help solve problems caused by rapid urbanization and industrialization. It is questionable if a court can do that anyway, but certainly not when it focuses on the individual psyche.

Traditional social work is a failure because its analysis is wrong. We are no more successful with our psychiatric approach than Jane Addams and Louise de Koven Bowen were with their benevolent Protestantism. Freud may be useful in explaining individual dynamics or ego psychology, but the Freudian model is useless in explaining the social pressures on the poor in this society. With its focus on individual personality, on the cause and effect between biology and social demands, it tries, as do most psychological theories, to adjust the individual to the existing environment, despite or regardless of its insufficiencies.

Before we try really to do something about family court, we are going to have to throw a lot of Freud out the window.

Short of a national family policy there are still some partial solutions. First of all, social behavior problems have no place in court unless they're criminal. Criminal problems belong in the court. Social behavior problems should be dealt with in the community; that's the place for more caring relationships. That is also where it may be possible to influence or change institutions. Social services should not be located in the basement of a court, but in schools, hospitals, in local health centers. There should be community facilities to deal with neglected and abused children who are really in trouble, and neighbors, or family centers, willing to take a child for a night if that's urgent. There should be help and counseling for the parents and probation services. The Marie Poplises may be beyond help, but the Lillys may not be.

7

She Would Benefit from Treatment

"A kid caught between two angry parents, it's like putting a child between two slices of bread." The state superintendent of social services in a large northeastern state is talking. "When there's a serious neglect or abuse problem reported to our office—doctors and social workers must report in this state—we go right to family court. But we have such a shortage of staff—and the hospitals know it—that they may go straight to court and bypass us. When that happens, the parents get very angry.

"In this business, everybody seems to get angry. The parents, the doctors, even the social workers. I'm a social worker myself and I know how I react sometimes. Abuse cases stir up so many emotions among professionals, especially hostility, that it's often hard to handle."

At that moment, a young woman in a white rain hat and matching coat bursts through the door. "Are you going to let us talk?" she says. "After all, we're the ones on the front lines."

"Sure," says the superintendent. "Call everyone in."

The three staff protective workers, all women, walk in. Annie, the girl in the white hat, pushing ahead; the other two hanging back behind her.

They are all young, all graduate social workers, all with experience in private agencies. Annie has never worked anywhere but in private agencies before coming to the state. Neither has Mary Jo. Louise has worked for VISTA in a big-city slum. She is the most distressed. She sits blue-jeaned and cross-legged on an office chair, twisting her fingers while Annie leads off.

"We're so incredibly specialized here, just dealing with abuse and neglect cases. It's so depressing it drives us crazy," she says.

"Sometimes I just don't know what to do," says Louise. "Our clients' needs are so overwhelming. They need so much support." She pauses a moment. "So do we. Working with people like that every day, it's so frustrating, we get overwhelmed, too."

"Our working conditions are lousy," Annie says, "but the biggest problem is our clients. They're unmotivated. They're unvoluntary. I guess I'm accustomed to working in private agencies. You get used to the idea there that people have to be motivated before you can do anything for them. They have to want help. Well, I think that's true. How can you help anyone who doesn't want your assistance?"

"Some people just don't get any better," says Louise. "Most people don't get any better. It's just a head-banging experience. It must be for them, too. So many people are just beyond help. You're never going to make up for all their deficits."

"Even if they were motivated," says Mary Jo, "we have so little to offer."

"Anyway," says Louise, "aren't we just trying to help people function in a lousy system? I think at times we actually are irresponsible that way."

"What about trying to change it?" I ask.

"Oh, the issue of social workers trying to change the social system is just philosophical," Louise answers.

"And equally as frustrating," adds Mary Jo. "It's very difficult to change the system. You have to have a lot of time and energy. Besides, how am I supposed to make a living while I'm working to change it?"

"Anyway," says Annie, "we're working for a system that relates to Washington. We certainly aren't getting any help from there. I don't know if increasing social services is really the answer or if it's just a stopgap, but it's moot because there won't be any money under this administration."

"It's more than that," says Louise. "We all have a feeling of giving up. We all have a feeling of resignation."

DR. LUCY GLENN, a sweet-faced, fortyish, gray-haired pediatrician and director of the hospital's newly formed child-abuse team sits at the head of the table. Seated next to her is a nurse, then the hospital social worker, a protective worker from the New York City Department of Social Services, a psychiatrist, the director of pediatric psychiatry at the hospital, and several observers.

Dr. Glenn's program is modeled after Denver's, where a hospital team works together with a lay therapist to provide continual support and analysis to the parent accused of child abuse. "Of course they've had ten years of experience in Denver and we're quite new," Dr. Glenn says, "but I'm convinced they have the right approach."

Glenn has not yet recruited any lay therapists, but meanwhile the team gathered around the table has been set up to deal with abuse cases that come into the hospital.

The case this morning involves a four-year-old brought to the hospital emergency room by her uncle who was baby-sitting while the child's mother was visiting the grandmother. The uncle had claimed he was afraid the child had swallowed rat poison. While examining the girl, the admitting doctor had noticed suspicious-looking marks, the kind caused by belts and cigarette burns. He admitted the child to the hospital.

The mother had come in the next day. She was twenty-three and had three older children, eight, seven, and five. She was separated from her husband and claimed not to have noticed the marks before, though she acknowledged they looked old. She had a part-time job and said the uncle's girlfriend looked after the children while she worked. Sometimes she kept the kids out of school. She said she's had a hard time managing and is moving to another neighborhood to be near her mother.

Dr. Brill, the psychiatrist, a young, beautifully dressed man in his early thirties, spoke up. "She said she wanted psychiatric help, and we had a couple of appointments. But she doesn't seem very serious about them. Either she's broken them, or she's been delayed."

The social worker broke in. "She said she couldn't make it. She called Monday morning."

"Well," said Dr. Brill, "you can't treat people who don't want to be treated and who don't show up for appointments."

"I went to see her this morning," said the city protective worker, a young woman with a pockmarked face and long hair dressed in blue jeans and a large sloppy shirt. "You know I have a terrific case load and it takes me hours just to get out there. She wouldn't let me in. I went there yesterday, too. Alvin, the five-year-old, was alone. I talked to him through the door. I left a note and went to find her at her mother's. While I was there she called my office. It seems the uncle isn't an uncle. He's her boyfriend. She said he hits the kids. There's a report on her in our files, though. Somebody once called in a neglect complaint and said the kids are unattended and there's rat poison on the floor. She says there's rat poison because there are rats. She's afraid of the building and the neighborhood. Her apartment is clean, though, and there's a lock on her freezer because she said the kids crawl in.

"She showed me marks on herself from her father who beat her when she was a child, nearly raped her. Her mother is really a stepmother. She does seem to love the kids. The two older ones are her husband's and the two youngest have another father— he's dead. Maybe we could put the kids somewhere temporarily. She asked me if she could go to see a psychiatrist. When she was out yesterday and I found the kid alone I called my supervisor. My supervisor said we may have to take the kids away."

"Well," said Dr. Glenn, "that's very sad. If the mother is asking for help, what can we do?"

"She definitely is asking for some kind of help," the protective worker answered.

The chief psychiatrist, Dr. Wood, a well-dressed, slightly self-conscious woman in her forties, sat forward on her chair and addressed the group. "That's the first mother we've had who's asked for help. We should try to work up a treatment plan."

"There seems to be a lot of conflict in the stories," Dr. Glenn said. "The intern in the emergency room told the intern on the floor that the man who brought the girl in was her father. Then later he said it was her uncle."

"Even without the interview, there's enough material here to suggest caution." Dr. Brill was speaking. "We know the kids have been beaten. The mother must have known about it. I have some doubt about her desire for treatment. I think the kids should be taken away."

Dr. Wood now backed down from her previous suggestion. "We're not functioning ideally but purely as a diagnostic service," she said. "We can't treat her, we can't treat these cases. Our treatment orientation is still very traditional and we don't have the facilities. We have to be very honest and say we can't help her."

"The kids should be taken away," said Dr. Brill.

"Would it stand up in court?" asked the social worker.

"My supervisor said something about court action," the protective worker answered.

"Would the mother agree to letting the kids go to the grandmother?" the social worker wondered. "Informally, without papers."

"I don't know. I have to talk to my supervisor," said the protective worker. "She's been at Protective Services fifteen years. I can't tell you because it doesn't rest with me. I really have nothing to say about it."

"If the child has no medical reason for being here, I'm a little reluctant to keep her," Dr. Glenn said.

Going around the table, Dr. Brill had no objection to releasing the baby to her grandmother, but Dr. Wood said she'd "be reluctant to let the baby go until we made a diagnostic evaluation."

"We'll keep the baby as long as necessary," the nurse said.

"Well," said Dr. Glenn, "I guess she'll have to stay until the workup is complete. We'll have to get the mother in to talk to her."

"And the kids," said Chief Psychiatrist Wood.

"We asked the kids who hit them, but it didn't seem to bother them," the protective worker said.

"Maybe we can get the uncle out of the house," Brill added. "Get an Order of Protection against him."

Most big-city departments of social service have been over-whelmed in the last decade or two with the growing numbers of people who could use their services. As the number of people on welfare increases, so does the army of specialists who are there to help them—and still there are never enough. Every social-service department complains of the same thing—not enough resources. Not enough social workers, not enough protective workers, not enough doctors; the schools have the same complaints. So do the courts.

It is clear that the traditional institutional solutions to problems are not working anymore, and yet the number of people who need help seems to be growing. So people in the field, active in social work, legal work, etc., look for other solutions.

One of the problems is that research is usually limited to exploring reported cases. Another is funding. Since money sometimes becomes available for small projects, more pilot projects appear. Each has the same general goal: to help the individual mother face herself and solve her problems.

Despite the input of social services, the programs are all based on the medical model and diagnosis: child battering is a disease. The sick person is the parent, although the child shows the symptoms. The way to cure it is to treat the parent.

There is probably nothing wrong with the model. Most mothers could use a lot of help and reassurance. Undoubtedly the unself-confident mother is helped. However, the model assumes that if you want to get rid of child abuse, you will have to give every problematic parent a psychiatrist, or lay therapist, or surrogate mother. It also puts the emphasis on the individual's adaptation and overlooks the social problems—not enough money, poor housing, difficult living conditions, bad food, insufficient health care, no recreation—as simply not susceptible to treatment.

Other programs start and depart from the traditional model, like the parent and child therapy at Kings County Hospital in Brooklyn.

The Parents' and Children's Center in Boston has a program

that tries to intervene early by getting the abused child in day care immediately and the parents into some limited treatment. The Boston program, like the one at Denver, has a devoted staff, has had some real success, and has influenced others. Again they are focusing on changing the person, not the society.

One organization that claims success is Parents Anonymous, based on the Alcoholics Anonymous model. Started by a self-confessed child abuser in California, the idea has spread and a lot has been written about it. The basic idea is to have people with similar problems help each other. A telephone hotline in New York City run by Gertrude Bacon, an ex-family court judge, is there to help people literally in their moment of madness. The parents in Parents Anonymous seem to be middle class rather than poor, and white, which suggests there might be many more white and middle-class families who need help than we know about.

Most workups by psychiatrists for the court end with the observation: "She would benefit from treatment." Who wouldn't? With most of the several pilot programs operating—and even Denver must be considered a pilot program—there are two faults: the numbers are too low and the costs are too high. A general estimate of Dr. Fontana's inpatient-outpatient program at the New York Foundling Hospital in 1973 shows that thirty people completed it at a cost of $150,000. An evaluator for the city, which supplies partial funding, claimed it was not really a program, that there was no real attention to child-parent interaction, and that patients were so carefully selected—no drug problems, no alcohol problems; no severe mental health problems; no one with more than one child; no one living with a man—that it made evaluation meaningless, at least in terms of its contribution to dealing with child abuse.

Denver will not release any numbers, making it difficult to evaluate the program. Critics of the program point that out and add that they do not deal with inner-city residents and thus have a much more treatable population. The Boston Parents' and Children's Center has not treated many more than ninety since it started. Several programs in New York, like the one at Kings

County and another community drug program for people with mental health problems have, perhaps, together helped one hundred people.

A hard look at the programs shows that few come up with any answers. None of them can or try to make a dent in changing social conditions. In those terms, programs like the Head Start program in Mississippi or community-controlled day care in New York did more to get families and communities involved in child care and child development. Along with national health care and more money, that is probably the most effective way to prevent child abuse in the long run.

What is the value of treatment? The answer depends on what you are trying to cure. What is the objective of the programs, what is to be gained from treatment? If the answer, as it is in most treatment programs, is to help those with severe problems so they are less severe, treatment is useful. A caring mother-substitute for one who never had a mother must be counted a good thing. Every attention for people, parents or children who have never had much, has got to be a positive, human value.

But what kind of treatment services are there? Take what happens to the neglecting or abusing parent from the moment of reporting. First, in a really serious case, and particularly if the police are involved, the parent may be jailed. That reduces what little self-esteem the parent has and enforces the idea of helplessness. For people with strong egos, it may be the shock of recognition. The history of incarceration, though, is that it doesn't contribute to therapy.

If the case has been reported to a local department of social services, there is likely to be an investigation. The investigator is most often a recent college graduate with little or no experience with poor people.

If the child is removed, and if the agency that receives the child assigns a social worker to the case, the social worker is in a bind. Chances are she has an enormous case load. Should she try to help the foster parents, if there are any, or does she, as the court says she should, try to rehabilitate the family? The agency does not encourage her to help the parents from whom the child has been taken, like Lilly. So the Lillys of this world, unless they are lucky enough to find a social worker with some community agency, have had it. And suppose they do find one, a superior one as Lilly did. It takes unusual stamina to remove the roadblocks thrown up by the system.

In effect, there is little in the way of real social services and little in the way of psychiatric treatment.

Most psychiatrists, like most social workers, are traditionally oriented. They expect good patients. They expect clients who are well motivated, who are not hostile (at least not to them), who come on time, who keep appointments, and whose problems, most of all, are susceptible to treatment. Perhaps the social workers and psychiatrists are telling us the truth when they say that unmotivated, hostile, appointment-breaking patients can't be helped by traditional casework and psychotherapy. And no doubt most of the patients who won't come know it, too.

The problem with so-called treatment programs or even individual treatment, in the rare cases where people really get any, is that they are, as David Gil puts it, smokescreens, transferring the focus of public interest and attention from the massive abuse of society to the acts of individuals. "That is our specialty in America," says Dr. Gil, "the ability to interpret any problem as an individual problem, responsive to individual treatment. That way we can continue to believe in our social system. You might say that rationale is unavoidable in a competitive, inegalitarian system."

Child abuse is a response to stress and tension, reflecting the attacker's inability to cope. Few things create as much strain in daily life as poverty. When the economy gets worse and unemployment increases, so does the number of families in trouble. Toward the end of 1974, for instance, social-service agencies were overwhelmed. In Massachusetts, a state particularly hard hit by unemployment, family services reported an "alarming increase" in child-abuse cases. In one state office alone, they jumped 85 percent. The director thought "it could be reflecting the economy."

Under the circumstances, it would seem an abusing parent might benefit from treatment. But he would benefit more from a decent standard of living.

8

Institutional
Abuse

"Let me describe it to you," says the social worker. "It's an institution for delinquents, run by the state. The place is so beautiful, really beautiful, you'd be proud to belong if it were a country club. Lovely grounds. Pretty cottages. But it's sterile, empty. I don't get the point. Why send kids to such a lovely place and then let them rot inside?

"There are about one hundred kids there. I was surprised but about eighty-five percent are white. For one hundred kids between the ages of fourteen and seventeen they have four academic teachers, one remedial-reading teacher, two vocational counselors, and one teacher's aide. The kids go to school either in the morning or the afternoon. They get math, reading, social studies. All the subjects are taught by all the same teachers. The kids who go to school in the morning have nothing to do in the afternoon. The kids who go in the afternoon have nothing to do in the morning. They do have a swimming pool, shop, and a couple other activities. But most of the time they have nothing to do. They are bored. They're almost totally inactive physically. They certainly have no fun. Imagine never having any fun. If you're bad, anything you do wrong, you lose your privileges.

"For instance, my kid who's there is fourteen. He was cutting up in school, so they took his activity privileges away. They also told him he couldn't go home for the weekend and he got so mad he pulled a kitchen knife on the guy. So then they put him in detention. That's a locked cottage. He can't go to school, he can't go to shop, he can't do anything but watch TV. Or play pool by himself. And he wants to go home.

"Oh, yes, he's also on Melaril. That's a depressant for kids who act up.

"They have one psychiatrist who comes one half-day a week. He does initial evaluations and then sees whoever's stabbed whom. No treatment.

"My kid is there because he stays out late all the time and snatched a purse. His mother doesn't want him. She has two other kids, one older and one younger. There's no father, and she can't cope with him. But he's the one she left in the Dominican Republic when she came here with the oldest to look for a job. Then she had a third. You could say my kid was temporarily abandoned. They say he's got an IQ of sixty. And he's Spanish. So he was turned down everywhere, by every agency I tried. I didn't want to send him out of the city, but there was no choice.

"It costs around fifteen thousand dollars a year to keep him there. He's not learning anything. And nobody is trying to help him, or to help his mother deal with him. So what happens when he goes home? You tell me."

THERE are far more American children mistreated in institutions than suffer injury or neglect at home. But our value system as well as our politics make it easier to finger the parents than to blame the society.

Americans believe that each man is responsible for his own fate. We see success or failure as a measure of individual worth, hard work, or the lack of it, and we are not inclined to blame social class, color, race or sex for inequities in income, education, or achievement. A recent poll taken by CBS-TV showed that some 70 percent of white Americans believed the low status of blacks in this society was due to their laziness. Most blacks polled saw it as the result of discrimination.

Horatio Alger is one of our demigods, self-reliance is part of our creed. Proud as we are of the openness of our society, which is truly more open than most, we reserve special recognition for those who get from the bottom to the top. As former President Nixon pointed out on television once, he and Sammy Davis, Jr.

have a lot in common. Success is a great leveler. It makes all the rich equal. And all the poor, too.

It is easier to admire the people who make it up the ladder than to change the system that keeps too many down. Real changes, serious examination of institutions, come slowly in American society. Schools, public agencies, correctional institutions, labor unions have vested interests in the status quo.

The belief that individuals can determine their own fate and the willingness to blame the person rather than the system make it logical to raise the roof about a mother who hits her child with a belt buckle and turn our backs on a reformatory where caretakers beat a score of children every day.

The preoccupation with personal hygiene and individual morality rather than institutional values and standards allows us to remove a child from parents whose living quarters are dirty and roach-infested, but to fund with public monies a school for retarded children where toilets are overflowing, garbage is uncollected, and children are permitted to lie in their own soiled clothes.

We have perfected the double standard not just for men as against women, adults as against children, rich as against poor, but institutions over human beings. Does it make sense to take children from parents who beat them and put them in institutions where guards will strike them instead? Can we forbid a mother but permit a teacher to hit a child?

How would the family court view parents who locked their child in a dungeon with only a toilet as furniture and fed them bread and gravy every day? Yet it allows that kind of "discipline" in custodial institutions. What would a police officer do if he saw a father hit his son on the head until he injured his eardrum? But custodians treat children that way in reformatories. What would a probation officer say about a mother who switches her child from one set of foster parents to another every six months? Yet child-placement agencies do that as a matter of course.

If that kind of logic does not make us challenge our policies toward children, perhaps the numbers can. Dr. Henry Kempe estimates that some 60,000 children were physically abused in 1972. At the same time some 58,000 children were held in jails or detention centers, an estimated 50,000–70,000 in homes for retarded children, and 285,000 in state-sponsored foster care. In 1971, public juvenile detention and correctional facilities admitted and discharged 616,766 children—85,080 to correctional institutions and 531,686 to temporary care. These do not count youths "in need of supervision" or in community facilities.

Most of these children are mistreated just by virtue of being where they are, that is, institutionalized and locked up. There are few if any custodial institutions for children, or adults for that matter, where inmates are treated like human beings, given sufficient diet, exercise, recreation, and education. Certainly they are not given the human affection and attention that is a necessity for the healthy development of the human being. If children are not mothered properly by abusing parents, we might ask what kind of mothering they get in state training schools. And we might demand an accounting of how many are systematically mistreated and abused.

And while we are adding up the numbers, should we count the children in public schools who are physically punished by teachers? And what of the 300,000 or so "hyperactive" youngsters who are forced by school authorities to take drugs to stay in school? Could that be considered state-supported drug abuse?

While every state now has some kind of reporting system that requires various professionals to report child abuse, none requires reports of institutional abuse, which damages far more children. Compared to parents, child-care institutions wholesale child abuse. If we are really interested in our society's children, we would do more good by removing those abused in custodial institutions than removing those abused in their homes.

In August 1974, Judge Frank Williams, the new administrative judge of the New York City Family Court, shortly after he was sworn in, took the family court judges to visit communities around the city. He said they had no idea what was going on and available—or not available—outside the courtroom. Few people visit child-care institutions. They are certainly more inviolate than the homes of welfare recipients or reported child abusers and neglecters who must admit any social worker, parole officer, or protective worker who comes knocking at the door. Only investigative reporters or legislators go visiting reformatories, usually when they are looking for a juicy scandal. They inevitably find one.

In 1969 Howard James of the *Christian Science Monitor* crossed the country visiting children's jails and detention facilities and his report, later a book, makes even a hardened reader sick. Children beaten with truncheons, fists, belt buckles, hands; left hungry, humiliated, caged, put in dungeons, anything but cared for, and certainly not "rehabilitated." [1] In 1971, Larry Cole, visiting institutions in New York, Louisiana, Colorado, and California that he describes in *Our Children's Keepers*, found the same conditions, as well as children "hog-tied," hands to feet, and kept face down in solitary for days; children raped and sodomized by guards; three-year-old babies kept in cages.

Unfortunately these are not rare instances or horrible exceptions. Custodial care for children ranging from indifferent to abusive is the rule.

Several years ago, Milton Luger, then president of the New York State Juvenile Delinquency Programs, said:

> With the exception of relatively few youths, it would be better for all concerned if young delinquents were not detected, apprehended, institutionalized. Too many of them get worse in our care. The public is terribly shortsighted. They just want them out of the way.

Institutions, he pointed out, are society's wastebaskets, public garbage bins. You throw waste into wastebaskets, garbage into garbage bins. You think of it that way. Institutions are only carrying out the wishes of the public which, at the point of commitment, is hostile and punitive.

The caretaking institutions that mistreat children most are custodial institutions, state training schools and reformatories, detention centers, often called youth or juvenile centers, most special institutions for retarded children, and foster care. Many public schools also fall into that category, at least those that permit or practice corporal punishment and those that discriminate against poor and minority children by failing to educate them.

Take foster care. To the public that reads the *Daily News*, to those of us who cannot connect it to our experience, foster care means parents like the Boccios who were better to Roxanne Felumero than her own. The reality is somewhat different. Foster care is a custodial arrangement for children whose natural parents are dead, absent, ill, or deemed unfit. Theoretically, placement with foster parents is better than an institution, but foster parents often fall far short of the ideal. If individual foster parents can't be found, and often they can't be found for older children, difficult children, and minority children, the children are than placed in group or institutional homes.[2]

In 1970, approximately 285,000 children were in state-sponsored foster care. Some are orphans with no other options. Some are placed voluntarily by parents who cannot care for them. Frequently the arrangement is temporary, as it was for Lee Harvey Oswald and Jack Ruby. But most children in foster care have been forcibly removed from their homes. Foster care is frequently punitive in intent to the parents and except under unusual circumstances, that is, generally caring foster parents, it is inherently harmful to the child.[3]

The court takes jurisdiction and orders placement in anywhere from one-third to 80 percent of such cases. Children are most likely to be taken from their parents if the parents are young, on welfare, and single.

A review of court decisions on foster care shows:

. . . that removal over parental objection takes place most often where the court determines the parent's supervision and guidance of the child are inadequate, where the mother is thought to be emotionally ill, or where the child has behavior problems. Although highly publicized, cases involving child battering, where a parent has intentionally abused or injured a child, are in a distinct minority.[4]

There is a financial incentive to the state for court-ordered placements, because the Social Security Act allows partial federal reimbursement only when the placement is made by the court.

One problem with the decision to remove children is the vagueness of guidelines. Too much is left to the discretion of the individual judge, who is often not competent to make that kind of decision. The grounds vary from state to state but usually include some version of the best interests of the child, and the judge must often decide just what guidelines to apply. Anna Freud has suggested substituting "the least harmful" interests of the child as a more honest touchstone in evaluating alternatives.[5]

Studies of placement decisions show tremendous variation in what constitutes ground for removal. For example, in one study, three judges with five years' experience were asked to decide whether ninety-four children from fifty families should be removed and put in foster care or whether services should be provided to the families. The three judges agreed on the disposition in less than half the cases. In those cases where they did agree, the factors determining their decision were often different.[6] Studies with social workers show similar results.

To leave such decisions up to family court judges with such vague guidelines is especially risky when class differences are involved. Extramarital relations, the presence of illegitimate children in the family, a mother's lesbianism, even a dirty home is frequently grounds for removal, without any real consideration on the judge's part of how it will affect the children.

The separation of young children from their parents is critical. In fact, while many things about child rearing and child development are unpredictable and unknown, we do know that it is generally damaging to take a young child away from his parents. Theoretically, then, that should be done for only the most compelling reasons. And if we are not to make a mockery of justice, the child's alternative should at least be decent and less harmful.

Approximately 25 to 30 percent of the children removed are

ever returned to their homes. For them, the separation is a painful, traumatic event. For the 70 to 75 percent who never go back, the prospects may be worse.

For one thing, when children are removed because of some fault of the parents, the parents generally get no help from the agency, even though it is a condition of temporary removal to facilitate the child's return.

Most agencies lack such resources. Where there are any, they are directed toward handling the placement. Parents are really discouraged from visiting children in foster care, as Lilly was. The foster parents usually don't like it. Neither do the social workers because it inevitably upsets the child. Visiting their own children in foster care is an intimidating experience to most people who have had their children removed. The children are upset and angry with their parents. The parent feels guilty about the child. It's hard for a parent to explain that he's not allowed to come often. A social worker is always present. How can the situation be relaxed and natural?

When asked what their judgment is about returning a child to his natural parents, social workers will often note that the child cries when he sees the parents, that the child is upset by his parents, with the implication that this is unnatural and bad.

As it turns out, many social workers don't help foster families much,- either. The Massachusetts foster-care study mentioned earlier showed foster parents were not told when children had health problems or physical handicaps. Frequently the children's disabilities were not taken care of.

Most agencies are so short of help that foster families who discover problems themselves, especially in teenagers, do not get much help, either. The practice is generally to take the child, whatever age, and place him in another home. Carlitos, for instance, spent the first year of his life in three different homes with three different mothers. A colicky baby is not a welcome child. A child who is hard to toilet train makes too much work. A child who becomes a discipline problem is not desirable. Why should the foster parents keep them?

There is never any long-term plan. Foster children are not

supposed to become too attached to their foster parents or vice versa, because their situation is defined as temporary. Foster families who have requested adoption have frequently found that, as a result, the agency takes the child away from them.

Voluntary and private agencies often refuse or resist adoption because of their financial stake in the child. They are reimbursed, usually by city and state funds, for the children placed with their agency, which they then place in foster care. If the child is adopted, they lose the money.

Foster care, however harmful, is probably better than jail. The National Council on Crime and Delinquency estimates that more than 100,000 children a year who have not been convicted of any crime are held in jails and detention centers. In 1971, over 600,000 were admitted to juvenile detention and correctional facilities. Detaining children, even overnight, with more sophisticated violators of the law, often contributes to future delinquency. While some system is necessary to restrain the violent young, it should also protect the young from more violent adults.

There are legal distinctions between detention centers and training schools. In matter of fact, however, they all are jails.

Everyone who reads a paper or listens to the six o'clock news has heard or read about deaths, beatings, rapes, drugs, and riots in jails and detention centers. The usual response to a public scandal is to appoint a commission and do a study. People who are the victims of injustice don't need any more evidence. A welfare recipient doesn't need a nutrition study to tell her she is not getting enough to eat. A six-year-old Puerto Rican who can't speak English doesn't need an investigative report to tell him the schools are not going to teach him to read. A black boy in Detroit doesn't need the Kerner Commission to convince him that he is living in a racist society. But since most people still need evidence of what they already know, here's what custodial institutions for children are like.

Howard James observed the following incidents in 1969; regrettably conditions are still the same.

In Washington State, James discovered a twelve-year-old girl who had been molested by her uncle and was now spending twenty hours a day in solitary confinement with nothing to do while she waited for her case to go to court. The director of the facility agreed that the situation was horrible but said he had no alternative. The children he got were not properly screened and he had only one staff person to do the work of four. Even now, he said it was better than it used to be, when he had two-, three- and four-year-olds in jail. Now he told James he has only dependent and neglected children twelve years and up—children not guilty of anything, not even accused. Somebody has acted badly toward them. They have already been victimized. So they are put in jail.

In Atlanta, James visited a detention center located behind a new $18-million sports center and just off a new multimillion-dollar expressway. The facility, the director admitted, was always overcrowded. The inmates were children, dependent children, neglected children, including infants. "We try," one official said, "not to get kids under a year." Children from ten up are mixed together, the abandoned with the criminal. Toilets are always overflowing. Rooms built for one, house two. One boy was locked in solitary confinement without a bed; the director said they were short of beds. This so-called room smelled of urine, feces, and garbage. He had been kicked in the stomach by a guard, the boy said, for refusing to obey.

Since the center lacks classroom space, the children do nothing but sit for hours a day. Some children have been there for a year.

In Los Angeles, a juvenile center processes up to 2,000 children a month. The youngest is six years. It has room for 400 boys, 162 girls. It holds 500 boys, 200 girls.

In 1961, adequate detention homes were spending $10 to $20 a day. In 1969 there were jails for children budgeting less than $1.50 per person per day.

In many jails, the situation has not changed, especially where the sheriff is paid so much per inmate per day. The food is likely to be awful, and the sheriff pockets the savings.

The National Council on Crime and Delinquency says that detention centers should not be used to keep children for the convenience of the authorities, to protect officials if the children abscond or commit another offense, or to shock children into behaving. However, they are used this way.

In cities like Memphis, Philadelphia, Seattle, and Hartford, in states like Florida, Tennessee, and Indiana there are tiered cages in which children are placed to await court action; dungeons, yes dungeons, in the basement, consisting of a cement room with a steel cot and a blanket for children when they are bad; jails which have not been renovated since the Civil War; and corporal punishment, flogging. The boys may be given five strokes on their bare buttocks if they misbehave, and then thirty days in solitary.

Corporal punishment is fairly common in children's jails and detention centers. In particular, it is frequently used on runaways. An official in one jail compared the treatment of juveniles to that of runaway slaves in the eighteenth and nineteenth centuries. Runaways upset both citizens and officials, he said.

An Indiana inmate described a flogging to James, a description later confirmed by a staff member of the institution.

They took me into the room where we watch TV. I was told to bend over the table. A security man held the strap. Mr. Heyne [the director] and some others stood around watching. They told me to drop my drawers. I kept looking around, and the security man slapped my face. Then he hit me with the strap. I went down to my knees. That happened five times. I couldn't sit down for three days. I couldn't lay on my back for a week until the welts went away.[7]

In Florida an employee of the Division of Youth Services described a typical flogging at Florida School for Boys in Marianna as follows:

A young boy [was] taken into a stark, bare, dimly lit room where he was compelled to lie on a small cot and receive licks with a heavy leather strap. At the time the strap was being wielded by a man who was at least 6 feet 3 inches and weighed well over 200 pounds. . . .[8]

In *Our Children's Keepers*, Larry Cole describes a "school for girls" in Denver where children who "caused trouble" (which included running away) were locked in solitary, sometimes for as long as eighty days. Several girls became psychotic during their confinement. Girls were frequently handcuffed, their feet tied to their hands, and left face down on a bed in solitary for days. If they screamed, the director came in, grabbed the girl by the hair on the back of the head, and rubbed her face in the mattress. One girl who was handcuffed and tied managed to turn on the water in her room, flooding the floor. The assistant director gave orders that the girl was to be left lying in water.

In California, in a city juvenile hall, Cole found that babies who are lost and picked up by the police or remanded there for emergency custody are put in "isolation cubicles" (so they won't give anyone germs) in an iron crib with a hard net over it to make a cage.

In Louisiana he saw children in a state training school beaten with hose pipes, put in dungeons, and refused medical care. Boys who are there for sniffing glue are given Methedrine if they refuse to work. It may exist, but none of the institutions appear to have anything approaching adequate recreation or schooling.

Cole reported that the children in a Louisiana reformatory say they sit in school all day and play cards.

The emphasis in most institutions for putaways is not on helping children but on making them adjust to the institution while giving as little trouble as possible. If they conform, they'll be labeled improved. If they don't, they'll be punished. They may be beaten, confined, transferred to a harsher environment, have their activity and privileges taken away. Very few places have adequate staff. Many are sadistic, some are perverted. Children have nothing to do. They sit on beds in their underwear after supper. They sit all day and watch TV. They are subject to homosexual attack from other children, from guards, from supervisors. Their visiting privileges are severely limited.

In one institution children are allowed one three-hour visit per month from members of the family; in another, two hours of visiting a month. If they're "bad," they get no visits at all. That is the usual pattern.

Children are frequently employed for institutional maintenance and are taught no skills. What will they do when they get out?

What the children need most is help in learning how to read. What they get is "busywork," making beds or polishing floors. At best they can play cards or Ping-Pong with other inmates.

The children may be stored out of the way, but children, as one social worker put it, cannot be stored without deterioration. At best they become time bombs, exploding when they get out.

Many, if not most, publicly funded institutions for mentally retarded children are sickening. The Willowbrook School on Staten Island in New York was the subject of a TV exposé in 1973 by ABC-TV's Geraldo Rivera, a program that most viewers found horrifying. A legislative investigation followed. Then a lawsuit filed by parents charged that the place was a "human warehouse." Children remained in dirty, soiled clothes or often no clothes at all for days at a time. Some were put in solitary. The suit described as "inhumane and psychologically destructive" an environment where two or three patients died each week, often from choking on food.[9]

A panel of state representatives, local public agencies, and citizen groups investigated and found the school too large, ineffectively administered, and "grossly overcrowded by all accepted standards." There were 5,000 people living in space designed for 2,970.

Beds were "often literally inches apart." There was no training in basic skills. There were no programs for most of the patients.

The report concluded that "society itself and its support of archaic practices has contributed to the problem we face today," pointing out that Willowbrook and other large-scale facilities to house the retarded had been built to "protect them from society and society from them."

Despite the public scandal, despite the investigative report, despite the facts and figures cited in the legal brief, the judge ruled that while the mentally retarded have a constitutional right to reasonable protection from harm, they have no right to treatment either independently or on due-process or equal-protection grounds. Today at Willowbrook, very little has changed.

During July and August 1974 a Senate investigation of the Defense Department's Civilian Health and Medical Program of the Uniformed Services, known as CHAMPUS, showed that children of U.S. military personnel had been tortured in private psychiatric centers financed by the Defense Department. It came out during the hearings that sick children with personality disorders, institutionalized in private psychiatric facilities in Florida and Michigan, were shackled with handcuffs, beaten with bullwhips, placed in electric "shock collars," locked in a twelve-foot-square bomb shelter for long periods of time, and injected with massive doses of vitamins and with their own urine.[10]

Cole believes that the civil service, the unions, and the professionals are part of a conspiracy that prevents any humanizing change within our custodial child-care system. Born of struggle and exploitation themselves, both civil service and unions once offered hope and power to the poor and the powerless. Civil service was a much-needed reform to take the control of jobs under the spoils system away from politicians. Unions, which developed to protect workers from being exploited by industry, helped to end, among other exploitive practices, the use of child labor. Professional groups offered some assurance that higher standards of professional care and treatment would be applied. But in institutions affecting children, these reforms have petrified into a system as rigid and brutal as those they were instituted to correct.

Civil service is now a roadblock to upgrading jobs and programs. According to Cole, "It has become next to impossible for progressive programs to be instituted in existing juvenile institutions because most civil service commissions demand that workers be fired only for misconduct and after lengthy administrative procedures." [11] In practice, this prevents change. A teacher who doesn't teach and a worker in a youth institution who doesn't care for children do not belong in their respective positions. They should not have to rape a child to be fired.

As for the professionals, medical and psychiatric professionals who work in public institutions have such abysmally low standards and are frequently hired in such ridiculous doctor-patient ratios, that it is almost impossible for them to perform any real service at all. Perhaps, as Cole suggests, class-action malpractice suits should be initiated against them.

The hideous abuse and neglect of our children in publicly supported institutions will only be remedied if the public objects. We are all part of that public and it is time to look at the institutions in our own cities and states and make a start.

9 Where Are They Now?

Harold Henry is in his middle thirties, medium height, slight of build, pale and nervous. He chain-smokes, the large ashtray on his cluttered desk is overflowing as he describes, somewhat unhappily, his view of family court. Henry has been a law-school professor and has worked in the federal government. He plans soon to go back. Right now he is working for a state investigatory commission studying juvenile justice.

"Family court just graduates kids to criminal court," says Henry. "They're all likely to be future lodgers at San Quentin or Attica. I mean that most sincerely. And it's painful to say. But it's about time we face facts. We just don't have the wherewithal to handle them. We don't have the money and we don't have the people.

"Besides that, we have poorly qualified judges and worse administration. Most judges don't want to be family court judges. They'd prefer to be appointed to the criminal court. And they have little training or experience for the job. So they lecture. It makes them feel good. Qualifications for a judge in the family court are usually ten years' practice before the state bar, at least that's what it is in New York. Often, there are no particular qualifications.

"The court needs some basic reforms. Aside from the day-to-day administration, what we need is a network of service alternatives.

"As I said, the judges lecture out of frustration. What can they do? There's nowhere to send the kids. Eighty-five percent of the placements are with private agencies—and there you have the whole problem of refusal. Private agencies want motivated kids. They want people who want to be helped. They don't want kids who act out. They don't want kids who are problems. Well, that's the kind of kids they get in family court. Those parents are not in court voluntarily.

"And then because of city budget priorities—I'd say that's true in all big cities today—they don't have the money to do the job.

"And services are just inadequate. I suppose psychiatric services are one of the biggest problems. Wherever they have them, it's a service to the judge, not to the defendants. And it takes so long to get even that done, it's often heartbreaking. Sometimes people have to wait for two weeks while they undergo an examination. In some cities, that process has been speeded up. But it's caused terrible hardship in others.

"For instance, not too long ago, I saw a mother with six kids who had burned the hand of one of them on the stove. Had it all wrapped up in bandages. It was the second time she'd caught him stealing. Middle-class people like us think that kind of punishment is grotesque. But then a dollar or two is not so critical in our budgets. For that mother it meant eating or not eating.

"Well, anyway, that's what her parents had done when she was a kid, so that's what she did. She'd gone out of the house and the child took her welfare money. I think it was her last three dollars and she just went crazy. So the judge decided to send her to the hospital for a psychiatric workup. Her kids were two, three, four, six, nine, and eleven. It was the nine-year-old that stole the money.

"It's crazy. That woman didn't need a psychiatric workup. She needed more money. The kids begged the judge not to put her in the hospital. They couldn't believe it when he said he'd have to. Well, believe it or not, they ended up in a shelter while she went off for two weeks for a psychiatric examination. I don't know what happened to her. That kind of psychiatric service is not treatment.

"I was talking about money. Every city agency in big cities

*today is competing with every other for a very precious dollar. I
don't see any changes.*

*"Of course the whole federal domestic policy is suicide. They
just don't understand that the local level is where the problems
are. That's where they have to be dealt with. On the street level.
That's where it happens, not in some bureaucrat's office.*

LEE HARVEY OSWALD, Jack Ruby, Charles Manson, Charles
Whitman, Anthony Spencer, Thomas Ruppert,[1] Ellery Chan-
ning. What do they have in common besides murder? These last
three were small-time, dime-a-dozen criminals, their lives part of
the pattern of big-city violence in the mid-twentieth century.

They were also part of the statistics of the mid-1960s when
crime in the United States was increasing in all age groups by
some 10.5 percent throughout the country and even more
among young age groups. For sixteen- to twenty-year-olds—the
Anthony Spencers, the Thomas Rupperts, the Ellery Channings
—it was up 11.1 percent.

The records show that as children some of our seven were
neglected, some were abandoned, some abused by their parents
or caretakers. Most of them spent time, some a lot of time, in
the kinds of institutions that are supposed to catch and prevent
delinquent and/or criminal behavior, or to "rehabilitate" or
help children with severe problems. Most of them were seen at
least once by psychiatrists. None were helped. They all came out
worse than when they went in.

The records of all but Whitman show that as children they
needed help desperately and didn't get it. Institutionalized for
varying lengths of time, they fell through the cracks in our
child-saving institutions, and many other people died because of
it. Their stories are monuments to parental and social neglect,
and the failure of the public correctional system.

Lee Harvey Oswald, who is alleged to have shot President
Kennedy, was born in New Orleans on October 8, 1939, two
months after his father had died, to a woman who had lost her
mother when she was two. Mrs. Marguerite Oswald was, by her
own account, a patriotic, hardworking, religious woman preoccu-

pied by questions of money and social class, resentful of authority. She had been married and divorced before she married Oswald's father. Lee Oswald had a stepbrother from his mother's first marriage and an older brother from her marriage to his father.

When Lee was born, Mrs. Oswald was working as a practical nurse. Unable to work and care for three small children at the same time, she put the two older children in a Lutheran orphanage and left Lee, who was a baby, with a relative. Mrs. Oswald never had much money and her finances had not improved by the time Lee was three, so she put him in the orphanage with his brothers. Meanwhile she married a third husband, Edwin Echdahl, who divorced her in 1948, charging cruelty.

Sometime during her marriage to Echdahl, Lee came to live with her. Lee had trouble as soon as he started elementary school. He was a poor reader and speller, and a shy, retiring child, remote and withdrawn. Evidently no one at school troubled to find out why. "If he had problems, we did not recognize them," the principal of his elementary school said later.

As a little boy Lee would come home from school at noon, make his own lunch, and eat by himself. When a teacher asked him if he could get on by himself, he is said to have answered, "I guess I can open a can of soup as good as anyone."

In 1952, Mrs. Oswald moved to New York with Lee to be with her eldest son. They lived with him for a month, but trouble developed between them, so Mrs. Oswald left, moving with Lee to the Bronx.

Lee was thirteen by now and we can assume he had not had much happiness in his young life. As his probation officer and psychiatrist both noted later, he resented his lack of a father fiercely. His mother had left him at birth for six years, and her later attentions were intermittent and sketchy. She was characterized by others as too wrapped up in her own problems to meet or even recognize Lee's emotional needs. When she was told he needed help, for reasons of her own, she refused it for him.

According to a diagnosis made when he was fourteen, Lee had a "towering rage against women" that was well hidden—along with his anger at the lack of a father—in his shy, remote personality. Perhaps if he had found himself in his New York school, it might have eased some of the pain. But he was already well behind his age in reading ability. In New York, as he later told his probation officer, he felt like an outcast with his blue jeans, his southern accent, and his poor school performance. So he didn't go to school much. Then he stopped entirely.

Oswald attended Trinity Lutheran school for three weeks. Then he was enrolled in JHS 117 as a ninth-grader. Between October and January, Oswald was absent from school some forty-seven days. He later told his probation officer he'd get up at nine and watch television all day.

Then the Oswalds moved again and Lee transferred to another school. But he never reported to this one. The attendance bureau tried to get Mrs. Oswald into family court to find out why the boy wasn't at school, but she didn't show up. Next they issued a warrant for her to appear in court with Oswald, but she came alone. She insisted Lee's troubles were a "family affair." The judge disagreed. Finally under court order she brought Oswald in and the judge ordered him to Youth House for a month for psychiatric diagnosis.

Lee was assigned a probation officer, John Carro, who later talked to the press about his impressions. It was evidently Carro to whom Oswald said, when asked about his mother, "Well, I've got to live with her so I guess I love her." But he showed no real relationship to her, according to Carro, nor she to him.

Lee went off to Youth House. Youth House, euphemistically called a detention home, is a children's prison in the Bronx. Like most such institutions throughout the country, it is an expensive (in this case five-million-dollar) tribute to the low standards and lack of concern we show for troubled children. Built in 1957 with a three-hundred-bed capacity, it was overcrowded nine days after it opened.

Like most such institutions throughout the country, Youth House got no attention until a local tabloid needed horror copy and then it became a public scandal. Three months after it

opened, for example, the New York *Daily Mirror* noted that
twenty-four boys had already escaped Youth House by picking
locks. "In an effort to do something about it, the Department of
Public Works has been asked to make a study of the
lock(s) . . . ," the *Mirror* said.

Along with the escapes there were deaths, riots, routine
beatings of the children by counselors and supervisors with fists,
belts, buckles, and chains. When released, children told of
forced sodomy by guards who liked to watch, and incidents
where children who wet or soiled themselves were forced to roll
in their own urine.

Oswald was sent to Youth House for a month where he was
seen by Dr. Renatus Hartogs. Ironically, Hartogs had been
looking unsuccessfully for research funds to study how to
prevent the outcome of dangerous tendencies in children.

Hartogs diagnosed Oswald as schizophrenic. He described
him as shy and withdrawn, hiding inside his resentment at the
lack of a father and consumed by a rage against women. He said
Oswald needed help.

Hartogs later told the Warren Commission he had found Lee
Oswald dangerous, with a potential for explosive, aggressive,
assaultive acting out that was rather unusual to find in a child
who was sent to Youth House on a mild charge like school
truancy. Hartogs suggested that Oswald be placed on probation
under the condition that he "seek help and guidance through
contact with a child guidance clinic."

Hartogs recommended that Oswald be treated while living at
home, and that his mother be treated too. If that was not
possible, he recommended that Lee be placed in an institution.

Oswald's probation officer later told the press, "I reported this
was a potentially dangerous situation. I'm not a psychiatrist but
I've been around the field as a youth worker. When you get a
thirteen-year-old kid who withdraws into his own world, whose
only company is fantasy, who wants no friends, who has no
father figure, whose mother doesn't seem to relate either, then
you've got trouble."

Oswald was now caught between his mother's unwillingness to
cooperate with the court and the lack of facilities where the boy

could either be placed or treated as an inpatient or outpatient.

Two recommended facilities turned him down because they had no openings. A third, the Community Service Society, could not get Mrs. Oswald to cooperate, and so they turned him down too. The Salvation Army, according to Carro, said Lee's problems were too severe for them to handle.

Unable to place him, the judge tried to arrange for outpatient treatment, but that proved fruitless also.

Lee's probation officer finally found an organization called the Big Brothers, a family counseling agency for fatherless boys, which agreed to help. Between December 1953 and January 1954 the agency called on Mrs. Oswald four or five times but she told them to stay away. She said Lee was all right and threatened to leave town if they kept bothering her. Finally the court wrote to her, but by then she had moved, and the letter came back, NO FORWARDING ADDRESS.

Should the probation officer, the court, the school, the doctor, the counseling agency, have assumed more responsibility? Should the judge have arrested Mrs. Oswald when she failed to show up in court? Could they have helped Oswald? Should they have tried to find a potentially dangerous child when he left the city? We can all ask ourselves.

In January 1964, after the Kennedy assassination, when everybody was asking who Lee Harvey Oswald was, it was clear, despite the soul-searching of New York City officials, that the case of Lee Harvey Oswald, examined and diagnosed by a psychiatrist ten years previously, was not unusual. Psychiatrists like Hartogs had been saying for years that many professionals are blind to symptoms of danger in children. Although others have put the figure lower, Hartogs said at the time that 15 percent of the children he saw at the Youth House were potential killers. "About four percent of the children in whom I have found dangerous traits have returned to the Youth House within one to four years on a charge of assault or murder," he later told *The New York Times*.

In addition, Hartogs pointed out the need for institutions designed especially for troubled children. A 1963 report urging the expansion of psychiatric facilities for children noted that there were 263 psychiatric beds in New York City hospitals for the city's more than two million children under nineteen years of age. Worst of all, they said, no city in the country did more for its children than New York. Oswald's former probation officer added that he would have even more difficulty placing an Oswald under psychiatric care in 1964 than he did in 1954 because in 1964 there were even fewer facilities.

Mrs. Oswald was not an attractive or sympathetic figure. Newspaper accounts mentioned her financial straits and noted she was envious of people with "class" and money and had trouble making ends meet. Some commentators called Oswald a victim of poverty.

Harry Golden, for one, then a columnist for the *New York Post*, wrote on February 10, 1964, that Oswald was a product of the "crippling effects of American poverty. This is not to insist if we had no poverty we would have no murders. It is to insist that many of us do not understand the quality of the neurosis poverty or underprivilege nourishes. The neuroses and megalomania bred in poverty are different from those bred in comfort." Psychiatrists like Arthur Green have said the same thing.

Jack Ruby, who shot and killed Lee Harvey Oswald, was born Jake Rubenstein on April 19, 1911, in Chicago, Illinois. He was the third of eight children. His father drank heavily and left Ruby's mother several times during Ruby's childhood. When Jack was twelve his father left for good. Ruby's mother lapsed into a series of depressions that took her in and out of mental hospitals. She was eventually diagnosed as paranoid and was committed.

Jake was put into foster care by the Jewish Foundling Society for the next two years. He completed one year of high school and then quit. Not much else is known about Ruby's early childhood. He evidently supported himself by small-time hustling in his teens. At the time of his trial, Ruby was described by friends as the victim of psychomotor epilepsy and an underprivileged youth.

Charles Miller Manson, who led his outcast family of LSD freaks on an orgy of horrifying butchery, was born out of wedlock on November 11, 1934, in Cincinnati, Ohio, to a teenage mother who was a prostitute. He never saw his father. When Manson was five, his mother went to jail for beating up and robbing dates she was hustling in riverfront bars. Manson went to live in a small town near Wheeling, West Virginia, first with his maternal grandmother, then with an aunt and uncle who had, according to later accounts, a "sour" marriage and gave him little affection. Manson said that his aunt was a harsh disciplinarian who punished him severely when he left the yard to play with other children.

When Charles was eight, his mother was released from jail. His uncle was ill with tuberculosis and he was sent back to his mother. He lived with her and a succession of her men friends in Cincinnati in a series of seedy apartments, spending most of the time alone, indoors. When Charles was eleven, his mother followed a boyfriend to Indianapolis and took Charles with her. In later years, she remembered getting drunk, putting him to bed, and leaving for the night.

At thirteen, Manson's mother tried to put him in foster care. At fourteen he rented a room and supported himself by making deliveries for Western Union and by petty thefts. He did that, he said, because his mother was living in sin. He told people he was ashamed of her.

That year his mother turned him in to the Indianapolis Juvenile Center. Charles was made a ward of the county and sent to the Bibalut School for Boys in Terre Haute, Indiana.

After ten months there, Manson ran away. He was now fifteen and was sent to Boys Town. A priest at Boys Town later said that Manson craved attention and affection. He evidently did not get enough. Within several months he ran away from Boys Town and stole, in succession, a motor scooter and a car. He was then sent to a reformatory, the Indiana Boys School in Plainfield.

In 1951 Manson ran away from Plainfield for the eighteenth time and was arrested in Utah for stealing a car. He was sent to the National Training School for Boys in Washington, D.C., and paroled in 1954.

So Manson spent his first thirteen years with a mother who rejected and neglected him, who drank, who prostituted herself, of whom he was ashamed, and with other relatives who also treated him harshly. He spent the next twelve years in either reformatories or prisons, one of which he ran away from eighteen times. By the time he was twenty-five, he had been convicted for a series of crimes ranging from car theft to violation of the White Slave Traffic Act.

Later, after he and his "family" of outcasts murdered movie actress Sharon Tate and four others at an isolated estate near Hollywood, in an orgy that terrified Hollywood residents for months, his life, like Oswald's, became a public curiosity. A friend said his roots had been in the prison system. When he left it, he collected a group of misfits like himself, mostly young girls from troubled families, several with early and unhappy marriages. He managed to hold them with his strange charisma, security, and affection. "That's all there is, man," he was quoted as telling friends. "If you don't have someone to love you, you don't have anything."

He despised the comfortable and successful, upon whom he finally took his revenge. As an adolescent, he was said to have been an unbending, lonely child, hiding his resentment and hostility behind an oddly ingratiating façade.

In a *New York Times* article entitled "One Man's Family," which appeared before the trial but after Manson's arrest, Steven Roberts noted that Manson's history, as well as that of his followers, showed gross neglect and abandonment by parents too unconcerned to look after their own, and the breakdown of family or any structure in which children can find security, affection or ideals.

One of Manson's girls got in trouble with the law soon after her mother's death when she was fifteen. A second said her father had deserted them when she was little and she had seen him twice in fifteen years. A third, the daughter of a wealthy San Diego stockbroker, said her parents were divorced when she was two.

Did anyone at the series of institutions Manson passed half his life in ever try to reach him? Or diagnose him? When they sent him from one institution to another, did they simply lock him up, in anticipation of the next time? What was the training he got at training schools? Of what was he reformed at the reformatories?

Manson took out his rage at life in a great splash of blood. His notoriety was such and his crime so repulsive that even the President of the United States commented on it. "Guilty," said Richard Nixon.

No President ever knew or cared about several other youths who made the papers in 1964 and 1965. They were little people, and so were the people they murdered.

In October 1964, three teenage youths went on a binge. The boys were all students at a special school for children who are disciplinary problems. They started in the bathroom, where they knifed a ninth-grader so badly he needed forty-odd stitches to close the wounds. They then attacked, beat, and slashed two men who had the bad luck to pass them in the subway.

One of the three had been released from Central Islip State Mental Hospital a little less than a year before, after a court ordered commitment of two years. He was released on convalescent status in custody of his mother.

On May 24, 1965, Lila Burns, a twelve-year-old girl who had been "emotionally disturbed" since the death of her father four years before, knifed a sixty-year-old woman in the subway and killed her. Lila had had school problems for some time. Expelled previously from her neighborhood school, Lila had been awaiting placement in a special school for months, because there were no openings.

On March 18, 1965, seventeen-year-old Manuel Christopher stabbed another seventeen-year-old to death in the subway. Manuel lived the first six years of his life with his father's sister while his father worked and his mother went to nursing school. When his parents separated shortly after, he went to live with another aunt. When questioned by the police his aunt said he slept until late afternoon, watched TV, wouldn't go to school or to work. The school authorities never checked on his truancy. He had been arrested twice before and released on minor charges.

In December 1965, a fire broke out in the Jewish Community Center in Yonkers, New York, killing nine children and three adults. Two years later eighteen-year-old Thomas Ruppert was found guilty on twenty-four counts of first-degree murder. As the papers described it, during the five weeks of the trial, the "youth's 18 years of deprivation and neglect was revealed, a chapter out of a sociologist's handbook."

Tommy had worked at the center briefly since his return from Hawthorne Cedar Knolls School for emotionally disturbed children, where he had been for a year and a half.

Tommy was the second of eight children. His father, a route man for a diaper service, was frequently ill and the family had trouble managing financially. His mother was sick too; at the time of the trial she was in the hospital with terminal cancer. His father could not leave work the day of the trial to come to the sentencing. In 1957 the SPCC brought a neglect petition against Tommy's parents and he was placed in a foster home a year later. There were problems between him and his foster parents and he was sent to another foster home, then later, to a third. At twelve he was sent to the Albany Home for Children. When officials there told him he might go home, he started to steal.

Three years later he was sent to Hawthorne Cedar Knolls where he stayed a year and a half until June 1965, when he was sent home. Six months later he set the Yonkers fire.

At Tommy's trial, an administrator at Hawthorne testified that the boy was disturbed emotionally, tried to please teachers at the expense of his classmates, and could not get along with boys his own age.

Tommy had previously set fire to his own home.

In June 1964, seventeen-year-old Anthony Spencer was arrested for rape and released on $500 bail. Although Spencer had a previous record the judge and the district attorney were unaware of it, because all prior cases were juvenile. In September, Anthony was picked up again. This time he confessed to several previous rapes, one of them a five-year-old child, and two murders, one of a schoolteacher in her forties, another of a woman of eighty-one.

On September 23, 1964, Jimmy Breslin, who covered the story for the *New York Herald Tribune*, quoted the police on the case as saying:

> You wonder who let him go. . . . His background alone, arson, raping a five-year-old child, that should have been enough to hold him. Talk to the boy for a couple of hours and you'd know he never should be on the streets. The psychiatrists must have spent five minutes with him.

Anthony Spencer was first picked up by the police when he was eleven for raping a five-year-old, and again on rape charges when he was twelve. At thirteen, because he set fire to a couch in his home, he was sent to Youth House, then to Bellevue Hospital for diagnosis, where he spent two months. He was diagnosed as mentally retarded and committed to the Wassaic State School for the Mentally Retarded. There he became one of 4,100 patients under the care of 20 psychiatrists. At fifteen he was released to an aftercare clinic and from there he was discharged. Two months after his discharge he raped a young woman at knife point.

His mother later said she never "had any trouble with him until he was thirteen. . . . That boy's sick and needs a doctor . . . he is oversexy."

School records show, however, that Anthony started having trouble at the age of seven. He appeared to be retarded. His teacher said he was a slow learner, was very difficult, and had a bad attendance record. The principal stated that the mother was hostile and frequently irrational and at times kept all the children—Anthony had three siblings—at home to do housework. Actually, Anthony was one of six children, not four; his two youngest siblings were his mother's children by another father, his real father having left his mother nine years before. His mother was on welfare.

While Anthony's first rape petition was pending in family court, he was referred to the Bureau of Child Welfare. The Bureau of Child Welfare social worker was told that Anthony bothered other boys and girls in school and had accused a teacher of sodomy. The social worker saw Mrs. Spencer several times. She said there was little chance of working productively with her. Mrs. Spencer had told her she was not responsible for what Anthony did. Anyway, she didn't know anything about it. She said he was well protected, well brought up, and not allowed out except to shop on Saturdays and to go to church on Sundays.

A psychiatric examination at Bellevue when he was eleven found that Anthony had an IQ of 54, functioned at a second- or third-grade level, was "impulsive," "without judgment," had no limits or controls of his own, and was likely to "clash" with his environment. The report recommended placement.

That was in December 1958. In January 1959 Anthony's case was dismissed in family court. When he was brought in for arson in 1960, the probation officer said relations between mother and children were good. At that time Anthony was examined again at Bellevue. The report said that he was immature, primitive, that his general mental development was retarded—showing diffuse organic impairment, marked feminine identification, unusually pronounced diffuse sensuality, and a need for gratification that found an outlet in fire-setting as a defense against the overt expression of homosexual tendencies. From Bellevue he went to Wassaic. Presumably, after Bellevue, until he confessed in the police station no one examined or questioned him again.

When the police picked Anthony up, though, he told one of them that he was sick, that he had this thing about raping women, that he had to do it, that something went through his head, that the only way he wanted sex was by rape and he wanted sex all the time.

Did Anthony ever tell that to anyone else? Did anyone else ever ask?

In August 1966, Charles J. Whitman, an ex-marine who was enrolled in the University of Texas at Austin, stabbed his mother, killed his wife, then went up to the top of a 307-foot water tower with a hunting rifle and shot forty-five people, killing fourteen. It was one of the largest mass-killings in the United States.

Dr. Dana Farnsworth, director of health services at Harvard University, a member of a panel later convened to study the case, said he was concerned about the increasing tendency toward violence in the country. Other committee members said they didn't know if ex-servicemen were more violent than others but recommended a program of deemphasizing "those hostile acts taught as laudatory in time of war."

Whitman had seen a university psychiatrist several months before the shooting. The psychiatrist's note indicated that Whitman was "oozing with hostility, most of which was directed toward his father." He said Whitman hated his father with a mortal passion, that Whitman's father beat his mother, that Whitman was very fond of his wife, but had previously assaulted her twice. He claimed his father was brutal to him when he was a child, had a terrible temper, was "domineering and extremely demanding," and that that was the cause of all his trouble. He said that when he beat his wife he was acting like his father when he beat his mother.

Whitman claimed to have overwhelming periods of hostility when he thought about going up on the tower with a deer rifle and shooting people. Under later questioning, the doctor said he had not considered that statement alarming. He had suggested Whitman come back for further consultation, but Whitman had not kept the appointment. The doctor's notes said, "He identified his father as being brutal." His parents had separated thirty days ago, and his father was calling him to try to persuade his mother to return.

Whitman, unlike Oswald, Manson, Spencer, Ruppert, Ruby, and the others cited in this chapter, was not poor. The staff psychiatrist at the University of Texas described him as an "all-American boy." Whitman, he said, was serious, studied hard, thought constantly of getting ahead, and got along wonderfully with his attractive wife.

Whitman's friends described him as a rather tightly controlled, rigid man. He was said never to make an involuntary move, to set up heavy tasks for himself, like a burdensome schedule in school, and then be unswerving in its pursuit. He was an Eagle Scout as a boy and a scoutmaster as an adult.

Other friends said he referred to his father frequently, and that Whitman claimed he had joined the marines to get away from him. He said his father beat his mother and others in the family. He was terribly afraid of being like him.

Whitman evidently suffered from periods of depression, something few people knew, during which his wife stayed home with him, fearing to leave him alone.

Whitman's parents had separated several months previously. According to a friend, this had really thrown him. For a while he considered giving up everything and becoming a bum.

His father later told the press that he could not believe what his son said about him. It was true, he said, that he was a strict father. "With all three of my sons, it was 'Yes, sir' and 'No, sir,' " he said. He had been an orphan himself, and therefore, he said, gave his sons all the advantages.

He also noted that his son had always been a "crack shot," raised as he was, in a house with a gun in every room. The father added that he himself was a great hunter and a "fanatic" about guns. The father's house, according to reporters, was expensive, well kept, and did in fact have guns hanging in every room.

Whitman also described his father to the university psychiatrist as semiliterate, but a perfectionist in other respects. The psychiatrist observed that Whitman had lived for the day when he might consider himself capable of excelling his father, that he had surpassed him long ago educationally but was trying to do so in "virtually all fields of human endeavor." When asked if he thought that Whitman came to him to ask him to stop him from going to the tower and shooting people, the doctor said no.

After Whitman's death the university psychiatrist agreed that a correct diagnosis might have prevented the killing. The case naturally received some comment from other psychiatrists, which was duly reported in the press. Dr. Lawrence Kubie of Johns Hopkins University thought that a doctor who thinks a threat is more than a fantasy has an obligation to intervene. But if he can't win the patient's confidence, Kubie said, the psychiatrist is confronted with a "gap in the medico-legal structure."

Perhaps Kubie was thinking about confidentiality, an essential ingredient in the doctor-patient relationship and one good reason a psychiatrist would hold back from notifying the police of a patient's possible bent for violence.

Dr. Frederick Wertham, who has written extensively about violence in our culture, agreed that there is a gap. He says this gap exists because society doesn't really care about violence and doesn't take advance warnings seriously. He pointed out that if a psychiatrist notified the police that a patient was going to commit violence, the police would say, "Tell us when he does."

A police officer was quoted as saying that persons diagnosed as psychiatrically capable of violence were medical, not criminal, problems. "It's up to the medical profession to see that they are hospitalized and treated," he said. "The police can't arrest people because they are ill."

The panel convened by Texas governor John Connally to study the Whitman case expressed concern that the Whitman incident and others like it suggested a growing tendency toward violence in the United States. The panel recommended a massive, nationwide study to find out if that was so and, if so, what could be done.

That was 1966. In December 1973 a sixteen-year-old charged with stabbing a fourteen-year-old during a subway holdup was identified as a former inmate of a state youth reformatory. Another sixteen-year-old who admitted killing a seventy-year-old grocer during a holdup was sent to a rehabilitation program for disturbed children. Five weeks later the program was said to be unworkable and was abandoned; the boy went home. A week later he walked into Bellevue Hospital's psychiatric ward and committed himself voluntarily, telling the doctor he was afraid he was going to hurt someone.[2] Where will those two young people be in 1983?

10

The Numbers Game

"Nixon, McGovern," the cab driver says, "what's the difference? I said a long time ago Nixon was trying to take over the country, and he nearly did. First of all that election was a fraud, fixed. He shouldn't have been there in the first place. Writing those dirty letters. Smearing Muskie. Smearing all those other guys so McGovern would be the candidate. Who nominated McGovern anyway? Not me.

"That's the problem. People don't have a chance to decide who's gonna run for President. Who decides? Who picked Nixon? Who picked McGovern? I say we ought to let twenty guys run and whoever comes in first ought to be President. And in second ought to be Vice-President. Most politicians are all crooks and liars anyway, and they're only interested in helping the rich.

"The rich people own this country. They always have. But they used to let you have a little something. Now they want it all. After thirty years working to keep this country going, what have I got? When a man works for thirty years, he's entitled to something. I think he's entitled to a house and every couple years a new car. And he's entitled to being able to feed and protect his family, and a one-month paid vacation.

"It's getting so a working man doesn't have anything anymore. We ought to have free medical care. Or what's the point? In China they got free medical care. What do we got? We got bills."

"Some people say that's socialism," I say.

"So," he replies. "As long as it's free, I don't care what they call it."

1 Reporting Systems

All fifty states in the United States have laws that encourage or require citizens to report child abuse. Most of them make it mandatory for police, hospitals, and social-service agencies to report also. New Mexico is the only state in which reporting is not mandatory.

In most states, the upper age limit is eighteen. Twenty-eight states have some form of central registry. Twenty-nine make failure to report a crime.

This legislation has been promoted by the Children's Bureau to protect abused children and prevent further abuse of these children and others in their families. Reporting legislation does not incorporate any strategies for prevention and treatment, nor does it require reporting of child abuse occurring in institutions like schools, foster care, detention facilities, training schools, or any public custodial institutions.

2 Public Monies

Since the 1960s, the U.S. Department of Health, Education and Welfare has taken the responsibility of devising policies dealing with child abuse and neglect through certain sections of Title IV-A (AFDC), Title IV-B (Child Welfare Services), and Title V (Maternal and Child Health Programs) of the Social Security Act. Total funding for these programs was $76 million in 1972. This represented an incredible increase in twelve years from $4 million in 1960 to $10 million in 1965 to $49 million in 1970 and $76 million in 1972.* Despite these expenditures only a fraction of this money, according to the Office of Child Development, went to programs that focused specifically on child abuse. Consequently, we have relatively little information

* Some of the figures in this chapter have appeared elsewhere in the book but are summarized here in one place to give the reader a broader understanding of the problem.

about many facets of child abuse, particularly what kinds of programs would be most effective in dealing with it.[1]

3 Incidence

There are 65 million children under eighteen in the United States. When we talk about the incidence of child abuse, we mean the proportion of all children under eighteen who are abused or seriously neglected. Estimates of the incidence vary enormously, partly because reporting is erratic regardless of state laws.

For example, 11,000 cases of abuse were reported to state registries in 1968. By 1972 those reports had just about doubled. But that does not mean that the numbers had doubled and the incidence increased, since it is unreasonable to talk about an increase in a phenomenon unless there is an accurate accounting over different periods of time. What has increased is the awareness, interest, and concern in child abuse. This has led to more legislation requiring reporting and therefore to an increase in reporting levels.

4 Limits

Dr. Henry Kempe, a pioneer in the field of child abuse, has reported that 60,000 children were seriously abused in 1972. That is the figure quoted most often by the Senate Subcommittee on Children and Youth.

An upper limit of between 2.5 and somewhat over 4 million severely abused children was the estimate of David Gil, sociologist and Brandeis professor, basing his figures on a study he did for the National Opinion Research Center in 1965. Gil has said that he thinks the actual number of cases that year was probably much less.

An upper boundary of 500,000 has been estimated by Richard Light, research associate at the Kennedy School of Government, a maximum one-third as large as Gil's.[2]

These figures are for abuse only. There is no survey data for the incidence of child neglect or sexual abuse, although studies in both New York State and New York City indicate that neglect and sexual abuse occur more than twice as often as physical abuse. Light believes that one child in every one hundred in America is physically abused, sexually molested, or severely neglected.

5 Profiles of Abusing Parents

In a study to determine what policies might be most successful in preventing child abuse, Light and others have tried to develop a profile of the abusing family. Using Gil's data, Light has concluded that the variable that shows up most frequently as somehow related to child abuse is the father's unemployment. This confirms the findings of most professionals that the kind of financial and emotional stress related to unemployment is also related to child abuse. Besides unemployment or very low income, abusing families tend to live in poor housing, to be twice as likely to have four or more children, to be in poor mental and physical health, and to live in social isolation.

As noted earlier, Gil's study showed that 30 percent of abused children lived in female-headed households; 46 percent lived with a father in the home; 20 percent with a stepfather. More than 2 percent lived in foster homes, 0.3 percent with adoptive parents, 12 percent in homes without the child's mother. Ten percent of the mothers were single, 20 percent separated, divorced, or deserted or widowed. The homes of nonwhite children were less frequently intact. Gil suggests that this data shows an association between child abuse and deviance from normal family structure that appears to be especially marked for nonwhite children.

Although other studies show that parents of abused children tend to be very young, Gil's does not.

All studies including Gil's show that education and occupation levels are lower than the general population. So are income levels, with the lowest for nonwhite. Over 37 percent of the families in Gil's survey were on public assistance at the time of the incident. Nearly 60 percent had been on public assistance at one time or another.

6 *Bias*

Of some 3,000 cases collected from New York City's central registry and analyzed by reporting sources, only eight cases were reported by private physicians. Other cities report similar findings. This particular reporting bias inevitably leads to a heavy emphasis on low-income families and tells us nothing about the rest of our society.

7 *Foster Care*

There were 326,700 children under eighteen in the United States in foster care in 1970, of whom 284,500 were under the partial or complete auspices of public welfare agencies.

It is estimated that there will be 364,000 children in foster care by 1975. Since there were 287,000 in 1965, that represents a projected 27 percent increase in ten years and an increase in the annual rate from 4.0 per thousand in 1965 to 4.7 per thousand in 1975.

Approximately one-fourth of these children return to their parents. After one and a half years the chance of a child being returned to his own home drops drastically. The average weekly payment for children in foster care is somewhere between twelve dollars and forty dollars, depending on the state.

Most departments of public welfare have a 30 to 40 percent annual staff turnover. At 29 percent, attrition in Massachusetts appears lower than most. Still, social workers there reported that in 12.5 percent of the foster-care cases they couldn't describe the foster home because they had never visited it. They knew from their records though that 25 percent of the children placed had been in three or more homes.

The agency also knew that 40 percent of the children were disabled in some way—in the use of limbs, hearing, speech. Almost a fourth had never been evaluated, much less treated. Most foster parents had not been told that they were getting disabled children nor given help, once the children arrived, on how to treat them.

Twenty-three percent of the children were placed because of

mental illness of the parent, 13.6 percent for neglect or abuse, 8.5 percent were abandoned.

In the study, some 37 percent of the parents could not be located to be interviewed. Of those who were, most said the option of day care or a homemaker had not been available when the children were placed. More than one-fourth did not see their children while in placement. Less than 30 percent visited their children for six months or more. Almost 20 percent said they had been prohibited from seeing their children by the social worker.

Despite a department policy that children should not be put in homes with more than six children, 16 percent were. In 1972, according to the *New York Law Journal*, it cost $4,400 yearly for permanent foster care, of which one-half is for administration.

8   *Families*

United States government statistics on families go back to 1940. Since 1940, 85 percent of American families are of the husband-wife type. But while the percentage of such families has stayed relatively stable, the numbers have increased. For instance, in 1940, 27 million out of 32.2 million families included a husband and wife. By 1973, the figures had changed to 46.3 out of 54.4.[3]

It is the numbers, not the percentages, that count. Female-headed families have made up 10 to 12 percent of the total since 1940, but there have been more of them each decade.

During the 1960s, families headed by women increased twice as fast as they did in the 1950s, growing from 4.5 to 5.6 million. By 1973 they had jumped another million, to 6.6 million. The increase has been concentrated among families of divorced or separated women, and the numbers are going up all the time.

The problem of female-headed families is disproportionately a black problem. In 1973, 10 percent of white families were headed by women, but among black families the figure was 35 percent.

This substantial increase in female-headed families has been attributed variously to the sharp rise in separation and divorce since the 1960s, the rapid increase in employment for women, the absence of husbands during military service, and the continued rise in unwed motherhood. It seems too early to tell how much effect the women's liberation movement has had. Other factors that have probably contributed are sporadic high-unemployment rates for black males and the generally low pay when they are employed. The first makes it less likely for unemployed black men to marry; the second makes it less likely for black women to marry.

Along with the jump in female-headed families is the jump in the last two decades of children who live with their mother only, from 8 percent to 14 percent. Again, this is a greater problem for black children. In 1973, 52 percent of black children under eighteen were living with both parents, while the figure for white was 85 percent.

However, decreasing birth rates have lowered the proportion of preschoolers living at home, from 3.3 million in 1960 to 2.4 million at present.

The other significant change in family composition involves families that include three generations; they have dropped in the last decade to less than 5 percent.

9 Mobility

Every year some 20 percent of all Americans move to a different place. For families, moving causes more problems for low-income people and more for blacks than for whites.

Blacks are more likely to move, but they move shorter distances. The latest figures show that 20 percent of blacks moved yearly as compared to 18 percent for whites. However, 17 percent moved within the same county, compared to 11 percent of whites, while whites had higher rates of migration to other counties and between states.

Among men, mobility shows a clear relationship to employment status with local mobility higher for the unemployed. Education is related also. College graduates are more likely to move than high-school graduates and high-school graduates are more likely to move than elementary-school graduates, but the latter are more likely to move locally than the other two.

The husband's mobility usually interferes with the wife's employment and/or career.

Along with connections between mobility, status, and pay, the single most important factor related to families and mobility is the relationship of moving to children's progress in school.

In terms of school, moving is definitely harmful to children whose parents are not college graduates, but it does not seem to hurt children whose parents are. We don't know whether this is because well-educated parents tend to have children who do well in school, because they send their children to better schools, or both.

Although moving frequently may not hurt their school records significantly, sociologist Lionel Tiger claims that the constant moving around of management in large companies takes a terrible toll of families and particularly of wives. In an article in *Fortune* magazine Tiger quotes the wife of one executive who claimed that her husband's various assignments forced them to move seventeen times in twenty-five years. Complaining bitterly that each time she had to start life over, the woman said, "No one but my husband knows about my past or cares about my future." [4] Somehow her plight seems to epitomize the sadness of the mobile American.

10 *Mothers Who Work*

There has been an enormous increase in the number of women who work, particularly the number of married women. In 1962 there were 16.1 million families in which both husband and wife worked, or 45 percent of all husband-wife families in which the family head was working. By 1972, the number had increased to 21.3 million, and the percentage to 55.

In 1950, less than one-fourth of all married women were working and only 12 percent of women with children under six. By 1972, over 40 percent of all married women were in the labor force, including 30 percent with children under six.

Another way to look at the numbers of women who work is to

view them from the point of view of their children. In March 1972, there were 65.3 million children under eighteen. Almost 26 million, or close to 40 percent, had mothers working or out looking for work. Of these children, 5.6 million were under six. Eight hundred thousand of those preschoolers lived in families headed by women.

Obviously women who head families are more likely to have to work. Thirty-eight percent of the children in husband-wife families had working mothers, compared to 51 percent in families where a woman was the head.

Black children are more likely to have a mother who works. Fifty-one percent of black children had working mothers compared to 37 percent of all white children. In black husband-wife families, children of fathers who worked were more likely to have mothers who worked too, although this was not true among whites. The difference is probably due to lower earnings among black men with families, which puts greater pressure on their wives to go to work.

Among female-headed families, however, 55 percent of white children had working mothers, compared to 44 percent of the black. This is due to the larger number of preschoolers in black families and to the greater numbers of less-educated black women, making it more difficult for them to get jobs.

Most women who work, particularly low-income women, have trouble making satisfactory child-care arrangements. The children inevitably suffer for it.

11   Family Income

Whether white or black, families headed by women have much less income than families headed by men. Of 5 million white children who lived with their mothers only in March 1972, the family income was less than $3,000 for 30 percent and between $3,000 and $4,999 for 24 percent. Of the 2.9 million black children in fatherless families, 39 percent were living in families with an income of less than $3,000 a year and 33 percent with an income between $3,000 and $4,999.

12   *Infanticide*

According to Urie Bronfenbrenner, professor of child development at Cornell University, infanticide in the United States has been increasing since 1957. Infant homicides accounted for 2.2 percent of total homicides in 1964, but the rate of 5.4 deaths per 100,000 was higher than that for all persons fifty-five and over. The 74 percent increase from 3.1 percent in 1957 placed infanticide in 1964 at the highest record level since 1945.

11 Who Will Parent the Child?

Judge Zuckerman died last year of a heart attack. He died shortly after this interview and after the press attacked him for the way they claimed he mishandled a case.

"Before I became a family court judge," Zuckerman said, "I was a director of family services in the Midwest, and before that, I was a social worker.

"Because most cases we see in family court in this city and in most big cities are black and Puerto Rican, most child-abuse cases we see involve blacks and Puerto Ricans. But sick people are sick all over. In family court we only see the lower socioeconomic groups. The better educated don't get to court. For instance, fighting parents, if they're middle class or wealthy, would not ordinarily bring their problems here. They would go to a lawyer. Italians might go to their church. Poorer people don't have such access in the first place.

"How do I see my role? Well I'm not here to punish people. I'm here to help. I try to talk to the children. I try to find out what's really going on. I try to see if the textbooks are right. Are abusing parents victims of abuse? Sometimes.

"One problem is that many parents use too much discipline, excessive force. A lady asks me, 'Judge, are you telling me I don't have the right to beat my child? How am I going to make him listen?'

"I'm not as interested in an abuse finding as in neglect because then I can order tests. If the mother will admit that because of inadequacies she can't cope, we can do more with that. I think in our anxiety to protect kids from abuse we go to *extremes rather than establishing the jurisdiction to help parents.*

"The main problem, anyone will tell you, is that we don't begin to have enough facilities. We are lacking in services and those we have are lacking in quality.

"For example, suppose a mother comes in who has put her kid's hand on a hot stove to punish him; this happens to be very common. Usually the child is placed while the mother is 'rehabilitated' either as an outpatient or in a state hospital. It turns out the hospital really can't provide treatment. Most state hospitals have serious money problems today, anyway. They'll send her back with a report that says, 'She needs and could benefit from continuous therapy, which will have to be provided on an outpatient basis.' Now where is she going to get it? In the so-called community? With the size of everybody's case loads, it's almost out of the question. There is such a turnover among social workers and therapists that her chances of getting any real help are minuscule.

"Has my social work background helped? Well, it's helped show me what social work can't do.

"Do I ever really help people? Occasionally. I have many cases of people on drugs. When I have a neglecting parent who's an addict, I say I'll consider returning the child only if they show me he's off drugs. Sometimes it works. If they want the child, parents can really pull themselves together.

"But it's not always so easy. The most difficult case I've had was a neglect case involving addict parents. A couple of years ago an aunt filed a neglect petition alleging that her brother's two children were frequently beaten by their addict mother. The father was then in prison. There was plenty of evidence that the mother was not caring for the children; the mother admitted it, and also admitted she was an addict. We placed the children with the aunt. One child was eight. Another was less than a year. That was in August 1970.

"Well, the mother was hospitalized. The aunt kept the older child but couldn't handle both and turned the baby over to neighbors. She did not ask or notify us about it.

"Then the mother came out of the hospital. The aunt gave back the older child. The baby was still with friends. The father came out of jail and enrolled in college. They are both doing well and they have brought a suit to get the baby back. I don't know what to do. The law in this state is very clear that parents have the right to get their children back unless it is in the best interest of the child to be placed.

"Some people would say, 'Well, addicts. They've done it once, they'll do it again!' But that goes against our whole philosophy of rehabilitation. On the other hand, the baby has spent his formative years with other parents. He's three now and doesn't know his mother and father. What will that do to him? That's the crux of the problem of custody.

"Then, besides the problem of facilities, there is the problem of gross discrimination. The Jewish agencies want to take Jews, the Catholic agencies want to take Catholics; the Protestant agencies don't have many facilities. They're all too selective. They don't want kids who are really trouble. Well, kids who are really trouble are mostly just what we've got. Agencies financed with public funds should open their doors. It's a disgrace.

"So is foster care. So are adoption services. We don't have the money to buy or create enough of them. But when we have real emergencies in this country, we get the money. To send men to the moon, for example, but not fill vacancies. In this court, out of four hundred and six probation positions, we have fifty-four vacancies. We can't fill them because there's no money. It's a comedy of errors. No, that's wrong. It's a tragedy."

CHILDREN are in trouble because families are in trouble, and families are in trouble because the other institutions which helped keep them together have also been falling apart. In America, less than 5 percent of the population has more than two generations in a household. The extended family hardly exists. Communities, even neighborhoods, are likely to be collections of strangers where no one knows the next-door neighbor's name. Religion has lost much of its moral force.

A host of factors increasingly isolates children from parents and parents, particularly young, stay-at-home mothers, from the rest of life. The separation of work from leisure, the separation of generations, the increased mobility of our population, the relaxation of many of the old forms and standards, and the American emphasis on individualism have all weakened the social fabric. Without strong parental guidance backed up by society, children look for other models, and increasingly these models are their peers. Meanwhile, the loosening of marriage bonds, the increase in numbers of the one-parent family, and the increasing pressures on women to work put a particular burden on the mother, especially the young mother who often has two jobs: raising her family and supporting them as well.

The growing number of divorces, the devaluation of mothering, and the pressures on families have been accompanied by a new and frightening phenomenon: often neither parent wants to care for the child. Such diverse figures as the youth services director in Maryland, the chief juvenile court judge in Denver, and a professor of child development at Cornell University have testified before Congress and elsewhere to this alarming trend— the wholesale abdication of parental responsibility.

Everyone, whether poor, middle class, or wealthy, is affected. The size of the welfare allowance and the contempt with which society holds welfare mothers have made it difficult for a poor woman to be proud of her role in raising her children. And the women's liberation movement, while increasing a woman's sense of self-respect, at the same time has deemphasized the importance of the maternal role. Leontine Young warns, "There are women who want work and women who have to work and the exceptional woman can do it. But the amount of energy needed is astronomic. It also presupposes a different kind of society if children are to be protected."

We don't give any value to mothering, just as we don't give any value to unpaid work. If a woman stays at home and takes care of her children and her household, that is not considered work. If she goes out, gets a job, and hires a housekeeper, however, the housekeeper's job is considered work. Most likely the housekeeper will have to make other cheaper arrangements for her children. Meanwhile, the less respect we have for our parental roles, the less respect our children have for us, and the less of a bulwark we have left in the family.

The end result of our mobility, the social disorganization, and the break between generations has led to another kind of family crisis. Many, if not most, young women today, women of all classes, when faced with caring for their own children simply don't know what to do. The crisis in transmitted values is a breakdown in knowledge. The "mothering instinct," like many other so-called instincts, is one of those aspects of culture and socialization that, just like ethnic recipes, must be passed from one generation to the next.

It is astonishing to hear young women today, or even women who are middle-aged, talk about their ignorance and anxieties when confronted with their own infants. A young lawyer who had her first child in her mid-thirties says, "Believe me, my Doctor of Law degree was no help. I saw that baby and I simply didn't know what to do. I solved the problem. I got a housekeeper fast and went back to work."

The lawyer is typical of the uprooting in America. Her mother was not around, her grandmother was dead, her husband's mother lived in another city. Many women could identify with her.

A young woman painter tells a similar tale. "My mother was born in Russia and grew up in Baltimore. My father grew up in Poland. I grew up in Chicago. I am now raising my children in Worcester, Massachusetts. Why Worcester? Well my husband's company sent him there. My sister lives in Spain. So when I gave birth to my first child, my mother was in Madrid."

With all that shifting about, with all that lack of cohesion in her life, who was to teach her how to mother? Who was to help her raise her kids?

"If my mother had been here," said the painter, "she would have had very little to pass on in the way of maternal advice. She was the first generation of American women too early in recent history to pursue a career comfortably, but recent enough to dislike raising children. Maybe there is something in the

American experience. It's curious, now that I think of it, but her mother had a feminist bent, too. The way my mother tells it, while my grandfather, a recent immigrant, was scraping boat bottoms in the Baltimore harbor, my grandmother, who never quite learned to read in English, was off picketing bakeries for using sweatshop labor. The owner would come to the bakery door in his white apron and he'd yell at her, 'Go home. Go home, you troublemaker. We'll take care of the union. You take care of your kids.' "

Another woman, describing the isolation of her early married life, said, "I had my first child at the Bethesda Naval Hospital because my husband was in the Public Health Service. We lived in this middle-class project they called a garden apartment. I had a hello–good-bye acquaintance with my two nearest neighbors. When I came home with the baby I had a private nurse for a week. She wouldn't let me near the baby because that was her job. When she left I was as green as ever.

"One of my neighbors had two little kids. They were both under three. She kept them spotless, just like her house. They ate under layers of bibs. She wiped them from stem to stern about six times a day, and if they got dirty, she yelled like hell. As little as I knew about kids it was clear she was not a good model. Today, in fact, I can see she was desperate for help. But so was I. I would have given anything for a visiting nurse."

White people often assume that blacks have mammies lurking in the next block just dying to take their babies off their hands, that is clearly a myth. Many black people have migrated from the South to the North, from the farm to the city, or from one city to another, following work. For all practical purposes, their relatives are as inaccessible as if they were in Poland. Others may have relatives around the corner, but chances are that relatives like Lilly's mother have problems enough of their own. If that were not so, there wouldn't be so many young working mothers whose meager earnings must also pay for unsatisfactory child care.

Shirley Carroll is one of them. A strikingly attractive black woman whose personal history is a triumph of ego over environment, Shirley says, "I don't want to speak for all black people, just for myself, but I sure didn't have a family to help care for my kids. I left home to get away from an alcoholic mother. My father took off long before I did. I was married, working, and had had a baby by the time I was eighteen, and I can tell you my mother was sure not gonna mammy my child. She couldn't even take care of herself. And I had to work. Unless I went on welfare, and I was just determined not to do that. So I left my baby when she was three months old with a friend's aunt in Queens. She boarded her for ten dollars a week. I lived in Brooklyn, so I couldn't even get her at night. I'd pick her up on weekends. My friends said my baby'd never know me. And I felt just terrible about it. But I had no choice.

"Anyway, I didn't know the first thing to do with that baby. I was just plain scared of the whole thing. And babies get on your nerves so. Well, because I was so young and had her at a city hospital, they sent me a nurse-midwife, a kind of visiting nurse. Man, did she help! I don't even want to think what would have happened without her.

"One thing about welfare, though. A lot of jobs pay so little there isn't much point working. I was making so little money that often I thought I'd be better off just collecting that old check. That's what a lot of my friends did. They'd say, 'The hell with it, I'm getting less money working.' In the end I just couldn't do it. It would have meant never getting out of Brownsville. If I'd gone on welfare I'd probably still be there today.

"I get awfully sick of women's lib, though. It's got nothing to do with me. It's got nothing to do with black people. I had to work or go on welfare, kids or no kids. Some girls who can't do anything else feel like they need to have kids. The kid at least means they can do something. Of course they usually have too many, and on welfare almost any is too many, and then they're stuck, like my mother was, and they just start drinking and taking it out on the kids."

Shirley has described many of the stresses that contribute to child abuse. Mothers who have children too young, who don't know what to do for them, but for whom the child represents an accomplishment—at first. Then frustration, loneliness, and often alcohol or drugs. But she has also supplied a simple clue when she mentioned the visiting nurse—help.

Dorothy Davis is another woman who got help with her child from a visiting nurse. "If you ask me," Dorothy says, "child abuse is due to frustration. And I know what I'm talking about."

Dorothy is a large, voluble, black woman who runs a day-care center in New York City. "I started off dirt," she laughs. "Now I'm a consultant. So if you're consulting me, I'll tell you. When I got pregnant with Gregory, I'd already had three. The youngest was eight then. And here comes number four. Shut the door. Well, it's not my religious belief to stop having kids that way. So I had to have him. But I was so depressed I didn't know what I was going to do.

"I guess I'm lucky because the aides in the hospital I was at said maybe they could help me. Of course I ain't no shrinking violet. I made it pretty clear how I felt about the baby. I mean I just said, 'Listen, I really don't want this child. I already got three. I've been on welfare all my life and now when I finally got a job, here comes number four.'

"They asked me would I like a nurse to help out. So I had a visiting nurse. She came twice a week the first three weeks and mostly we'd just talk. Well, I knew how to take care of babies. But boy did I need someone to talk to. If I had trouble, I'd call her on the phone. We had a real relationship. She was white, but that didn't make no difference. It was really cool. She taught me to love that baby and she helped me to like myself. Do I appreciate it now!

"Like I said, most child abuse comes from adult frustration. The baby-sitter complains, the fees go up, the mothers take it out on the kids. Welfare tells you you can't get no more money, you whip the kids' ass. The landlord won't listen to you 'cause you're a woman, the apartment falls apart, the school sends for you, you beat the hell out of the kid. It ain't the kid needs help. The problem is, how do you help the parent?"

One way to solve the problem of isolated motherhood is to have fewer children. And all American women, rich and poor, are having fewer. Legalized abortion and the greater availability of contraceptives and family planning have given women more options. That choice plus the efforts of groups like Zero Population Growth, the women's liberation movement, and a new, perhaps more realistic, attitude toward children and parenthood have made many young people think about why they are having children—something few past generations have done.

As Shirley noted, many women have babies for the wrong reasons. The mother is then trapped. If she is strong and particularly if she has a tough ego, if she is lucky and gets some help, she will do something with her life that will allow her to like herself. She may decide, like Shirley, that welfare will make her feel worse in the end. However, eighteen-year-old Shirleys are rare. That is often a difficult evaluation for a young girl to make. And unfortunately, despite the figures, many young unmarried girls are still having babies.

The mothers most likely to hurt their children are not, the majority of them, psychotic. They are lonely, isolated women with a heavy dependency on their children. Many of these mothers have very low feelings of self-esteem. Most have had a bad relationship with their own mothers and have no model to follow.

The nature of our society compounds these problems. We have all moved about a great deal. Except in very tight family units, there is a break in family lore, particularly information about child rearing. It gets lost in the move from one country to another, from South to North, from country to town. Something happens to transferrable cultural values that previously were passed from one generation to another. Some of it was lost a generation back. There is no one nearby to pass it on. We are, so many of us Americans, lonely, isolated, cut off from our own past.

That is, undoubtedly, the reason there are so many "how to" books in America. Written instructions from strangers replace tradition, particularly in the field of child rearing. There are literally hundreds of books written for the lay mother every year telling her what to do with her kids.

For years, we would have all been lost without Dr. Spock. Spock came on the scene when the breakdown in communication became most apparent, particularly when educated women were learning to be dissatisfied with the way they had been brought up. But separated from their own mothers and from anyone with mothering experience, they all looked about desperately for advice.

Spock spoke directly to their worries. In retrospect, it seems he was less concerned with teaching women how to mother than with teaching them how to avoid guilt. He realized both the ambivalence of his readers and the bewildering variety of their child-care choices, and concentrated there.

Part of the problem for parents is the number of possibilities to choose from, the many kinds of child-rearing practices, and no context of family traditions to help parents decide which way of disciplining—or not disciplining—the child will do.

The American emphasis on individualism exacts a price. Anything goes. Do it your way. Or like your neighbors, which may be very different. One mother keeps her child spotless. The other mother says it is bad to make children concentrate on staying clean.

Do you toilet train your child early, before the age of one? Or is it better not to pressure them? Wait till they are two or even three. Don't toilet train at all. The child will work it out. Let the baby suck his thumb. And drag a filthy blanket around. Don't let the baby suck his thumb. Give the baby a pacifier. Or don't give the baby a pacifier. Be permissive. Be strict. Do what feels most comfortable. Go to work. Stay at home.

Whatever we wish to make of our own lives, however important it is *not* to sacrifice ourselves to our children, we cannot deny the importance of love and nurturing to the infant and of care to the growing child. Harry Harlow's experiment with monkeys and with wire surrogate mothers showed more than a decade ago what happens to the young monkey who has no loving contact with a parenting adult. Jane Goodall, in *In the Shadow of Man*, shows us the difference in behavior between mothered chimpanzees and those who are the victims of maternal neglect. And doctors and psychiatrists, René Spitz, Anna Freud, Robert Coles, have been writing for years about what happens to human infants deprived of maternal love. They do not grow up emotionally intact. They grow up stunted, at the least. They become behavior problems, delinquents, withdrawn, unhappy human beings, socially deviant. Some, like Charles Manson and Lee Harvey Oswald, become murderers. They do not make good parents. They do not make good citizens. They do not lead happy lives.

Other countries might offer some models for America. England, with its national health-care system, for instance, has the visiting nurse. We could easily adopt that model for all women when they give birth. To give every mother some help when she needs it most might eliminate a lot of problems later on. The visiting nurse might be the most useful way to give aid and comfort to mothers in our society. As a federal program it could also be a way to employ women who have developed their own mothering skills at the expense of skills like, say, typing, have something valuable to pass on, and need work.

In other societies where women have achieved some greater degree of liberation—China, Israel, Russia—institutional child care has taken different forms. Particularly in societies of high consensus, like China, where everyone sees the central issues and values of life more or less similarly, women's liberation takes a different turn. Women can't stay home because the economy needs them. But the society provides for the care of their small children. There are day and residential nurseries in China that care for children of all ages and sizes, starting with the newborn. They differ somewhat depending on local circumstances. In many cases, particularly in the country, grandmothers may still care for the very young.

There is naturally a great deal of regimentation in Chinese day-care arrangements. According to Ruth Sidel in *Women and Child Care in China*, children are taught not only to sing in unison but even to move their bowels at the same time. However, the custodians or teachers in Chinese nurseries also exhibit a lot of warmth, love, and physical contact with children at the same time. In newborn nurseries, according to Sidel, mothers often come in one or two times a day to nurse their own infants.

Since the dominant attitudes in a society usually emanate from the middle class, it is important to look at what is happening to middle-class attitudes toward mothering, in particular that deemphasis that has inevitably accompanied women's lib. As women concerned with their own fulfillment have begun to question more closely their relationships with men and work, they have got to give women's historical preoccupation with children a searching look.

They have had to think through the question of what unshared parental responsibility has meant to women's lives and the toll it has taken of other energies. They have had to try to get out in front of themselves.

Now, however, the women's movement must consider how to liberate all women in the society without depriving the children of necessary parental care. Reducing sexual stereotypes by encouraging both boys and girls to cook, sew, and play with fire engines will still not solve the problem of who stays home with the kids—assuming one parent stays home.

Some few unusual men with unusual occupations who have taken custody of their children in divorces or who for special reasons have decided to assume the child-caring function will provide interesting examples of what happens when the father takes over. And they may teach us something. But most American men are not about to trade the assembly line for the line at the Laundromat, or the role of chief corporation counsel for chief bottle washer and chef. For one thing, a woman's work doesn't pay. That makes paying women for household and child care in some form, tax credits or direct payment, a number-one priority for all women. And while the women's movement must continue to talk and work with men about sharing their family work and lives, they must also convince them of their obligation to join with women in pressing for social and institutional solutions to child care.

We might start by conceding that motherhood has been devalued and by taking a new look. Women who choose to stay home with their children the first several years should get some help in mothering, and they should not be made to feel guilty because they are "only mothers" and not "liberated human beings." Ironically, many professional women end up wishing they had spent more time at home when their children were small.

All of us, in fact, should be able to make that choice by pressing for institutional arrangements that allow us some flexibility and freedom. If women want to stay home with their children, they should be able to do so without penalties. If they want or need to work part-time, they should have part-time day care available. If they want or need to work full-time, there should be the same choice.

And let's have enough flexibility in national programs so that they can be adapted to local needs. We need most of all, for the children's sake, to make sure we do not have a highly institutionalized segregated child-care system that would limit people by class, income, or color. We want to make sure our children are lovingly cared for.

There are many older people in our society, men and women, who would like the chance to be with and care for young children. It would be good for grandparents and children, too. Our foster-grandparents program has been enormously successful. Why not try it in schools and day care?

We might also consider whether day-care centers and nurseries could be schools—for mothers as well as children, and for fathers, too. Some cities, like New York, have thousands of children already in publicly funded community-controlled day care. They are fighting with city, state, and federal authorities to keep it from becoming a segregated, institutionalized system for welfare mothers, and sometimes they must fight to keep any day-care funds at all.

The next fight for those concerned with child welfare should be a national lobby for a new child-development bill. It should be publicly funded, community-controlled day care, and it should be removed from the welfare system. It should, gradually, include parent education and child health care. And it must not be for poor people only.

In addition, we should start pressing now for national health insurance, which provides quality medical care for all. It should include prenatal care and instruction in infant and child care. We should consider some version of the British visiting-nurse system that provides supervision and help for a period of time for all mothers.

There are many other battles for child welfare we will have to wage in the next few years. We should start with restoring value and significance to the idea of nurturing, recognize that all our children need it, and create programs and institutions that will help us give it to them, without sending those of us who don't want to go, back to the nursery. If we're worried about the cost, we might look at it this way: The less care a child has in the early years, the more society will pay for it later on.

12   Conclusions

The judge is famous, white-haired and handsome, dressed appropriately in a tuxedo, and the audience, a collection of well-known lawyers and jurists, equally well dressed and good-looking. The occasion is social: the retirement of a juvenile court judge known for her activism in the field of juvenile rights. The subject is juvenile justice and the right to treatment.

"Three days ago," the judge says, "the President of the United States announced the end of the crisis in our cities. At the same time, The New York Times *noted another jump in the cost of food.*

"My usual speech is about the underlying promise of treatment as the aim of the juvenile court; the unfortunate lack of resources, meaning lawyers, treatment facilities, social workers, probation officers; and the result, assembly-line courts and warehouse institutions.

"Our biggest cities are full of children bred casually, borne begrudgingly, growing up to delinquency. Living on the streets destroys the ability to empathize.

"We would like to but we don't know how to implant in these people middle-class sensibilities. We rely on the services syndrome, the medical bag, the therapeutic approach.

"I read recently that most American people, eighty percent, are ready to crack down on the remaining twenty percent, in a mood to confine crime to the ghettoes.

"We talk a lot about crime and its relationship to economic and cultural deprivation. I suggest the answer is income redistribution, I suggest the answer is a guaranteed annual wage, given to a family to raise its children as it sees fit.

"The family is the most effective child-development agency around when it wants to be and can function that way. A child needs a family, a poor child as well as a rich one. The poor are confronted with the same problems that confront the rich, but not with the same resources.

"I suggest we distribute the money directly, without government intervention.

"We have become addicted to custody, putting people away, and then pretending it is rehabilitation. Instead of more custodial institutions, we need more jobs, more housing, and integration.

"I'm not sure this is possible in our lifetime. It would, however, do more for poor children than the best juvenile-justice system and the most carefully insured right to treatment."

IT IS CLEAR that many children in America suffer physical and emotional abuse due to acts committed or omitted by parents and other caretakers. In the past several years the problem has become more aggravating to professionals in social welfare and to others for whom children are an exclusive concern.

There is still relatively little research in this area. But from those studies that have been done, the statistics show certain distinct trends.

The first is that physical abuse occurs at all levels of our society, among rich and poor, but the incidence seems significantly higher among those people trapped in the rut of poverty and discrimination.

Some take the view that child abuse is deviant behavior. Many investigators, legislators, and often the general public tend to view those who hurt children as sick, perhaps crazy, individuals whose acts are symptoms of their disease. This view is encouraged by the media, which makes a crusade of the more sensational cases, like that of poor Roxanne Felumero. By turning the full and continued glare of press coverage on the swollen body of a tortured three-year-old, by presenting sentimentalized views of her foster parents, and by giving space and voice to the often calculated hysteria of professionals who take such opportunities to beat their own drums, the public is dangerously misled as to both the causes and dimensions of the problem.

Other writers and observers, including this author, believe that the more outrageous and sickening acts of violence against children—beating, kicking, torturing and the like—are extreme examples of so-called normal attitudes and practices toward children in our society. Many child abusers act this way because they are sick emotionally and have no control over their behavior. Others, acting from the deprivation, stress, and frustration of daily life, are more likely to take out violent feelings on their children than are those who live more comfortable, hopeful lives.

The higher incidence of child abuse among poor and minority groups is due only in part to overscrutiny of the poor and over-reporting to central registries of the deprived. Common sense, as well as all our statistics, tells us that life is more painful, more stressful, more enervating, to say nothing of more physically crowded and uncomfortable when you have too little money, too little opportunity, and too little hope in life.

Besides the greater chance of poor mental and physical health and a greater tendency of their parents to take frustrations out at home, poor and minority children are more likely to live in one-parent families. Their parents have less ability to make satisfactory child-care arrangements if they work, or to ever get away from their children and responsibilities if they care for them at home.

Any serious examination of American society shows that physical discipline of children is widely accepted in our culture, whether by individual parents in their own homes, in schools, or in various child-care settings. Child abuse, like infanticide, abortion, or any other such phenomenon that has existed in almost every known human society, either as a response to the demands of the gods or as an answer to the burden of child bearing and child rearing, cannot be considered an individual aberration. It is a serious mistake to regard the father who beats his child with a belt buckle, or the mother who burns a child's hand, as a deviant individual in a society that loves and cherishes its young.

American society has a complex attitude toward youth, composed of admiration, love, anger, and envy. Our values are inherited from all those immigrant, largely Protestant and pioneering, values that go to make up our country, and the dominant American theme is success. We believe that the best man wins. Those who can't keep up get left behind. We regard the unsuccessful as outcasts and their children as worse. Still, while we are busy compiling records of individual parents who harm individual children, we have no system for recording the far more wide-scale neglect and abuse of children in schools, detention homes, foster-care settings and public institutions, or the emotional and physical deprivation of thousands of others due to inadequate medical care, substandard housing, and poor education.

While it is true that common sense would support the findings that the poor and deprived have more frustrations and are more likely to take out their frustrations on their children, and while it is true, too, that our culture has an ambivalent, frequently hostile view toward the young, we are faced with some special circumstances that are making family life more difficult for all Americans today and increasingly difficult for children. If we are really interested in helping abused and neglected children, we will have to do a good deal more than pass laws to enforce reporting.

Despite the attempts of various women's and communal groups to reexamine and perhaps restructure our concept of the family—all of which is useful and long overdue—the family has been, throughout history, the vehicle for bearing, nurturing, and supporting the life of the society. The family is charged with the primary economic and human responsibilities. It remains the irreducible unit of social responsibility and has a complicated reciprocal relationship with what we call society. In some countries, like China, the state has accepted more responsibility for functions that used to be private and within the family. At the same time, it has more direct say in what individuals and individual families do. Other countries have adopted policies, including health care and family allowances, which give families and children more support. America seems to lag behind.

When society has trouble, particularly economic trouble, the family is the first to feel the shock waves. The social and economic ripples of evolving capitalism affected all seventeenth- and eighteenth-century Europe, throwing people out of work and home and on the mercy of the emerging modern state. Children suffered the most from the new economic arrangements, particularly those whose slavelike labor helped to build the new industries and new states.

In America the family has been in real trouble for the last several decades, many of the problems being due to the nature of the American culture and experience. While industrialization, the effects of technology, and the blight of the media have all adversely affected contemporary life, it is particularly the negative aspects of mobility, the emphasis on individualism, and the value placed on success that have most weakened our society at the same time that they have contributed to our national and personal success. If it is one thing more than others, it is the emotional and geographical mobility that has left us, as Vance Packard calls us, "a nation of strangers," with only the thinnest and shallowest of roots.

America is a nation of immigrants. Everyone has come here from somewhere else and is always picking up and moving on. Consequently, many of those institutions that once provided stability are crumbling. There are few places left in this country that represent old, established communities. Even neighborhoods and neighbors come and go. The extended family, which once gave the young the advantage of another age's experience, has almost disappeared with the need of the next generation to make its own way. The church is almost defunct. Religion today, at least among the young, has become ecstatic and cultist. Whether it can develop into any kind of real life-support system remains to be seen. Marriages are on and off, increasingly off. What was once regarded as a lifetime commitment now lasts only as long as it works for both parties. And for an increasing number of people it works less and less. Ironically, as technology has freed more women from drudgery and the women's movement has worked to free women from the secondary role they have historically played, more women have been freeing themselves—at the expense of the family—without paying enough attention to who will care for the kids.

Whatever affects one member of the family eventually affects the others. And since so many other institutions converge on it, families are inevitably influenced by policies that other institutions—government, industry, schools—adopt.

In 1973 the Senate Subcommittee on Children and Youth held hearings on the American family. Almost without exception those who testified spoke of the lack of thought that went into how various government programs affected families.

Dr. Edward Zigler of Yale University spelled out the particular effects of some of those policies. Government policies such as highway construction and urban renewal that cause miles of road to be built and old neighborhoods to be destroyed is part of our phenomenon of flux. The national corporations whose policies are to move personnel every three or four years profoundly affect families in much the same way by taking away the supports that families once relied on. So, too, Zigler noted, do the media, which spread the message of American affluence to those who can never have it. And finally there is the lack of facilities for child care for those parents who must work and must find child-care arrangements they can afford.

It is time to start reorienting public policy in America to the support of the family, the health of the children, and the success of the whole society, rather than the wealth and comfort of a few.

First there is the problem of work. What little we know about child abuse and neglect, we do know that the most common factor in all child-abuse cases is the joblessness of the father or his absence from the home. The latter is often due to the former. Work in this society is considered the badge of adulthood and paid work is considered the only possible legitimate activity for a mature adult. People who work without pay, like housewives and women who care for their own children, or people who are un- and underemployed, like the old and the sick, are not considered to have full identities. Children whose families cannot provide for them can almost by definition be said to have problems—including poor mental and physical health—and to be prime candidates for neglect and abuse, if not by their parents, then by a neglecting society.

There has been so much rhetoric about full employment in this country that it seems unnecessary to repeat it. Jobs, for everyone who wants them, at which people can decently support themselves and their families, should be our first goal. Older people might be usefully employed in child-care settings, instead of being segregated from the rest of society and warehoused, usually to their detriment and ours.

Women who work at home, particularly those who care for children, should be decently compensated, and suitable economic child-care arrangements should be provided for those who want to go outside their homes to work.

The second problem is decent, livable housing. It is beyond the scope of this book to draw up a national housing scheme. Since, like full employment, we have been talking about it for decades, there are plenty of thoughtful, existing plans. It is not the knowledge or technology that keeps us from providing it. It is the national will.

It is clearly impossible for low-income families living in big cities to bring up children decently in deteriorating housing with insufficient plumbing and heating, defective wiring, in the company of roaches and rats. Parents cannot be considered neglecting if they can afford nothing better and if, in the existing market, decent housing is more than they can afford.

Next we need some form of income redistribution. The same small percentage of people in this country continues to control most of the wealth. Scandinavia and countries like England, Australia, and New Zealand have been more willing to come to grips through their government with economic disparity than we have—as have more outright socialist or communist countries like Cuba and China—and to give their citizens not only a sense of working dignity, but a feeling of a share in their country's life.

Fourth, universal, quality health care, free, paid for by some sort of tax levy, is an urgent need. It should include free family planning and contraceptives and be available to teenagers on request.

Prenatal care is obviously of prime importance if we want all of our children to start life healthy. Poor diet and poor health of expectant mothers has been demonstrated to cause brain damage and mental retardation in children, as does insufficient nourishment early in life. It is shortsighted not to correct this through public policy since the individual suffers and the society is likely to pay over and over again for people whose mental and physical health disabilities start at birth.

In addition to proper prenatal health care, pregnant women should be offered an intelligent short program in infant care. For women with no children, it should be compulsory and free. This should be followed, once the baby is born, by free visiting-nurse services for everybody, not to identify cases of suspected child abuse, but to help women who know nothing about children or women who just welcome the chance to express concerns and get some support. People who care for children should have access to continuing education in child development, whether through formal or informal classes and/or discussions at day-care centers and neighborhood schools. There should be places in the community where people who want and need help with their children can come and get it. Real family education in a sympathetic environment would eventually eliminate much of the need for family courts.

Abortion, like contraception, should be free on demand.

The whole day-care system should be expanded with federal support and local direction. There should be day nurseries for those women who must or want to work and can't afford or don't want to leave their children in individual care. There should be after-school programs for the children who have no one at home to care for them.

The day-care centers and schools should also be centers of family help, where people who have similar problems can get together for mutual support.

The family court system should have all support services such as probation, mental health services, and social work services removed and located in the community, particularly as regards neglect and abuse. Families reported to registries should be investigated by one set of protective workers and then referred to another for whatever help is deemed necessary. Cases in which a parent seems psychotic or in which the child appears to be in real danger should be handled in a separate manner. Children who must be removed from their homes immediately should be placed on a crisis basis in a community facility, perhaps connected to a day-care center or emergency center adjunct to the school. Communities should develop, with federal and state funds, their own mental health services staffed with professionals and paraprofessionals located in the community, and crisis centers for people needing immediate help. Children should *not* be removed from their families unless they are in danger at home. In particular, ameliorative services like homemaker services, which have proved to be effective and yet are still in short supply, should be expanded.

Foster care should be reexamined and new criteria applied. If it is thought absolutely necessary to remove children from the home, there should be a reasonable cutoff for the amount of time they can be left in foster care. When children are removed from their families, every real effort should be made to prepare the parents for the child's return. If that return is considered dangerous to the child, subsidized adoption should be facilitated. Children should not be switched from one foster-care setting to another without review.

Corporal punishment in schools and all caretaking institutions should be forbidden by law with realistic sanctions against teachers or caretakers who employ them.

We all have our blueprint for a better world. There are plenty of institutions that need radical revision, including the schools. It is hard to know where society should begin. Certainly all child-custodial institutions have been overwhelmed. However, whether any or all of these suggestions can be implemented—after all, we have talked about many of them half a century or more—we had better face up to the fact that passing more laws against child abuse and establishing more central registries is not going to help. It will accomplish very little except another computerized information system and more labeling of people as they go through life.

By the time most families in trouble come in contact with the law, it is too late to help, and the children who might have had a chance at home have already lost out.

It is abundantly clear that our prisons don't work, our courts don't work, our social-service systems don't work, and most of our schools don't work either. It is time for a social revolution. If not, we can confidently expect that for children, as for families, life in America is just going to get worse.

Notes

Chapter 1

1. Boyce Rensenberger, "The King of Myths," pp. 36–133 passim.
2. Sigmund Freud, "A Child Is Being Beaten," pp. 172–201. Freud said patients were more embarrassed by and more reluctant to talk about their sadistic feelings about children than they were about sex fantasies.
3. David Bakan, *Slaughter of the Innocents*, p. 70. Bakan has a useful discussion of literature as a key to unconscious feelings and fantasies about children, and a discussion of the ubiquity of infanticide and abortion.
4. Robert Graves and Ralph Patai, *Hebrew Myths: The Book of Genesis*, p. 175.
5. Bakan, op. cit., pp. 28–29.
6. " 'Spare the rod and spoil the child' was a dictum backed by the Bible and expressed in 1633 in the *Bibliotheca Scholastica*. There was a time in most Christian countries when children were whipped on Innocent's Day to make them remember the massacre of the innocents by Herod. Beatings to drive out the devil were a form of psychiatric treatment especially applicable to children and where epilepsy was attributed to demonical possession, the sufferer was thrashed soundly to expel the demon. There was a sacred iron chain in India expressly for this purpose." Samuel X. Radbill, "A History of Child Abuse and Infanticide," in *The Battered Child*, eds. Ray Helfer and Henry Kempe, p. 3.
7. E. S. Stern, "The Medea Complex: The Mother's Homicidal Wishes to Her Child," *The Journal of Mental Science (The British Journal of Psychiatry)*, 1948, 94, pp. 324–325, as quoted in Bakan, op. cit., p. 30.
8. William Graham Sumner, *Folkways*, pp. 267–277.
9. Bakan, op. cit., pp. 30–31.
10. "During the first half of the nineteenth century, Rev. J. M. Orsmond reported on this condition in Tahiti. (His manuscripts were published by his granddaughter in 1928 under the title *Ancient Tahiti*.) More than two-thirds of the children were destroyed 'generally before seeing the light of day. Sometimes in drawing their first breath they were throttled to death, being called *tamari'i hia* (children throttled).' " Ibid.
11. Sumner, op. cit., p. 266.
12. Bakan, op. cit., pp. 36–37. See also O. H. Werner, *The Unmarried Mother in German Literature*.
13. Jonathan Swift, "A Modest Pro-

217

posal for preventing the Children of Poor People from being a Burden to their Parents and Country," in *Satires and Personal Writings*, ed. W. A. Eddy (London: Oxford University Press, 1965), as quoted in Bakan, op. cit., p. 39.

14. Charles Darwin, *The Origin of the Species and the Descent of Man* (New York: Modern Library, 1936), pp. 429–430, as quoted in Bakan, op. cit., p. 40.

15. Quoted by D. Tenant, "The London Ragamuffin," *English Illustrated Magazine*, June 1885, cited by G. F. Northall, *English Folk-Rhymes* (London: Kegan Paul,

Trench, Trubner, 1892), p. 550, as quoted in Bakan, op. cit., p. 41.

16. *Encyclopaedia Britannica*, 9th ed., 1890, vol. 13, p. 3, as quoted in Bakan, op. cit., pp. 42–43.

17. George Devereux, *A Study of Abortion in Primitive Societies* (London: T. Yoseloff, 1960), p. 161, as quoted in Bakan, op. cit., p. 44. Devereux's italics.

18. Sumner, op. cit., p. 269.

19. "Infanticide in Japan: A Sign of the Times?" *The New York Times*, December 8, 1973.

20. Sumner, op. cit., p. 270.

21. Ibid., p. 272.

22. Ibid., p. 267.

Chapter 2

1. Margaret Mead, *Blackberry Winter*, pp. 194–195.

2. The age of seven has theological implications, too. After that, children are assumed to have rational capacities and therefore can take communion.

3. Heroard, *Journal of the Childhood of Louis XIII*, edited by E. Soulie and E. De Barthelemy, 2 vols., 1868, as quoted in Philippe Ariès, *Centuries of Childhood: A Social History of Family Life*.

4. See Ariès, op. cit., for the much greater freedom of sexual expression, which disappeared, along with the growth of the bourgeoisie.

5. In 1969 the National Commission on the Causes and Prevention of Violence, headed by Dr. Milton Eisenhower, reported that the rate of violent crimes in cities is especially high among men fifteen to twenty-four, and that arrest rates in the ten-to-fourteen age group showed dramatic and disturbing increases. In 1973 the New York City Police Depart-

ment's Crime Analysis Section showed that juvenile crime in the city for ages fifteen and under increased from 43,160 in 1966 to 58,801 in 1971. See Donald Singleton, "The Violent Children—A Shock Report," *New York Daily News*, January 30, 1973.

6. *The Fleischmann Commission Report on the Quality, Cost and Financing of Elementary and Secondary Education in New York State.*

7. Bernard Bard, "Schools: A System in Trouble," *New York Post*, May 11, 1973.

8. Ibid.

9. Untitled Study, New York State Office of Education Performance Review, released April 3, 1974.

10. Leonard Buder, "Education Study Hopeful of Poor," *The New York Times*, April 4, 1974.

11. "The Beaten Generation," *Time*, June 12, 1972, pp. 37–38.

12. Ibid.

13. E. L. Doctorow, *The Book of Daniel* (New York: Random House, 1971).

14. Lesley Oelsner, "Survey Urges an Overhaul of Court Procedure Here," *The New York Times*, May 31, 1973.
15. Sheridan Faber and Elizabeth Shack, "Juvenile Injustice."
16. Douglas Watson, "Maryland Juvenile Facilities Fail to Reform Lives," *The Washington Post*, July 2, 1973.

17. Ibid.
18. See "Juvenile Justice," by Stephen Wizner, *The New York Times*, January 2, 1971.
19. New York City Family Court Act, sec. 718 (b).
20. Jean Strouse, "To Be Minor and Female," pp. 70–116.
21. Alan R. Gruber, "Foster Home Care in Massachusetts, 1973."

Chapter 3

1. Frances Fox Piven and Richard A. Cloward, *Regulating the Poor*, p. 183.
2. Ibid., p. 130.
3. U.S. Congress, Senate, *American Families: Trends and Pressures, 1973*, Hearings Before the Subcommittee on Children and Youth, p. 187.
4. Ibid., pp. 19–22.
5. Piven and Cloward, op. cit., p. 224.
6. *American Families*, op. cit., p. 53.
7. Ibid., p. 183.
8. Piven and Cloward, op. cit., p. 7.
9. Karl de Schweinitz, *England's Road to Social Security: From the Statute of Laborers in 1349 to the Beveridge Report of 1942* (Philadelphia: University of Pennsylvania Press, 1943), as quoted in Piven and Cloward, op. cit., p. 24.
10. Ibid., pp. 22–23.
11. Beatrice Webb and Sidney Webb, *English Poor Law History, Part I: The Old Poor Law* (Hamden, Conn.: Archon Books, 1963), p. 29, as quoted in Piven and Cloward, op. cit., p. 12.
12. Paul Mantoux, *The Industrial Revolution in the Eighteenth Century: An Outline of the Beginnings of the Factory System in England* (New York: Harper & Row, 1962), as quoted in Piven

and Cloward, op. cit., p. 28.
13. Hammer, U.S. Atty., v. Dagenhart et al., 247 U.S. 251.
14. Anthony Platt, *The Child Savers*.
15. Mary E. Humphery, ed., *Speeches, Addresses and Letters of Louise de Koven Bowen*, p. 299, as quoted in Platt, op. cit., p. 91.
16. Ibid., p. 92.
17. Emile Durkheim, *Rules of Sociological Method*, pp. 65–73.
18. Enoch C. Wines, *The State of Prisons and of Child-Saving Institutions in the Civilized World* (Cambridge: Harvard University Press, 1880), as quoted in Platt, op. cit., p. 49.
19. *Sixth Biennial Report of the Board of State Commissioners of Public Charities of the State of Illinois* (Springfield: H. E. Rokker, 1880), p. 104, as quoted in Platt, op. cit., p. 107.
20. *Tenth Biennial Report of the Board of State Commissioners of Public Charities of the State of Illinois* (Springfield: Springfield Printing Company, 1888), pp. 131–132, as quoted in Platt, op. cit., p. 112.
21. John H. Wigmore, ed., *The Illinois Crime Survey* (Chicago: Blakely Printing, 1929), pp. 713–725, as quoted in Platt, op. cit., p. 159.

Chapter 4

The material in this chapter is taken from newspaper clippings, reports of the case, particularly from the *Daily News*, and the "Report of the Judiciary Relations Committee on the Handling of the Roxanne Felumero Case, June 19, 1969."

1. New York City Family Court Act, sec. 344.
2. New York City Family Court Act, sec. 346.

Chapter 5

1. David G. Gil, *Violence Against Children.*
2. Henry S. Maas and Richard E. Engler, Jr., *Children in Need of Parents* (New York: Columbia University Press, 1959), p. 356, as quoted in Robert H. Mnookin, "Foster Care; In Whose Best Interest?" p. 611.
3. David Fanshel, "The Exit of Children from Foster Care," *Child Welfare*, 50, February 1971, pp. 65–81, as quoted in Mnookin, op. cit.
4. Kermit Wiltse and Eileen Gambrill, "Decision-Making Processes in Foster Care." Unpublished paper, School of Social Welfare, University of California, Berkeley, 1973, as quoted in Mnookin, op. cit.
5. Lilly's story is taken from her caseworker, Miriam Muravchik, a social worker with the Legal Services Division of Mobilization for Youth, and from Muravchik's published account of the case in "The Child Abusers: The Story of One Family," pp. 28–32.
6. Vincent De Francis, *Child Abuse: Preview of a Nationwide Survey.*
7. Edgar J. Merrill, "Physical Abuse of Children—An Agency Study," in *Protecting the Battered Child.*
8. Gil, op. cit., pp. 49–70.
9. Thomas McHenry, Bertram R. Girdany, and Elizabeth Elmer, "Unsuspected Trauma with Multiple Skeletal Injuries During Infancy and Childhood." See also Elizabeth Elmer, *Children in Jeopardy.*
10. U.S. Congress, Senate, *Child Abuse Prevention Act, 1973*, Hearings before the Senate Subcommittee on Children and Youth of the Committee on Labor and Public Welfare, pp. 13 ff.
11. Ibid., p. 15.
12. David G. Gil, "Violence Against Children," *Journal of Marriage and the Family*, November 1971, pp. 637–648.
13. Anneliese F. Korner, "The Effect of the Infant's Level of Arousal, Sex, and Ontogenetic Stage on the Caregiver," pp. 105–121. See also Anneliese F. Korner, "Individual Differences at Birth."
14. Doctors Ray Helfer and Henry Kempe were among the earliest pioneers to bring child abuse to the attention of the American public. Their books on the subject include *The Battered Child* and *Helping the Battered Child and His Family.*
15. Arthur H. Green, "Physician's Approach to Child Abuse, Views of a Child Psychiatrist"; and "Psychological Effects of Child Abuse and Neglect."
16. Arthur H. Green and Richard Gaines, "Patterns of Self-Destructive Behavior in Child Psychiatric Emergencies."
17. Theo Solomon et al., "Final Report, The Mayor's Task Force on Child Abuse and Neglect," p. 27.
18. Leontine Young, *Wednesday's Children*, p. 36.

Chapter 6

1. B. F. Steele and C. B. Pollock, "A Psychiatric Study of Parents Who Abuse Infants and Small Children," in *The Battered Child*, eds. Ray Helfer and Henry Kempe, p. 105.

Chapter 8

1. Howard James, "Children in Trouble," *Christian Science Monitor*, April 5, 12, 19, 26, 1969; May 10, 24, 1969.
2. See Robert N. Mnookin, "Foster Care; In Whose Best Interest?" for a good review of the subject.
3. Ibid. Mnookin has an interesting discussion of the government's exercise of its power to remove or indenture poor children over parental objections, going back to colonial times, see especially p. 603.
4. Ibid., p. 609.
5. Joseph Goldstein, Anna Freud, Albert J. Solnit, *Beyond the Best Interests of the Child*. An inter-

Chapter 9

1. Sources for Lee Harvey Oswald biography: *The New York Times*, December 3, 4, 5, 7, 10, 1963, January 28, 1964, February 10, 14, 1964, September 3, 1964; *New York Post*, December 1, 2, 5, 8, 9, 1963, November 24, 1964; *Journal American*, December 2, 1963.
Sources for Charles Manson biography: *New York Post*, December 4, 1969; *The New York Times*, December 7, 1969; Steven V. Roberts, "One Man's Family," *The New York Times Magazine*, January 1, 1970.
Sources for Charles Whitman

2. Sylvia Porter, *Pittsburgh Press*, September 15, 1974.
3. Robert Lefferts, "Radicalism and Repression: The IWW and American Society."

esting discussion of custody under various circumstances. Anna Freud's suggestion that children involved in divorce actions should not be allowed to see the parent with whom they are not living ought to stimulate discussion.
6. Michal H. Phillips et al., *Factors Associated with Placement Decisions in Child Welfare*.
7. James, op. cit.
8. Ibid., April 26, 1969.
9. *The New York Times*, February 28, 1973.
10. *Boston Globe*, July 22, 23, 1974.
11. Larry Cole, *Our Children's Keepers*, p. 126.

biography: *The New York Times*, August 3, 4, 1966, September 9, 1966.
Sources for Anthony Spencer biography: Confidential report; *New York Herald Tribune*, September 23, 1964.
Sources for Thomas Ruppert biography: *New York Herald Tribune*, January 27, 1966; *New York Post*, June 9, 14, 1967.
Source for Jack Ruby biography: *The New York Times*, December 15, 1963.
2. *The New York Times*, December 23, 1973.

Chapter 10

1. Richard Light, "Abused and Neglected Children in America: A Study of Alternative Policies," pp. 556–560.
2. Ibid., pp. 560–567.
3. All figures in sections 8–12 are from Hearings Before the Subcommittee of Children and Youth of the Committee on Labor and Public Welfare, *American Families: Trends and Pressures, 1973.* It is a very useful document both for figures and for its various analyses of what is wrong with government policies toward children and families.
4. Lionel Tiger, "Is This Trip Necessary?" pp. 138–182.

Bibliography

Ariès, P. *Centuries of Childhood: A Social History of Family Life.* Translated by Robert Baldick. New York: Random House, Vintage Books, 1962.

Bakan, D. *Slaughter of the Innocents.* Boston: Beacon Press, 1972.

Cole, L. *Our Children's Keepers.* New York: Grossman Publishers, 1972.

De Francis, V. *Child Abuse: Preview of a Nationwide Survey.* Denver: American Humane Association, 1963.

Durkheim, E. *Rules of Sociological Method.* New York: Macmillan, The Free Press, 1950.

Elmer, E. *Children in Jeopardy.* Pittsburgh: University of Pittsburgh Press, 1967.

Faber, S., and Schack, E. "Juvenile Injustice." Office of Children's Services, Judicial Conference of the State of New York, New York, 1973. Mimeographed.

The Fleischmann Commission Report on the Quality, Cost and Financing of Elementary and Secondary Education in New York State. 3 vols. New York: The Viking Press, 1973.

Freud, S. "A Child Is Being Beaten" (a contribution to the study of the origin of sexual perversions: 1919), in his *Collected Papers,* Vol. II. New York: Basic Books, Inc., 1959.

Gil, D. G. *Violence Against Children.* Cambridge: Harvard University Press, 1970.

Goldstein, J., Freud, A., and Solnit, A. J. *Beyond the Best Interests of the Child.* New York: Macmillan, The Free Press, 1973.

Goodall, J. *In the Shadow of Man.* Boston: Houghton Mifflin, 1971.

Graves, R., and Patai, R. *Hebrew Myths: The Book of Genesis.* New York: McGraw-Hill, 1963.

Green, A. H. "Physician's Approach to Child Abuse, Views of a Child Psychiatrist." Unpublished paper.

────── "Psychological Effects of Child Abuse and Neglect." Presented at Brotherhood in Action, New York, February 7, 1973.

────── and Gaines, R. "Patterns of Self-Destructive Behavior in Child Psychiatric Emergencies." Unpublished. Reprint requests to Division of Child and Adolescent Psychiatry, Downstate Medical Center, Brooklyn, N.Y. 11203.

Gruber, A. R. "Foster Home Care in Massachusetts, 1973." Commonwealth of Massachusetts, Governor's Commission on Adoption and Foster Care, 1973. Mimeographed.

Helfer, R., and Kempe, H., eds. The Battered Child. Chicago: University of Chicago Press, 1968.

────── Helping the Battered Child and His Family. Philadelphia: J. B. Lippincott and Co., 1972.

Judiciary Relations Committee, First Judicial Dept. "Report of the Judiciary Relations Committee on the Handling of the Roxanne Felumero Case, June 19, 1969." Mimeographed.

Katz, S. When Parents Fail: The Law's Response to Family Breakdown. Boston: Beacon Press, 1971.

Korner, A. "The Effect of the Infant's Level of Arousal, Sex, and Ontogenetic Stage on the Caregiver," in The Effect of the Infant on Its Caregiver, eds. M. Lewis and L. Rosenblum. New York: John Wiley and Sons, 1974.

────── "Individual Differences at Birth." American Journal of Orthopsychiatry, 41(4), July 1971.

Kozol, J. Death at an Early Age. Boston: Houghton Mifflin, 1967.

Lefferts, R. "Radicalism and Repression: The IWW and American Society." School of Social Welfare, State University of New York at Stony Brook, 1972. Mimeographed.

Light, R. "Abused and Neglected Children in America: A Study of Alternative Policies." Harvard Educational Review, Part I, vol. 43, no. 4, November 1973.

McHenry, T., Girdany, B. R., and Elmer, E. "Unsuspected Trauma with Multiple Skeletal Injuries During Infancy and Childhood." Pediatrics, 31, 1963.

Mead, M. Blackberry Winter. New York: Simon and Schuster, Touchstone Books, 1972.

Merrill, E. J. "Physical Abuse of Children—An Agency Study," in Protecting the Battered Child. Denver: American Humane Association, 1962.

Mnookin, R. N. "Foster Care; In Whose Best Interest?" Harvard Educational Review, Part I, vol. 43, no. 4, November 1973.

Muravchik, M. "The Child Abusers: The Story of One Family." *World*, October 10, 1972.

Phillips, M., et al. *Factors Associated with Placement Decisions in Child Welfare.* Child Welfare League of America, Inc., 1971.

Piven, F. F., and Cloward, R. A. *Regulating the Poor.* New York: Pantheon, 1961.

Platt, A. *The Child Savers.* Chicago: University of Chicago Press, 1969.

Rensenberger, B. "The King of Myths." *The New York Times Magazine*, October 14, 1973.

Sidel, R. *Women and Child Care in China.* New York: Hill and Wang, 1972.

Solomon, T., et al. "Final Report, The Mayor's Task Force on Child Abuse and Neglect." December 15, 1970. Bound report.

Strouse, J. "To Be Minor and Female." *Ms.*, August 1972.

Sumner, W. G. *Folkways.* New York: New American Library, Mentor Paperback, 1940.

Tiger, L. "Is This Trip Necessary?" *Fortune*, September 1974.

U.S. Congress, Senate. *American Families: Trends and Pressures, 1973.* Hearings Before the Subcommittee on Children and Youth of the Committee on Labor and Public Welfare, 93rd Congress, September 24–26, 1973. 22-949-0, U.S. Government Printing Office, Washington, D.C., 1974.

——— *Child Abuse Prevention Act, 1973.* Hearings Before the Subcommittee on Children and Youth of the Committee on Labor and Public Welfare, 93rd Congress, March 26, 27, 31, and April 24, 1973. 95-591-0, U.S. Government Printing Office, Washington, D.C., 1973.

Werner, O. H. *The Unmarried Mother in German Literature.* New York: Columbia University Press, 1917.

Young, L. *Wednesday's Children.* New York: McGraw-Hill, 1964.

Catalog

If you are interested in a list of fine Paperback
books, covering a wide range of subjects
and interests, send your name and address,
requesting your free catalog, to:

McGraw-Hill Paperbacks
1221 Avenue of Americas
New York, N.Y. 10020